NP

We Learnt About Hitler at the Mickey Mouse Club

We Learnt About Hitler at the Mickey Mouse Club

A Childhood on the Eve of War

ENID ELLIOTT LINDER

ICON

ABOUT THE AUTHOR

Enid Elliott Linder (1928–2007) was a famous West-Country artist, specialising in silhouette drawings. As well as being an artist she was also a writer of considerable ability and brought a perceptive artist's eye to her written work. Following her evacuation from London in 1939, she lived the rest of her life in Torquay, Devon.

Enid Elliott Linder had a remarkable, almost photographic memory, which is reflected in her writing and the original illustrations that accompany the text.

This memoir has been compiled and edited by her niece, Elaine Cox, who is a lecturer at Oxford Brookes University.

Published in the UK and USA in 2021
by Icon Books Ltd, Omnibus Business Centre,
39–41 North Road, London N7 9DP
email: info@iconbooks.com
www.iconbooks.com

Sold in the UK, Europe and Asia
by Faber & Faber Ltd, Bloomsbury House,
74–77 Great Russell Street,
London WC1B 3DA or their agents

Distributed in the UK, Europe and Asia
by Grantham Book Services, Trent Road, Grantham NG31 7XQ

Distributed in the USA
by Publishers Group West,
1700 Fourth Street, Berkeley, CA 94710

Distributed in Canada by Publishers Group Canada,
76 Stafford Street, Unit 300
Toronto, Ontario M6J 2S1

Distributed in Australia and New Zealand
by Allen & Unwin Pty Ltd,
PO Box 8500, 83 Alexander Street,
Crows Nest, NSW 2065

Distributed in South Africa
by Jonathan Ball, Office B4, The District,
41 Sir Lowry Road, Woodstock 7925

Distributed in India by Penguin Books India,
7th Floor, Infinity Tower – C, DLF Cyber City,
Gurgaon 122002, Haryana

ISBN: 978-178578-609-9

Typeset in Stempel Garamond by Marie Doherty

Printed and bound in Great Britain
by Clays Ltd, Elcograf S.p.A.

CONTENTS

ILLUSTRATIONS

All illustrations are originals by Enid Elliott Linder, drawn for this book

I

A Message from India

In the summer of 1932 most people in Great Britain had never heard of Adolf Hitler. The sun was still shining brightly on the British Empire and the days seemed long and golden, especially to a four-year-old child like me. My two-year-old sister and I lived below stairs with our parents in the servants' quarters of an ancient riverside mansion in Richmond. Our father was the butler there and our mother was the cook.

Memories of that time and place still come echoing down through all the years to haunt my mind. I see once more the forbidden garden and hear again the droning of bees in the tall roses, the sound of water splashing from a bronze fountain and the laughter of two exotic children who had come to stay in that imposing residence by the river, quite unaware that there were two other children living below them in the deepest and most hidden part of the house.

Queensberry House, which has long since been pulled down, stood with its feet almost in the water beside the River Thames, just a few hundred yards downstream from Richmond Bridge. Our bedroom was in the many-corridored, gaslit, stone basement, where daunting shadows lurked in every corner. It was a place just made for ghosts, particularly when white mists wreathed in from the river, turning the lofty trees, the wooden boathouse, and even the old coach houses tucked away by the court-yard into vague and eerie shapes. Images or reality; the line between them is flimsy like a veil.

Something happened there, in Richmond, that sum-mer, that was to change the course of our lives. A strange sequence of events played out under the bluest of skies, in an England that has gone and can never return.

～＊～

Our father was a tall man with a good figure and bearing. His hair was almost as dark as our mother's but was wavy at the front. He had blue eyes and the sort of smile which made you feel warm and important. When he was not on duty upstairs he played with my sister and me a great deal and made up funny stories for our delight. From our earli-est days he regaled us with rambling tales of his own youth and boyhood – it was almost as though he was surprised to find himself grown-up, and was still wondering how he had come to be changed from a jolly country boy into a mannerly and dignified butler. Coming down through the service lobby dressed in his tails and with his 'upstairs' face still in place, he was a different man altogether.

Our mother did not look at all like a cook, even when she was dressed in her highly starched white coat-overall and apron, handling her ladles and wooden spoons with expertise. Her eyes were dark and thoughtful, her skin was pale and cool, and she wore her glossy dark hair cut in a fashionable bob. She was gentle and petite. She was also quietly studious, teaching me to read at an early age and taking time to answer my innumerable questions. Like my father, she had been a farmer's child, but had been orphaned early in life. She had been put into private service by the orphanage when she was fourteen, despite the fact that her bright intelligence had earned her the chance to become a pupil teacher.

My sister, Joan, spent quite a lot of her time when she was young corralled in a wooden playpen in a corner of the huge basement kitchen. There in the rosy shadows between the gleaming fire range and the tall wooden dressers, she would amuse herself for hours with her wooden alphabet bricks, a sawdust-filled doll with orange hair, and a chewed cardboard book full of yellow lions and tigers and people waving union jack flags. She had velvety brown eyes, honey-coloured hair which went curly in the rain, and dimples. The kitchen maids, and even the smart-as-a-pin housemaids were always picking her up and cuddling her, risking their starchy caps being pushed askew and their stiff white collars being dribbled on in the process of receiving one of Joan's soft baby kisses.

I had green eyes and freckles and very dark straight hair which never did anything interesting. I had long legs like Father, long eyelashes like Mother and, whenever I was thinking deep thoughts, an expression on my face which caused maids to remark: 'be careful now – if the wind changes you'll get stuck like that!'

In the early days I sometimes heard our mother say to people: 'what a blessing Joan has always been such a good baby. Heaven knows what we would have done otherwise.' I would feel a little put out on hearing this, for nobody ever remarked on my goodness. To a child who was bursting with curiosity, living below stairs in a world peopled almost entirely by busy servants, and where there were numerous forbidden doors and secret stairways, the achievement of staying good always required a great deal of self-restraint on my part.

My mother would sometimes let Joan play with a wooden spoon and two or three of the jelly moulds made of shining copper, which were shaped like fish or rabbits or castles. They normally lived on one of the dresser shelves. In that big, busy room the noise my sister made with them could hardly be heard: it seemed to drift to the top of the arched stone ceiling and get lost up there. The ceiling stones near to the fireplace end were all blackened. My mother thought the stain had probably been caused by rising smoke and fatty steam from days, long gone, when sides of meat had been cooked there on a roasting spit. A number of curious pieces of black metal and little wheels were still fixed in place in the wide chimney and on the chimney breast.

Each of the high wooden dressers could hold a full dinner service on the lower shelves. The drawers and cupboards below stored all the cooking crockery, baking equipment and other large utensils. On rainy days I was sometimes allowed to 'tidy out' the dresser drawers, or, at least, the shallow ones. A space would be cleared for me in a quiet corner of the scrubbed stone floor and I would lay out, in order, all the jumbled-up bits and pieces that were so necessary to the running of the kitchen but were difficult to keep tidy: things like piping-bags, corks, string for trussing birds and rolls of meat, metal meat skewers, wax candles and pudding cloths. In other drawers were bunches of keys, tradesmen's order books, indelible pencils, bills and invoices and a box of white chalks. The chalks were used for writing on the flagstones near the fire, the times when certain pots should be removed from the boiling end and drawn aside to simmer. Sometimes there would be chalked messages saying things like 'DO NOT BANG,' when there were soufflés in the oven.

But my favourite indoor occupation was to sit perched up on a high stool, with a cushion on it, at a corner of the long, scrubbed kitchen table, and either draw pictures of what I saw, or just watch my mother cooking.

One morning, when I was doing this, I became aware that an unusually large number of staff and other people were gathering together in the kitchen. Even the housemaids, who usually spent so much of their time looking after the mysterious kingdom upstairs, were down in the kitchen with us. The kitchen maids were present, naturally, because they belonged there. One of them, with floury forearms, was carrying on making pastry while the other was turning the handle of the mincer with her right hand and pushing a cold saddle of mutton into it with her left. I knew that later on three big mutton pies for the servants' hall would emerge from the oven. Then I saw the scullery maid emerge from her steamy den with her red hands hidden under the brown sack-cloth of her outer apron. Thomas and William, the footmen, were there in their shirtsleeves and aprons, having just come from washing glasses in the pantry. The chauffeur, also in his shirtsleeves, had come in from hosing down cars in the cobbled courtyard. His wet wellingtons stood side by side on the kitchen doorstep and beside them in a neat row, stood several pairs of gardeners' boots: the head gardener and his men had come into the kitchen in their socks. There were even two tradesmen standing over by the fire range. They wore loose, fawn, linen coats over their black three-piece suits. They had come to enquire about orders and stayed to drink tea. Their bowler hats hung on the coat rack behind the door.

Everyone was gulping down hot tea, poured for them by one of the kitchen maids. They all seemed to be talking at once and all the voices were more highly pitched than was normal. It seemed that some very special people were coming to stay at Queensberry House and for lack, as yet, of adequate information; the atmosphere in the kitchen was a frenzy of speculation. 'They're very important indeed,' one of the footmen said knowingly, 'he's a sultan and his wife's a sultana.' Everybody burst into laughter. Even Joan in her playpen over in the corner, caught the mood. She jumped up and down and threw back her head and laughed out loud, showing off all her pearly milk teeth and her dimples.

During all the jollity our father entered the kitchen, followed by Mr Parsons. It seemed to me that the old pantry-man's eyes were rolling slightly. Father accepted a cup of tea in his own special cup, and then informed everyone that it was not a sultan and a sultana, who were coming, but an Indian Maharaja and his wife, the Maharanee. They would be staying for at least three months as house guests and were already on a ship bound for England. Also coming with them, he added, was an entourage of about two dozen other people, consisting of relatives, companions and personal servants.

At this last piece of information, everybody's eyes started to roll, just like Mr Parsons's. Father told them then that as far as he knew no extra staff were being taken on. At this point he reminded everyone that they had a good and thoughtful employer, prodding their memories about the 'special arrangements' made every year so that they could have a good Christmas. Now it was their turn to do well by their employer. There would of course be a 'present' for each of them at the end of it. He finished by saying that it was just as well they all had a little time ahead of them before the arrival of the Indian royal party, because a great deal of preparation lay in front of everyone. I saw his quizzical glance at our mother and wondered what it meant.

After this, everything seemed to go back to normal for a while, except that everybody was extraordinarily busy and I had to be extra careful not to annoy anyone or get in their way.

❧

At night the wind coming off the River Thames moaned along the vaulted stone corridors outside our bedroom and whistled under the door. The gaslights on the corridor walls created welcome little islands of light, but they were surrounded by wide lakes of darkness. I found it a very scary thing to go along to the lavatory at night. Not only might I bump into William or Thomas, the footmen, in their pyjamas, but I might even see old Mr Parsons creeping around in his long white nightshirt.

The indoor menservants slept down with us in the basement. The housemaids and kitchen maids slept up in the attics. I did not know where the attics were because I was not allowed upstairs. But late one evening, when, unable to sleep, I had wandered into the kitchen in search of my parents, I had found them sitting before the fire drinking tea. The fire in the long range had been banked up for the night. The two kitchen maids and the scullery maid, all with lighted candles in saucer-shaped candlesticks, were saying goodnight. They then went through a door in the service-lobby wall, which was referred to as 'the back stairs'. I saw their candle flames flare and flicker as if they had walked into a draught. The sounds of their soft-soled shoes became fainter as they mounted many stairs within the wall. Then everything was silent except for the slow ticking of the mantelpiece clock and the sound of the coals shifting as they settled. I wondered why the maids had to sleep so far away from the rest of us, and mount those creaking stairs at night, all alone.

The gardeners and chauffeur slept in little rooms over the coach houses. To reach the entrances they had to ascend a flight of rickety wooden steps on the outside of the long building. At one end was an old hay loft in which were stored a blue-covered ottoman chest and several tea chests. They contained most of our personal possessions, apart from the few things that were kept in our enormous bare bedroom, such as Father's trouser press, Mother's hat boxes and our most prized possession of all, the gramophone. There was a tiny moss-grown window high up in our bedroom wall, through which a greenish light filtered if it was a sunny day. Whenever our father lifted us up we could see, at eye level, the long kitchen gardens where we were allowed to play, provided we did not annoy the gardeners. They were all-powerful in the kingdom of the gardens.

The kitchen-garden walls were built of mellowed rosy bricks which seemed to soak up and hold the sunshine. In one of them there was a small green door with a dented and tarnished brass knob and a big keyhole. On the occasions when the door was unlocked, I would run to it and gaze through the archway at the beautiful, but forbidden, garden on the other side. In it was a small, round, wooden summerhouse with a grey thatched roof, and a big shady tree with a circular wooden seat built around its trunk. There was also a fountain, with water droplets that blew sideways if there was a breeze. Smooth lawns swept gently past beds of roses, to a barrier of dark railings silhouetted at the river's edge.

Sometimes, in the distance, I would see people in summer clothes walking along a path on the other side of the railings. If the weather was very hot many of the women would carry gaily coloured parasols and the men would carry their jackets over one shoulder and tilt their hats forward. From the river there often came the hoot of pleasure steamers. They had rows of white circles on the sides and grey smoke would stream out behind their tall funnels. Sometimes a band would be playing on one of the decks and there would be singing and laughter, made soft and echoey by the water and the trees. Now and then the sound of gramophone music would drift across the silver river as punts or rowing boats glided past the trailing willows.

Quite often, I would recognise snatches of melodies, like 'Goodnight Sweetheart' or 'You Forgot Your Gloves.' I had heard them before on the occasions when all the daytime meals had been served and cleared up and all the other servants had, for one reason or another, gone out for a while. Then our parents would carry our gramophone into the long servants' hall and, after winding it up, and with us watching from the end where the piano stood, they would slip into each other's arms and quickstep, or foxtrot, all around the wide parquet floor. These happy times together were always brief. Our parents would still be in their working clothes. Mother's apron strings and Father's coat tails would fly out into the air as round and round they whirled. And their eyes would shine.

1. Mother's apron strings and Father's coat tails would fly out into the air.

Our father's domain included the butler's pantry, which had barred windows, a wooden-lined sink with rubber-tipped taps, and in the centre stood a baize-topped table and four chairs. In the corner was a big metal safe, and two entire walls shone with a dazzling array of silver, all locked away behind plate glass: shining silver chafing dishes, tea and coffee services, galley trays, candelabra, cutlery, salvers, cake baskets, jugs, dishes, soup tureens, wine coolers, there was even a silver samovar for making tea.

Even though he had the two footmen to clean the silver, Father often hung his day coat on a hanger behind the pantry door and, donning a green baize apron to protect his outer clothes, he would roll up his sleeves and dedicatedly polish the loveliest or most intricate pieces himself. After brushing out the dried pink paste with the softest of brushes, he would then rub in the shine by applying a steady, warm, circular pressure through the polishing cloth, with the padded parts of his thumbs. 'It's love that makes silver stay beautiful,' he would say, holding up the precious object for his inspection, with the light behind him.

My father told me that the samovar was used at breakfast times. Then the people upstairs would serve themselves without the aid of servants, he said. At around half past seven in the mornings I had seen the footmen carry large trays of burnished silver up the service stairs. Father said that these were taken into the breakfast room and laid out on long buffet tables which were draped with starched white linen cloths.

I was surprised to learn that the family and any guests could come down to breakfast at any time up to half past ten, and, provided they looked respectable, could appear in their dressing gowns if they chose. During this meal, no footman or other servant was allowed in the room. Apparently, this was customary in many large establishments of the gentry. So once Thomas and William had set out all the food on the side tables, they had only to sit or stand outside the door in case they were needed. Usually they were hidden behind a screen. The idea, so my father explained, was that if some people didn't feel very well in the morning they may not want to be seen by servants or to be fussed over.

It was common knowledge too, that the upstairs people ate their breakfasts sitting at a long refectory table, after helping themselves to what they fancied to eat. The display was always the same: prunes, green figs and porridge to the left, beside freshly squeezed orange juice, tea, coffee, jugs of milk and cream, racks of toast, dishes piled with freshly made butter pats, and baskets of hot rolls that had been specially made for breakfast. Keeping hot in the silver chafing dishes would be scrambled eggs, bacon, kidneys, mushrooms, sausages, sautéed potatoes, fried tomatoes and, always, a good supply of fried bread, made succulently golden and crispy in the same big iron frying pan that had been used for the bacon, but with a bit of beef dripping added.

In other closed silver dishes would be pairs of plump kippers and fillets of smoked haddock, poached in milk and butter. Beside them, in a special high-domed dish, would be a great mound of kedgeree. To the right of the display would be a cold ham that had been freshly boiled and prepared the previous day. Hams were always sent up whole, never partly carved away. Every morning what was left over from breakfast was devoured in the servants' hall, between pieces of homemade buttered bread, by more than a dozen indoor and outdoor servants, who always seemed to be ravenous for their snack by eleven o'clock or thereabouts. Their own breakfast had been at around six o'clock and a lot of hard physical work had been performed since then.

Queensberry House was almost an entire little world unto itself where food was concerned, so much was produced in its own garden or kitchen. Upstairs at breakfast there would be bowls of fresh fruit including, when in season, bunches of grapes straight from the warm, moist, atmosphere of the many-scented greenhouses. As a final touch, from the kitchen, a big, rich, Dundee cake would be set upon a doilied silver stand beside the cheeses. This, too, was a traditional item that must be provided every morning at breakfast.

When I asked my father why all the people didn't end up with tummy ache, he laughed and said that they worked a lot of it off playing tennis, golf and polo at places nearby like Richmond Park, Roehampton, Hurlingham and Windsor. I had no idea what he meant then, but most things we talked about when I was small, he spoke of again a great many times throughout my childhood, so that I almost knew them off by heart.

He told me that most of the big houses of the gentry, where those big breakfasts were an accepted way of life, were right out in the country where there was also hunting and shooting in season, the care of farms and woodlands to be overseen, and many other country pursuits and responsibilities to be undertaken. 'They work quite hard in their own ways,' he explained, 'and their worries are different to ours.' He told me, with feeling, that we should never envy or resent people like them, because they provided work and security for hundreds of thousands of people who might otherwise be unemployed, or else working in ugly factories or living in squalid surroundings.

Having spent my entire life until then in the cloistered and protected world of private service and having rarely been taken beyond the high walls of a Big House or private estate, I could not imagine what an ugly factory or squalid surroundings might look like. But seeing the look on my father's face as he said the words, I gathered that they were something very different to Queensberry House.

2

Behind the Green Baize Door

Our father was not always the stately and dignified person we saw when he mounted the gaslit service stairs to go on duty in the great house above us. When no other servants were near and he was alone with just our mother and us, he was loving and playful and full of fun. Among the many stories he told my sister and me, as we grew older, our favourites were nearly always about his boyhood. He told us that he was a Shropshire lad, born and brought up in the deep, still countryside near a place called Whitchurch. All through his boyhood he had quite expected that when he grew up he would become a farmer, like his father and grandfathers before him, at Allport Farm. His stories reflected many of the things and people he saw all about him in that Shropshire landscape at the turn of the century.

Whenever he could make the stories funny, he did so, and we listened to many tales about mischievous tramps, rascally poachers, irate farmers and supercilious squires. But he also told us about how he and his seven brothers and sisters worked in the fields when they were not at school, often, it seemed, falling out of apple trees, sliding down haystacks or being fished out of ponds. Hay-making, stone picking, crow scaring, cleaning or making corn stooks by day, at night they would tumble, exhausted but happy, into two huge beds where they slept top-to-toe under the sloping upper ceilings of the farmhouse. As they settled down, the rustlings and scratchings of the mice and birds who lived under the cosy thatch above them, would set them all whispering and thinking about ghosts and hob-goblins until, sufficiently scared and thankful for all the company they had in bed with them, they would fall asleep as peacefully as the farm animals in their straw.

But in 1916, he told us, his country-boy existence had come to a sudden end. He was fourteen years old then. Advertisements had begun to appear in the country news-papers asking for personable youths, well below the age of military service, to be trained as hall boys and then as foot-men in some of England's big country houses and stately homes. The reason there was a shortage of footmen, he explained, was that Great Britain was at war with Germany and most of the footmen had gone away to fight in the Great War, on something he called the Western Front.

The money being offered for the trainee hall boys and footmen was good. His parents' farm had been going through a lean season. His mother had several other chil-dren still at home to be provided for. Almost before he knew what was happening to him, he found himself bundled onto a steam train with a small tin trunk beside him, bound for a place he had never heard of. The label on the trunk was addressed simply Keele Hall, Staffordshire.

The top-hatted coachman, who met him at Keele Station, told him that the country house he was being taken to belonged to a relative of Tsar Nicholas II, the reigning monarch of 'all the Russias', and also that high-ranking members of the aristocracy came frequently to Keele Hall as visitors or house guests.

In all his boyhood he had rarely been further from the farm than the nearest village where he went to school. Only occasionally had he accompanied his mother to the market town of Whitchurch: sitting in the rumbling horse-drawn cart beside mounds of vegetables, rattling churns and covered baskets of dairy produce, eggs and honey, had seemed to him then like a great adventure. So when he was first shown around Keele Hall he was overwhelmed and intimidated by its size and grandeur: 'huge hanging lamps, each one glittering like a thousand icicles, marble pillars and floors, silken carpets on the walls, vast shimmering mirrors, banks of chrysanthemums everywhere, each flower with petals as stiff and white as frozen snow'.

Our eyes would grow round with wonder as vivid pictures formed in our minds from the words he uttered, and when he told us that the grandeur had frightened him so much that he would have run away if he had been able to, we nodded our heads in agreement.

His employers had provided him with the first complete new outfit of clothes that he had ever possessed; a Norfolk jacket and knickerbocker trousers of dark grey worsted cloth, worn with black woollen stockings, black leather boots, a white cotton shirt and grey woollen tie. As a hall boy one of his many tasks was to hurry along corridors the length and breadth of the vast building, carrying messages from one department to another. He also helped the other boys clean all the boots and shoes of the family and their guests; the flat silky bootlaces were first removed and then pressed with a hot flatiron before rethreading. He also ironed out the creases in the daily newspapers before they were carried upstairs on a silver tray by one of the footmen. Brown paper under the hot irons would have absorbed the newsprint's inkiness, so that his employer's hands stayed clean.

Gradually he was taught to wait at tables, upon upper servants in the stewards' room and, a bit later, was shown how to brush, sponge and press the butler's various suits of working clothes. He was told that these humble tasks were all part of the training of those who aspired to become top footmen, valets and butlers, fit to work in or take charge of English upper-class homes, or even those of the aristocracy. The trainee boys were reminded that if they rose high enough, through diligence, they might one day be able to travel with their employers and see something of the world. Then, instead of remaining country boys all their lives, tipping their caps in awe at local squires, they would have made something of themselves.

Our father was nearly sixteen when he was promoted to third footman. He received two suits of splendid livery for dress wear, plus another set of clothes which resembled the brocaded and ruffled uniforms worn by 18th-century flunkeys. These, he was told, were for use on special occasions such as grand dinners and balls and he was instructed in the art of caring for and powdering the silver wig which completed the outfit. Lastly, he was given a rise in wages, which meant that he could increase the amount of money that he sent home to his mother every month by postal order. It was only in 1920, when he met our mother, then fifteen, at a servants' ball, that he began to think about saving for his future.

꧁꧂

Our mother usually only told us things in 'snippets' when she spoke about her life as a child, and later as a young woman. But gradually over the years a picture emerged. It was a very different one from that painted by our father, about his happy youth. She told us that her name had once been Mary-Jane Hartley and that she had been born in 1905 in a chill stone farmhouse, high on the border between Lancashire and Yorkshire. The house was known as Lower Dean Head Farm, a place of cold stone floors and a wind which blew continuously over the wide, bleak moor, moaning in the chimney tops and whistling through the jagged holes in the dry-stone walling that surrounded the farm.

The only memory she had of her mother was from a sepia photograph in an oval frame which hung on the parlour wall; a gentle-faced young woman with big, dark eyes, like her own, and dark hair parted in the middle. Her grandmother, who looked after her and her older brother, Richard, on the farm, told her that her mother had died from a broken heart when the children's father had deserted them all. Before long, the grandmother also died and the children had no one else to turn to. The last she saw of the farm was from a pony trap that took them, joltingly, along the stony road that led down from the moor. It was driven by strangers. They told the children that, because they were not real orphans, they could not be taken to an orphanage. Richard was a strong boy, they said, and a place had been found for him. But nobody wanted a five-year-old girl, so she must be taken to the workhouse. She never saw or heard from her brother again.

She might have stayed in the workhouse a long time, but one day a widowed lady who was looking for a suitable child to take home as a companion chose her from a row of other little children brought forward for inspection. She was taken to a house near Burnley, where she had four happy years of warmth and security. She was also dressed prettily by the lady, who she called 'Aunty Polly', and was coached in her lessons and taught good speech and manners. Aunty Polly, who was a Roman Catholic, made an arrangement with the nuns of a Catholic orphanage that if she should die or become ill, then little Mary-Jane, even though she had been christened a Protestant, should be taken into their care and protection: and that is what happened.

The orphanage had been so in need of money that when she was twelve, during the Great War, she had become one of the many female orphans sent out to work part-time in the cotton mills. But she enjoyed the work and still thrived at school, she said, going early to the top of the class and soon helping to teach the little ones in classrooms bereft of teachers by the war. Her headmaster hoped she could become a pupil teacher, but in 1919, when she was fourteen and legally old enough to work full-time, the nuns informed her that a man calling himself Robert Hartley had traced her to the orphanage and was downstairs asking for her. He was now set up in business as a clog-maker, he had told them, and as Mary-Jane belonged to him legally until she was 21, he was now claiming her back so that she could come and live with him and work for him. But, on seeing the look of bitter hatred that came into Mary-Jane's dark eyes, not to mention the fear, the nuns said they could help her to 'disappear', if she chose, to a place where her father would never be able to find her. She quickly agreed and it was soon arranged for her to be taken into private service in the adjoining county of Cheshire. The nuns told her that, as it was important for a young girl to have a secure roof over her head, she should direct her intelligence to climbing as high as she could within private service. If she could become a housekeeper or cook she would never want for anything, even if she never married.

The rung of the ladder from which she began her climb saw her as a mob-capped scrubbing maid in the laundry wing of a big country mansion in Cheshire. But, she consoled herself, situated as it was in the depths of a large private estate and with the gates guarded by the lodge-keeper and his wife, there was very little chance of her father finding her again. As an added precaution she was no longer even Mary-Jane: she had given herself the fashionable name of Mabel instead.

By the time she married our father she had become a lady's maid to a titled lady, after gradually 'bettering' herself in a series of grand houses, and even a castle. He, by that time, had become a polished first footman and valet to a Cheshire lord. They were good-looking, healthy and very much in love. They had splendid references and great hopes and ambitions for their future life together, working jointly as a butler and a lady's maid.

It was as such that they had, apparently, obtained a very superior position in central London, quite soon after their marriage. Their London employer was the favourite daughter of a multi-millionaire. She had lost her first-born son in infancy shortly before our parents went to work for her. He was the only child she could have. Being a gifted musician, she sought to assuage her grief in music, in travel, and by becoming a minor society hostess, particularly to celebrities from the world of theatre. Her home was a small Georgian house just a few yards from Harrods on the one side and Hyde Park on the other. She was a very generous and thoughtful employer to our parents, who then

2. Our parents worked in rich and elegant surroundings.

became her personal servants. She liked them so much that she had planned to take them with her on a world cruise that would last six months. First class berths aboard the Liner had already been booked for the autumn of 1927, and our mother was already accompanying her mistress on a giddy round of shopping and beginning the packing of cabin trunks.

By the July of that year, however, our mother was not feeling well. One day she visited a doctor, and then walked back across Hyde Park to the house. Several times she had to sit down on a park bench because she was feeling so faint. Back at home, and in some agitation, she immediately sought out our father. He was in the drawing room, where their mistress was sitting at the grand piano, with a young man called Noël Coward alongside, helping to produce some songs for the forthcoming *Charlot's Revue*.

Father stopped his collecting up of music scores, which were scattered all over the room, and followed our mother below stairs. There she told him that she was expecting a baby. 'A baby! What on earth is a lady's maid supposed to do with a baby?' So often was the tale retold throughout my childhood, that her exclamation of despair became lodged in a compartment of my brain normally reserved for other fateful historic sayings, such as 'A horse! A horse! My kingdom for a horse!'

Their employer, on being informed that I was 'expected', had excitedly offered to become my godmother as soon as I arrived, and to pay for my education and all my childhood needs. But, as with all good fairy godmothers, there was a condition attached. Her suggestion was that she should put off the cruise until the following year. In that way they would still be able to accompany her. But in order to do this they, in turn should put their child out to be fostered as soon as practicable after the birth. In that way they could all have the cruise, as promised, the child would have a good life with all that money could reasonably buy, and our parents could go on enjoying one of the best positions in London.

Our mother later told us that after much anguished soul-searching, she felt that she could never desert her child as her father had done to her (for that was how she saw it). At the same time, she knew that her refusal to have her baby fostered, a practice that was not uncommon among upper-class servants, would mean the end of her husband's plans to better himself still further in London.

She also knew that the only employment available to a married butler with children was in the country, the place her husband had struggled so hard to gradually advance himself away from. His heart was by then firmly in London. He had fallen under its spell when, as first footman to the Cheshire lord, he had spent several London seasons at his employer's town residence in the elegant Carlton House Terrace beside the Mall.

It was a paradox. Her husband loved children yet did not relish the idea of sacrificing a good career for one of them. She herself was not, at that time, all that fond of children, yet she could not bear the thought that one day a child of hers might think bitterly of her. She had admitted to herself that she not only hated her father for deserting her, but also felt a deep anger towards her mother for being so weak as to die of a broken heart, leaving her children deserted for a second time: 'She should have stayed alive and fought for us,' she once said with surprising passion. It was one of the rare moments when she did not have her feelings under firm control.

So our parents reluctantly gave their notice to their London employer and a way of life came to an end. I was born the following February in one of a pair of small tied cottages in the middle of some wide Warwickshire fields, during a blizzard. Several days of swirling snow had almost buried the hedgerows, and the small country lane which led from the cottages to the Elizabethan manor house where our father now worked. Through the small iced-up panes of the two adjoining cottages it was almost impossible to see the glowing oil lamps of the people who lived within, and who had been up half the night. Our father, afraid for his wife, who was having difficulties with the birth, finally wrapped himself around the head and shoulders with a horse-blanket and, with a lantern held on high, struggled through the waist-deep fallen snow and the flying snowflakes, across three fields and over two submerged stiles, in order to take the short cut to the only telephone in the district, which was at the manor. Conditions were obviously too bad for the doctor to come by car from the nearby village of Hatton, or even on foot, but over a crackly line he said he would try to make the journey on horseback.

When our father, back at the cottage again, finally saw the doctor through the window, 'looking like a snow-man on a snow-horse', I had already been safely born; delivered by the wife of the groom who lived next door, with the groom standing at the bottom of the twisting wooden stairs shouting up instructions. 'Three guineas that little trip from the doctor cost me,' our father would joke, 'and our Enid already born.' It was not the last time that he was to call me 'cussed'.

Our mother often reminisced that, looking very incongruous in the firelight and shadows of that rustic bedroom, was the beautiful treasure-cot, draped in ruffled lace, which now contained her first-born child. It had once belonged to the little boy of their erstwhile employer in London. She had given it to them as a parting gift.

❦

Nobody ever told us what our father's reaction had been to our mother's decision to keep her child. He himself never mentioned the incident – not at any time during the hundreds of family stories he related over the years. It was from our mother we learnt that she had only turned herself into a cook working alongside her husband after some mysterious trouble had come their way after my sister Joan was born.

Even at Queensberry House I was still too young to understand that it was because of our parents' outstandingly good references from past employers, plus certain information relayed along the 'golden grapevine' of upper-class employers, that they were being allowed the most unusual practice, and favour, of bringing up a family below stairs. The condition had been that their children must be kept in order and out of sight and hearing.

At Queensberry House, temptation was all around me. On those days when the gardeners unlocked the door in the kitchen-garden wall and, carrying their various gardening implements, plodded into the forbidden, private garden through the arched opening, I would experience an almost irresistible desire to creep in unseen behind them and hide.

Standing on the barrier of the threshold, I would watch the men slip away into the shrubberies or the rose garden. Sometimes they would disappear behind the summerhouse or the trees, or even, if still in view, become transformed into black shadows as, silently engrossed in their work and standing as still as statues, they were silhouetted against the shining silver band of the river.

When the sun was at its highest they would troop back to the servants' hall for their midday meal. Occasionally they would forget about locking the door and leave it standing open. It was at these times, especially, that the deserted garden did its best to lure me inside with its heady perfume of roses, its tall shimmering trees full of whispering leaves, its droning bees and splashing fountain. I would stand there as if under a spell, mesmerised by beauty, wanting only to lose myself in its enchantment. Not knowing why I was not allowed inside the garden, I would turn away and go back to the semi-underground work-regions of the great house, where I belonged.

Underneath our basement bedroom was an even deeper realm, a network of cellars, where the wine was stored. When my father first took me down there I saw hundreds of dusty bottles, lying in wooden racks. Some were festooned with ancient cobwebs, their labels mottled or blackened with age. Others lay in padlocked metal cages. There were no gas lights down there and Father had to do his selecting, testing and decanting, plus many other jobs, by candlelight. He carried matches, tapers and two lighted candles in candlesticks, whenever we went down.

At the bottom of the stone steps I would watch while he lit at least a dozen other candles that stood in wax-dribbled niches in the arched brick walls. When they were all alight, their flames burning tall and bright in the cold motionless air, the wine cellar would seem to me like a fairy grotto. It was one of my favourite parts of the house. Even Father sometimes seemed jollier than usual when we came up again from the cellar.

At the end of one of the north corridors was a huge, chilly larder. It had draughty mesh windows, a stone floor and black slate shelves. Every bit of food that had to be kept cold was stored in there, under domed fly covers made of muslin, wire mesh or glass. There were always two or three wooden mouse traps on the floor with either Cheddar cheese or dead mice in them. I felt sorry for the mice, just as I did for the dead furry hares that hung upside down from ceiling hooks in another cold larder next door. They had blood-streaked enamel cups strapped over their faces. Rabbits hung in there too and, in season, all sorts of pretty game birds: pheasants and woodcocks, partridges and snipes.

Between the butler's pantry and the huge kitchen was the large, square service lobby, on the wall of which hung a row of numbered bells on springs. Too often they rang several at a time, or even all at once, or so the two footmen used to grumble. Although I am sure that I would have noticed if they ever really had rung 'all at once'.

What really fascinated me, though, was the flight of plain wooden stairs that ran from the lobby to a short, gaslit landing, where there was a green baize door. The footmen, dressed in their green livery with silver buttons, and usually carrying laden silver trays, used that door a lot. Watching them from the semi-gloom of the basement quarters, I noticed that whenever they mounted the stairs with their trays and, half-turning, pushed upon that green baize door with their shoulders, a very different sort of light could be seen. It would flash brightly for a moment and then vanish as the door closed again.

I wished very much that I could go up and find out what was causing that unearthly light. But the green baize door was an area that was very strictly forbidden to me. There again, I did not know why, but the very vehemence of the prohibition made it seem one of the most exciting parts of the house. All I knew about upstairs was that some mysterious people lived up there, who devoured mountains of food and were still ever-hungry for more. There was also somebody up there, who was referred to below stairs as 'His Lordship'.

In the kitchen the maids looked fresh as forget-me-nots in their blue cotton dresses and white caps and aprons. Unlike the kitchen maids, our mother wore no headdress. Her dark hair held back by a brown tortoiseshell slide, and her black strapped shoes and black stockings, made an interesting contrast to the dazzling whiteness of her crisply starched coach-overall and bibbed apron. Backwards and forwards she would go between the preparation table and the hot fire ovens, with the broad stiff bow at the back of her apron strings following her around like a big white butterfly. In her overall pocket she always carried a sweet-smelling swan's-down powder puff wrapped in a square of pink chiffon. I often sat on my high, cushioned stool by the table and just gazed at her, thinking how pretty she was.

Early each morning at Queensberry House, an earthy green smell came into the kitchen when the gardeners brought in large baskets of fruit and vegetables for the maids to prepare and Mother to cook. Our mother used a little red book called *Menus Made Easy*. She liked to experiment and I often saw it propped upon a dresser. All the necessary ingredients were prepared by the kitchen maids before the actual cooking began. I would sit fascinated as things were pounded and chopped, peeled, skinned, de-pipped, ground, grated, mashed, whisked, beaten and sieved, slices shelled, shredded or crushed or, possibly, minced or whipped. All such preparation was done from start to finish by hand, and that was just the beginning.

The cooking range stood in an opening under the chimney of the old original fireplace and was about eight feet wide, at least. The fire never went out, even at night, and when meals were being prepared it was coaxed into full red roaring life by means of a complicated and ingenious arrangement of flues and dampers in the chimney and ovens. When the gaslights had not yet been lit by the tapers in the early morning, it would be so dark and shadowy in that basement kitchen that the range appeared like a long black dragon, sleeping against the end wall. With his big, red, fiery eye that never closed, he would watch us cross the flagstones. Only the gaslights could destroy the dragon's power.

All the top of the range was taken up by boiling or simmering cooking pots with rattling lids. A large, black, iron kettle lived there all the time. It was never off the hob because that was where the pots of tea were made that seemed to keep everybody going. The kettle sang breathy little tunes as wisps of steam drifted up to the high mantel shelf where the wooden clock stood – Mother usually looked worried after glancing at it.

The deep, dark ovens, which blasted forth delicious hot smells when opened, were usually crammed with sizzling roasts, rich steaming casseroles and savoury meat pies that oozed dark brown juices through their crisp pastry lids. Herbs and shallots, mushrooms and wine, these aromas were all mixed up with the sweet smells coming from bubbling fruit tarts, spice-laden cakes and treacly puddings. The cold puddings were made with masses of whipped cream, ratafia biscuits, purees of fresh fruit, pounded chestnuts and Bavarian creams, all sorts of things that tasted delicious when licked off the end of a wooden spoon. After these creations had been turned out upside down onto serving dishes and then decorated, they looked pretty enough to be worn as Sunday hats. The bouquets coming from the rich liqueurs that some of them contained were almost enough to knock me off my stool.

Rubbish and parings from the kitchen were taken along one of the corridors to the boiler room, where a big black 'donkey-boiler' the shape of a long suet pudding opened up its fire mouth at one end and ate all the rubbish up. All the pudding cloths, tea cloths and glass cloths were draped on a wooden clothes horse in there to dry. In the corners were piles of dusty coke, heaps of shiny black coal and great mounds of spidery logs, which the gardeners had trundled in on barrows ready for the winter.

Outside the boiler room was a flight of shallow steps, bordered ornamentally above by a stone balustrade with a wide flat top. Beside this were dark shrubberies, through which a cobbled pathway meandered off along the side of the house. I was not allowed to go along it. Sometimes I would climb up onto the top of the balustrade out of everybody's way. Lying there on my back, I would gaze up at the sky and at the tall chimneys on the rooftop high above me. The chimneys looked very old and I knew I was very young, but together we would just dream time away as the ever-changing clouds drifted slowly over us. From the shrubberies beside the house came a pungent smell of rotting leaves. From the thick walls of the old house itself came a fainter, but more persistent smell, of earthiness and decay.

꽃

When the Indian Maharaja and his Maharanee, and all their entourage arrived at Queensberry House later in that summer of 1932, the busy maids and menservants seemed to be racing up and down the stairs all day long, fetching and carrying and sometimes grumbling. Mainly, though, they were excited and stimulated by this new experience – or so it seemed to me. Listening to their chatter, I gathered that upstairs in the forbidden part of the house, there now lived even greater numbers of mysterious people. Beyond that green baize door at the top of the stairs, there were beautiful brown-skinned ladies dressed in coloured veils, which Mother said were called *saris*, who wore lots of bangles on their arms and jewels in their noses. The Indian women servants were 'very fussy', said one of the other housemaids, in a giggling whisper. They took 'brass bowls full of scented water' with them to the lavatory, so that they could wash themselves afterwards. There were also Indian men up there, I heard, dressed in white pyjamas: 'Tall, dark strangers,' one of the housemaids called them.

This sort of talk was all extremely interesting. But then I heard something that made me sit bolt upright on my stool. It seemed that the Maharaja and Maharanee had brought their two children with them. Someone said they were a little prince and princess. More importantly, someone else said that they were just a little bit older than I was.

3

Three Gifts from the Maharaja

Green moonlight was filtering in through our mossy little bedroom window. Awakening in my narrow bed that night, I thought about the Indian children sleeping somewhere in the great house above me. I wondered if the moon was also shining on them. It was strange and exciting to think that there were now four children lying within the walls of Queensberry House. In all my life I had had very little to do with any other children except my sister, although I did not realise at the time that this was in any way unusual. I just knew that I could not sleep for wondering about the young boy and girl who had come all the way from India, on a ship. Maybe they would play with me.

The next day I found that I could no longer see into the forbidden private garden, because the door was locked. It was kept locked all that summer. But I often heard the high-pitched laughter of the children coming from the other side of it. I pestered the gardeners so much to lift me up, that in the end they put an upside-down water butt beside a low part of the wall where a pear tree grew. They told me I could peer through the leaves, providing I was neither seen nor heard by anyone on the other side.

When I first saw the children, they were playing over by the big tree. They were dressed all in white. The boy was riding round and round the tree on a white tricycle. The girl was sitting on the grass playing with a toy monkey which had golden fur and pink ears. A woman wearing a blue sari was sitting on the circular seat under the tree, obviously supervising their play. Because their laughter carried, I came to know when they were playing outside. Then I would run to peep through the keyhole in the little green door and rattle the knob. But the door never budged. So, from among the leaves of the pear tree, I would watch them.

The fruit was ripening on the boughs, the days were shortening and withered rose petals were blowing across the lawns, and I felt it was no longer enough just to watch them. I suddenly realised that I badly wanted them to know that I was there, living in the same house as they were, almost playing in the same garden with them. I dared not risk calling out to them, or I should have been in trouble with the gardeners. But a great leap forward in my thinking processes now took place. All my previous naughtiness had been unintentional. Now, for the first time, I did something deliberate. I decided to let them know that I existed, not as something rustling in the shadows, that must not be seen, but as a real-life child with thoughts and feelings.

Climbing down from the water butt I sped into the house, through the basement corridors and out through the boiler room door. It had just occurred to me that if the gardeners brought logs in through that entrance, then the cobbled pathway might also lead into the forbidden garden. It did. Triumphantly, I ran down past the glorious beds of roses. Close up, I found that the roses grew much higher than I had imagined; some of them were actually taller than I was. Also, the grounds were much larger than I had seemed to observe from the other side of the wall. When I finally got to the big tree on the far side of the lawns where the children usually played, there was no sign of anybody at all. I ran around the circular seat in case they were hiding on the other side: nothing. Although my ears were still filled with the recent echoes of their laughter, the garden was empty and quite silent, except for the flapping wings of two or three large birds which flew up from one of the tallest trees.

There was a grassy part of the garden between where the roses ended and where the row of dark railings began. I could hardly see where I was going because of the tears that were beginning to distort my vision, but I stumbled over there so that I would be out of sight of the big house. There, where nobody could see me, I wept. It was not merely through my immediate disappointment: I ached with a kind of hollow loneliness for something that I did not quite understand.

Bees were droning in the heavily perfumed air. Over the high roses I could just see the thatched roof of the summerhouse – it looked golden in the blazing sunshine. The fountain tinkled like fairy music and through the railings I could see the silver river. I dried my eyes. Then, just as I was wondering whether to extend my search a little further or hurry back to the safety of the big kitchen, a group of grown-ups came along the river path. They stopped to look at the elegant house, its three-storied walls and ornamental parapets dreaming in the bright sunlight among the dark shrubberies beyond the lawns. After looking at the house their gaze fell upon the roses. Then they saw me. My first instinct was to hide: I was not supposed to be there. But the only sanctuary was the summerhouse and that was several yards away – too far for me to run to it. 'Hello,' one of the grown-ups said, bending over and speaking through the railings. 'You're a lucky little girl to live in that lovely old house.' 'Yes, I am,' I agreed. Apart from my parents, it was the first time anyone had ever spoken to me as an individual. It gave me a strange new feeling, which I liked.

As they continued on their way along the river path, I drew myself up straight, intrigued by the fact that they had obviously taken me for a child who had every right to be there in the garden. Slightly happier now, although shaken by such an unexpected encounter with people from the world outside Queensberry House, I made my way stealthily back to the boiler room, walking with my knees bent in the belief that it would make me less visible. But as I went I saw that on the hidden far side of the grounds, four Indian men were playing tennis on a grass court, while others watched. Some of the men wore white bands across their foreheads, and there was something else very strange about the way they were all dressed. Forgetting all caution, I ran to the kitchen as soon as I entered the house – full of what I had seen: 'Mummy, Mummy there's some funny men in the big garden, playing with bats and balls, and with their shirt tails hanging out!'

That afternoon my parents gave me a strict 'talking to' about my naughtiness. They not only looked sad while they did it, I thought, but they also seemed uncommonly agitated. I could not understand their extreme reaction: it was not as if I had picked the flowers. In spite of this confrontation though, I was deliberately naughty again quite soon afterwards.

Very early one afternoon, when the kitchen was all a-clatter with the sounds of a five- or six-course luncheon being cleared away and washed up after, and the tables and tops being scrubbed down, and preliminary preparations being made for tea, I decided that everyone was sufficiently preoccupied not to notice what I was doing. Slipping into the dark and deserted service lobby, I crept up the forbidden stairs. Then, with some difficulty, I pushed open the mysterious green baize door. The flash of unearthly light I had often glimpsed so briefly from the basement now shone steadily all around me.

Beyond that forbidden door, I saw what seemed to me like a world in reverse: a pillared fairyland of shimmering white marble. High up in the ceiling, above a curved marble staircase, was a dome made of coloured pieces of glass. Sunlight was streaming through it and staining every shining surface with dapplings of translucent colour. Crystal chandeliers were also catching the sunlight and turning it into rainbows of their own. Too bedazzled even to draw back in fright I just stood there, round-eyed and open-mouthed, immobile as any statue.

3. Behind the green baize door.

Still dumbfounded and motionless, I watched in dismay as the two footmen and my father came out of a wide double doorway across the circular hall, and saw me. As the white-gloved and liveried footmen held open the doors, a throng of people with ringing voices emerged into the hall. I saw my father put his hand quickly to his forehead before crossing the dazzling marble expanse in giant strides. He scooped me up in his arms and carried me downstairs, telling me what a bad girl I was. Yet all the time his voice was so tender that I sensed he would rather have been showing me even more wonderful and beautiful things upstairs. Downstairs he made me give a solemn promise that I would never do such a thing again, and later on, seeing the strange look which crossed my mother's face when she heard about my latest escapade, I knew that I would keep my promise.

Not long after this I witnessed a great commotion in the kitchen in the very middle of one lunch time. One of the footmen had brought down a message from the Maharanee. An early course of the meal had been some sort of fish, accompanied by a pretty pink sauce. I had watched the sauce being made from a great many shelled shrimps, pounded together with anchovies and other things. Now the Maharanee was asking for a sample of it to be sent up to her in a sealed jar. This was quickly done.

My mother was tense and edgy, wondering what was wrong, and even the maids were a bit twittery. Then my father came down. His eyes were sparkling. He explained that, apparently, the Maharaja was having two Rolls Royce limousines specially made for him while he was in England. The Maharanee had excitedly decided that the shrimp sauce on her plate was the exact colour she wanted for the upholstery of the cars. All the grown-ups below stairs seemed in a very good mood for days afterwards.

Also, I think it made our mother feel like quite a famous cook, when she realised that there would soon be two Rolls Royces driving around India with pink upholstery that was the exact colour of her special shrimp sauce.

Throughout what was left of the summer I still peeped, at intervals, over the wall. I never lost hope that one day some sort of contact might be made without actually disobeying any rules. I never spoke or called out to the children, and they never gave any sign of having seen me. But just to know they were there was like being part of a bigger world, somehow, and I liked it.

Then one day in autumn I was told that the Maharaja and all his entourage were going home to India. The long holiday was over. That meant, of course, that the children would go home also. That summer had been for me a very special, almost magical, era. Now it was ending. I must have looked as sad as I felt, for my mother put her arms around me one teatime and told me there was a present each for Joan and me in the bedroom. The two presents had been sent down to us from 'upstairs'.

The first thing I saw, peeping out through the bars of Joan's wooden cot, was the toy monkey with the golden fur and the pink ears. Somebody had brushed his fur and put a small child's necklace made of silver filigree and turquoise blue beads around his neck. Standing on the brown linoleum beside my bed was the white tricycle. Dangling from one of the handlebars was a small silver bangle.

There was no note attached to either gift. But I knew now that the Maharaja's children must have been aware that they had shared the same summer, in the same house, with the butler's children – even though we had never been allowed to meet. I pushed the silver bangle onto my skinny wrist, climbed on to the white tricycle and, simply bursting with happiness, pedalled wildly all around the echoing stone corridors of the Queensberry House basement, whooping with delight.

Several days later, just before they left for India, the Maharaja and Maharanee presented our father and mother with a very handsome gift of money. It was in return for what they described as 'very special service'.

Through listening to our parents' conversations shortly after this event, I became aware that they had, for some time, nurtured a special dream. In it we would all go to live in central London. Father, with his marvellous references from lords and ladies of the realm, would be given the pick of all the best waiters' jobs, in the finest places. He would surely become a headwaiter quite quickly, at somewhere very special, and he would earn so much money that we would all be secure.

We would have a home of our own for the very first time: a place where Joan and I could laugh and shout and run in and out of all the rooms. We would even have a front door, with a key. Best of all our mother wouldn't have to be a cook working alongside our father in order that we could all be together, either living in a tied cottage or below stairs, because he would earn enough money to rent somewhere that was not dependent on his job – a place where our security could not be threatened by my adventurous spirit. In their dream Father would go out to work for a set number of hours, like other men, and leave it all behind him when he got home. Our mother would stay at home as, apparently, most other mothers did, just looking after us all and making a lovely place for us to live in, happily ever after.

The only trouble with this dream, it seemed, was that they had never been able to save enough money to cover them while they made the transition from the old way of life into the new. The unexpectedly generous gift from the Indians had at last made it possible. On Saturday 28 January 1933, the four of us, all wearing our best winter clothes, sat excitedly in the swaying and creaking wooden carriage of a steam train. Filled with anticipation and optimism we watched ragged drifts of white and grey smoke fly past the windows and listened to the clickety-clack of the wheels, as we sped along the rails to central London, where the dream would begin.

Over on the mainland of Europe, a man called Adolph Hitler was within hours of being made Chancellor of the German Reich. But we were not aware of that. And even if we had been, it would have meant nothing to us.

4

The Dream Begins

As we emerged from the station into the ancient busy streets of what was then regarded, by many people, as the most important city in the world, the chimney pots on high were almost the first thing I noticed. In one glance upwards, I saw literally hundreds of them standing in black rows against the wintry sky, and from every one of them came outpourings of grey or brown smoke to add to the general murk. Soot was actually falling down out of the sky like a fine dust, and all around us I saw that every surface, both horizontal and vertical, was begrimed with a thick layer, most of it caked hard and solid. The acrid smell of the soot and the homely smell of chimney smoke was all mixed up with traffic fumes and the pungent aroma of horse dung.

Then there was the noise. The rumbling roar of the motor traffic was almost drowned by the grinding of metal-rimmed cart wheels on the road surfaces and the

47

clopping of horses' hooves. The yells of street traders, the ringing of bicycle bells and the plaintive notes of street singers and musicians, all intermingled into one great sound. It was as if somebody had suddenly opened the lid of a peculiar, and curiously strident, musical box.

Our new home in London turned out to be a two-roomed apartment in Homer Street in Marylebone. It was at the top of a six-storey late-Victorian building constructed of dark red brick with white facings. It was splendidly ornamented in a mixture of styles that I was too young to recognise as a combination of Gothic, Baroque and Queen Anne revival – but the whole effect was quite pleasing. Our apartment was number 67, the very last one in Crawford Buildings. It was high up among a panorama of sooty, grimy rooftops and large hosts of twittering London sparrows. Always before, if we had wanted to see anything from our basement window in Queensberry House, we had had to look upwards. Now, from the arched windows of our new home, we had to look down-wards – a long way downwards it seemed to us.

But there was plenty to look at and so many people to both see and hear. Apart from the cries of London, the street calls of traders and others as they went about their business in the early 1930s, and the constant hum of the busy traffic mingling with the varying sounds of horses' hooves, there was a seemingly never-ending ringing of countless church bells from steepled sky-lines both near and far. All these sounds were borne upwards to our high windows on the soot-laden breezes.

There were three round things up in the sky with us. One was the sun, another was the moon, and the other was the big round face of the clock above Marylebone Station. Straight over the rooftops, it was about three or four streets away, and it was on the highest building. Our father tried to explain its relative size to us by saying: 'You could put a double bed onto the face of that clock, and there would still be enough space left for a wash-stand and a couple of wardrobes, too.'

Between the clock and us, just below our eye-line was a vast plantation of domestic chimney pots – thousands of them in all different sizes, shapes and styles. They all seemed to be in constant use and all issued forth variously-coloured plumes or billows of smoke. Sometimes sparks came out of them as well. And just as all the people in the streets below wore some sort of head gear, so too did nearly all the chimney pots above wear funny hats. They were called cowlings. Some were hooded like cloche hats, or Y-shaped like pairs of trousers turned upside down, while others bent over like fat question marks. Some had weather vanes perched on top of them, many surmounted by sooty metal cockerels, running foxes or sailing ships, their ornamental shapes silhouetted flat against the sky when standing sideways-on to winds from the north west.

Most chimney pots had been fitted with lightning-conductors. Like raised batons above a hundred hidden orchestras, they pointed forever upwards from the smoke. Many of the chimney cowlings were designed to spin in the breezes, sending out feathers of smoke in all directions.

The cowlings on our own two chimneys were like that. On windy days they creaked and rattled as they twisted backwards and forwards on their high perch between us and the empty sky.

Our rooms seemed 'set apart' from the other 66 apartments in Crawford Buildings. There were five long, shallow flights of stone stairs and the same number of wide landings leading up to it. Their surfaces had all been polished to shiny smoothness by the thousands of boots and shoes which must have climbed them since they were first built. There were four brown-painted doors on each rectangular landing, all of which had neat doormats outside them and brightly shining door knockers, door-knobs, and door sills, all made of brass. The whole building was divided into three separate blocks, one of which was approached through an archway. The three blocks clustered around a wide tarmacadamed space at the back, which was known as 'the courtyard', and it was here that most of the children used to play – that is, when they were not out playing in the streets or in the parks.

Outside our own front door was yet another flight of stone steps, which led up to a flat, high-railinged section of the roof. My sister and I were practically the only children to use that rooftop eyrie. Peeping through the soot-blackened railings for the first time we saw all that part of London which was soon to become 'our territory'. From what we saw spread out below us we also realised how very central our new home was. It was situated in the middle of a square mile of busy thoroughfares and quiet tree-lined squares all bounded by four historic highways: Baker Street, Oxford Street, the Edgware Road and the Old Marylebone Road. At the north-east corner of that square of territory was Regent's Park, set amid the gracious Nash Terraces. To the south west was Hyde Park, Marble Arch and Tyburn. Each park was about ten minutes' walk from our home and we could see the uppermost leaves of the trees from our rooftop. The streets were soon to be our playgrounds and the parks our countryside.

We quickly discovered that within that area of Marylebone there were some of the most interesting contrasts to be found in London. From dingy cobbled Dickensian courts, gaslit alleys, pump-yards and stables, to internationally renowned shopping districts and the elegant Georgian Squares. From the old, forbidding-looking workhouse on the other side of Baker Street, to the smartly dressed tourists and sightseers who queued outside Madame Tussauds just a matter of yards away from the workhouse. Long shuffling lines of quiet, solemn-faced men waited outside the dole offices on the Marylebone Road just around the corner from Homer Street – while a few blocks away in the other direction, well-heeled shoppers promenaded beside the sumptuous and brightly lit window displays of the most fashionable and famous of West-End stores, and socialites drove in taxis or chauffeured limousines along Park Lane and into Mayfair.

But when the 'pea-souper' fogs crept over the city, all familiar sights and sounds disappeared or were distorted – baffling our perceptions and so misleading our feet that we could almost have believed that we had wandered, some-how, into another age. The fog-wreathed gas lamps, lit at noon, would glimmer dimly on high, like faint stars seen through mist. All motor traffic would come to a stand-still, and all that could be heard on the eerie highways were the muted clip-cloppings of hooves and the ghostly grinding of cart wheels as a few tardy wagoners hand-led their horses blindly back to cobbled mews turnings and stable blocks in order to bide their time. It was then that Marylebone seemed to slip back three or four decades into the days of Sherlock Holmes, and all the trappings of the 1930s seemed no more than a dream.

As soon as Joan and I were old enough we were allowed to roam the streets freely and to, more or less, go anywhere we pleased. Apart from the traffic, there was no serious danger to children. As well as us, most adults went everywhere on foot, so that even though we might seem to be alone, we were not really so. Those men and women – other children's mothers and fathers, uncles and aunts and so on – seemed like part of an extended family. If you did anything wrong they would 'tell you off', and if you were in trouble they would help you. Once when Joan fell into the boating pond in Regent's Park, before she had had time to 'go down twice', the grown-ups rushed forward and pulled her out. She refused to take her clothes off so that they could be wrung out, so they dried her as best they could with handkerchiefs and cardigans. Then a gentleman wearing a bowler hat and pinstriped trousers and other smart clothes, handed a ten-shilling note to the women so that they could help bundle us into the taxi that he flagged down for us, with his rolled umbrella, at the Hanover Gate. The taxi driver put his mackintosh on the seat. Later he opened the cab door for us outside Crawford Buildings. The other Homer Street children stared at us goggle-eyed as I proudly escorted my dripping sister in through the archway. None of us had ever travelled in a taxi before – or even a car – and apart from that one grand homecoming, most of us never did.

We also had the protection of the policemen, who went around mostly on foot or on bicycles. They were the friendly caped and helmeted men with bull's-eye lanterns, who always seemed to appear from the vapours at just the right moment whenever we were lost in a fog. To us they were like magical genies, who could do almost anything. They were also 'father-figures' to us, and all children were taught, at school and elsewhere, to respect them and look upon them as our guardians and friends. And they responded with great kindness.

When we first came to Marylebone we were still very young of course; I had my fifth birthday on the last day of February in that year of 1933, and Joan became three years old on 14 June. So in those early days we were taken on walks of exploration mostly by our parents. Joan sat comfortably in her blue pushchair but my legs had to go 'twenty to the dozen' along miles of ancient pavements. Nearly all of them were studded with the round metal lids of the coal cellars beneath, and all the road surfaces were made yellow with dried up and flattened remains of horses' dung. Beside the kerbstones, about half a mile apart at most, were drinking troughs for the horses. They were made of stone, or pink granite, and were usually inscribed with the names of ladies or gentlemen who had arranged for them to be placed there in memory of somebody. Sometimes there were small blocks of stone steps beside them where people, a little time before so Father said, had been able to dismount from and then remount their horses or carts. There were also drinking fountains erected at frequent intervals for the use of humans. They were made of the same pink and grey polished granite and had heavy metal cups hanging from them by stout chains. Those cups made the water taste cool and refreshing. Father conjectured that the water might even have been drawn up from hidden springs deep below the earth. Mother said we must always be sure to wipe the rims of the cups with our handkerchiefs before drinking from them.

To both my delight and alarm I saw that there were hundreds of children playing in the streets as we went along. Some of them were having fun on homemade swings, the ropes hanging from the ladder-brackets of the gas lamps. Others played skipping games in groups, chanting sing-song rhymes about people with names like Oliver Cromwell and Charlie Chaplin. Many boys and girls played competitive games with glass marbles, rolling them along the gutters, while others crouched down busily over coloured pavement chalks or played one-legged hopscotch, or darted around with squeals of excitement playing 'tag'.

Some boys proudly rode homemade scooters up and down the roadways, making a lot of noise and sparks as they purposely let the metal 'blakeys' on the bottoms of their boots drag along the road surfaces. They had all made their own scooters from sawn-up orange boxes, we found out, and the running-boards often had bits of stencilled words on them, like 'Empire Grown'. Many little girls sedately pushed their dolls along beside the house walls or area railings, in hooded high prams made of wood or wickerwork. There also seemed to be a great many games that were played with dirty-looking tennis balls. Quite a few children played at juggling, with as many as four balls at once. But most prevalent of all were the children chasing wooden spinning-tops along the flagstones, lashing them along with wooden-handled leather whips.

At first, I wondered what I would have to do in order to become a part of those noisy, and often grubby, groups of happy children. In the end it turned out to be quite easy. When not at school, sleeping, eating or running errands, they all seemed to spend their lives in the streets, 'out in the fresh air' as their parents put it, and they just pulled us into their games as a matter of course. I soon learnt to understand the way they talked and to realise that even though some of the poorest children had patched or tattered clothes – elbows sticking out of jumper sleeves and shoes or boots lined with cardboard to cover the gaping holes in the worn-through leather soles – they were often the most fun to be with.

The only time Joan and I were disappointed with our new friends during those early days was when our mother had taken us, and the Queensberry House tricycle and toy monkey, down into the courtyard of Crawford Buildings to play while she prepared our midday meal. Feeling very hungry we failed to wait for her return but made our own way up all the steps to number 67. We left our toys behind us as we had always done in the kitchen gardens at Richmond. Our mother raced with us down all the steps again to retrieve those gifts from the Maharaja's children. But when we reached the courtyard they had gone, and we never saw them again. We cried bitterly at our loss. At the same time, I also realised why, despite our protests, our mother had taken the Indian silver necklace and bangle into her safe keeping 'until we were older'. It was all part of our first lesson in becoming proper 'London Children'.

❦

In the spring of 1933 I started school at St Mary's Church of England Mixed Boys, Girls and Infants. It was in Wyndham Place, two turnings along Crawford Street from Homer Street and three from Baker Street, and it was there that the widening of my horizons was accelerated. I not only learnt about other children, but I became aware of a thing called 'history'.

My school, it seemed, had been built more than a hundred years before: in 1824. It had already been standing there, in all its brown-bricked Georgian grace, when the lady on most of our pennies, Queen Victoria, had been a little girl. One of our playgrounds was in the courtyard at the back, but when it was rainy we got our fresh air as it blew sideways in great draughts through an open-sided basement under the building next to the row of miniature lavatories in the 'front area'. That cellar-like playground and its iron supports smelled of a very old London. Later, when I read the stories of Charles Dickens, I found it intriguing to think that the school bell in the turret above St Mary's had tolled out over the Marylebone rooftops all through the times of Oliver Twist, Scrooge, Fagin, Bill Sykes, Little Nell and all the rest. Sherlock Holmes seemed quite modern by comparison with Dickens and St Mary's. Even the public house across the road from the school, The Duke of Wellington, had, we were told, been built at the same time and commemorated the – then recent – battle of Waterloo.

Soon after I went to school I came to realise that our family was now what was known as 'respectable working class'. Just like the 'rich–poor' district we lived in, we too were beginning to have an identity. We had become 'real people'. The Maharaja's gift of money had gone into a post office savings account. Part of it had been used for the actual removal and then some more of it had gone towards purchasing enough second-hand furniture to fill our two rooms. Mahogany, rosewood, wickerwork: none of it matched anything else but it all jumbled together happily and comfortably, and we were proud of our new home. The gramophone lived in one of the cupboards with the records. The blue-covered ottoman chest, full of linen and smelling of lavender and orris root, which had been stored in the hayloft at Richmond, now stood under our living-room window. It made a cosy seat for watching the chimney pots.

Our mother had also spent ten shillings on a second-hand Singer sewing machine. It lived in a wooden compartment on top of its own polished table which had wrought iron supports and a treadle below. When our mother worked the treadle with her feet, a bullet-shaped shuttle full of cotton thread sped back and forth to form the underneath of the stitches. Apart from now being able to make or alter clothes for herself and us more quickly, she was soon making curtains and cushions, all in a matching warm and pretty-coloured chintz material, most of it purchased from Selfridges' hot and crowded 'Bargain Basement'.

'Warm and pretty' were the two words which soon described our home. It was bright and cosy and clean. It was soft with cushions and chintz covers, the starched white dimity curtains hanging daintily across the lower half of the windows. There was always at least one vase filled with fresh flowers and our rooms smelled of Mansion polish. There was lots of gleaming brass, polished up like pieces of gold. Even the black-leaded fire range shone like precious metal. When it was dark, our rooms were made even warmer by the yellow glow coming from the 'popping' gas lamps on the wall, and also from the golden flames leaping up from the burning coals and the rosy shadows dancing on the walls.

The fire range, which was like a much smaller version of the one in the Queensberry House kitchen, was actually in our living room as, so I found out, were all the other ranges in Crawford Buildings, for all the apartments were similar in design. There were also big, black, iron gas stoves in all the living rooms that I saw. But most women, like our own mother, liked to do all the 'proper cooking' in the fire ovens. They said that the food, especially the bread and cakes and the roasts, tasted better when 'cooked in the old ways'. Like ourselves, many of the families had originally come from 'in the country', brought to London because the fathers were looking for work. Many of the mothers had brought with them the ways of country women. One of those ways (as in our own home) was that, except in high summer, the fire ranges were lit every day. It was more economical to do so. The families of the city generation, however, were more likely to make use of the gas stoves, which were quicker and didn't require so much planning or polishing. I first noticed this disparity when I was with friends in the various apartments when the 'gas man' called. After emptying out all the pennies from the gas meters onto the living-room tables, and entering the amounts into his book, counting out the coins into piles of twelve, the amounts of 'rebate' that the gas man gave back to other mothers was always much greater where the families spoke like Londoners of long-standing.

Just like at Richmond, a big, black, iron kettle sat singing on our hearth or hob all day, little wisps of steam curling up to the mantel shelf above where the wooden-cased clock, the fire spills, the tea caddy, the candlestick (in case the gas mantle broke or the meter suddenly ran out of pennies) and the letter rack, all lived. We were shielded from the fire by a brass-railed nursery fireguard. Night clothes, underclothes or bed linen were often draped over the fireguard to warm or air, but only when our mother was in the room with us and keeping a sharp eye on it.

Within the fireguard wire-mesh confines stood the coal scuttle, bellows, poker, coal tongs, brush and shovel, and any other apparatus required for the lighting of the fire and keeping it burning – for the living-room fire was the heart and hub of the home. Some people had 'chimney curtains' hanging in frills or drapes from their mantel shelves. They were made either of cretonne or velvety material and their function was to prevent soot and smoke from discolouring the ceilings. Also, in times of high winds or heavy fogs, half the soot and all the smoke in the chimneys would come falling, thudding, or roaring back down them again, quickly filling the rooms with acrid smoke and setting everyone off coughing and opening the front doors for air. It was not uncommon to see a landing full of people after a particularly strong gust of wind had turned their living rooms into extensions of their chimneys. They would all then laugh and chatter to each other, especially about their bronchitis.

Most people had a big nail hammered into each side of their chimney-breasts. On one hung the toasting fork and on the other hung 'The Cane'. In nearly every household where there were children there was a cane hanging by the fire. They were hooked over at the top like Charlie Chaplin's walking stick but were thin and bendy. They were not stout or heavy enough to do any damage but could give a nasty sting. In fact, the canes were rarely used. They just had to be pointed at by parents and the children usually did as they were told.

The canes at school were used about once a month or so, usually on one or other of the boys. But the threat of it worked as a deterrent to misbehaviour. As a rule, any boy who had gone so far as to be punished in this way by a teacher or, in the case of real 'wickedness' by the headmaster (whose cane was rumoured to have big spikes sticking out of it – especially by returning caned boys) would usually not dare to tell their parents about it. The parents knew that the caning was rarely done unjustly, and so they would give their sons another 'taste of the cane' at home as well. 'That's for letting us down at school,' the boys would be told as they spat on their stinging fingers or rubbed the seat of their trousers. We did not witness these punishments of course, but the parents often told each other about it afterwards, and all children listened in to grown-up conversations. It was one of the main ways we learnt about our world.

At school we were taught 'The Three Rs', and it was at home that we were expected to learn the 'social graces' that would one day turn us into acceptable adults: such as having good manners, respecting older people, being honest, working hard, being thrifty and learning to dance.

All the children we knew, including ourselves, learnt to dance by copying their parents and practising with each other. Nearly every evening our gramophone, like a great many others in Crawford Buildings, was brought out of the cupboard, set upon the table, wound up and a new needle selected for it from a little tin box. Then we played or, later on, did our homework, to a musical background provided by our parents' collection of shiny black shellac records. There were dozens of them, mostly old love songs and dance tunes from their courting days in the Twenties.

Before we went to bed the furniture would be drawn back, the rugs rolled up, and our parents would quick-step or foxtrot all around the linoleum living-room floor. Joan and I, after watching awhile, would dance with each other or with our parents. Dancing was important to learn properly because, so we were told, that was the way most people got to know each other before they married. It was usually when we were learning to dance that our parents, especially our mother, would tell us about how they first came to meet. The story was told to us piecemeal over the years. But the pieces were regaled sufficiently often for an important part of the lives of those many people who had been servants in the Twenties and before to be revealed to us.

It had long been the custom for the servants of all the big country houses within a radius of ten miles or so from each other to hold regular monthly dances and social evenings to which the off-duty staff of all the other big houses were invited. Some servants travelled to the dances by country train and others went by bicycle. In the Twenties, as in the Thirties, 'ordinary' people did not own cars.

On the nights of the 'host' dances, which were held in the various servants' halls or recreation rooms, the music was provided by gramophone, piano and song. Trestle tables laden with food, tea, lemonade and beer would line the end walls. The sandwiches, pork pies, cakes, trifles and so on, although simple fare, were usually of top quality. The various cooks liked to compete with each other, aware that there could be no sterner judges than other know-ledgeable servants.

As soon as someone had wound up the gramophone and put a record onto the baize-covered turntable, the music would begin. Two senior members of staff would step forward to start the dance: usually a butler and a cook, or a steward and a housekeeper. When they had been 'once around the floor', all the other grades of servants both indoor and outdoor would join in and mix and mingle in the dance. It was the only time and place, so our parents told us, where the strict social grading within the domestic hierarchy was relaxed to some extent. It was quite possible then to see governesses dancing with first footmen and valets dancing with kitchen maids. Even nannies were sometimes seen dancing with gardeners or grooms.

All the men wore their best suits, sometimes with flowers in their buttonholes, which the resident garden-ers would 'eye' suspiciously, wondering if any of their own best blooms were missing. The women showed off their party frocks, often hand-sewn by themselves, with lots of tucking and fringes of drawn thread-work, and appliquéd beads. Both the men and the women would be wearing their slippery-soled dance shoes, which had been carried there in brown-paper parcels tied with string. The dust would rise as the jolly couples twirled round and round the parquet, stone or linoleum floor, to the rhythms of the quickstep, the foxtrot and the tango. Sometimes an older record would be put on and then everyone would gallop around the room to a rousing polka or join hands for the 'Sir Roger de Coverley'. New gramophone records were being added all the time.

Halfway through the dance came the time to stop for food. There was usually a scramble for the piano then, for it could be counted upon that several eager piano players would be present. The one who reached the piano stool first would place his or her plate of food and drink on the top while they thumbed through a dog-eared pile of sheet music. Then the popular songs of the day, interspersed with a few traditional airs, would be banged out on the keys and gradually, towards the end of the munchings, swallowings, laughter and general chatter everyone would join in a rousing sing-song. Everyone always knew all the words.

After the singing it would be: 'Everybody back into the centre for the "Ladies' Excuse Me" dance'. Those were the times when new scullery maids were dared to ask the butler for a dance, but never did. There were never any 'wallflowers' left sitting on the side. Everybody both young and old would dance. Although usually the older ones would 'give up' and sit down later in the evening and 'just watch' the proceedings from then on.

One or two elderly retainers, who still kept to the genteel customs of their original 19th-century employers by wearing gloves while dancing, might now be discreetly fanning themselves with those items. As the room became even warmer, matronly cooks or housekeepers could be seen covertly trying to wriggle themselves into more comfortable positions within their whalebone corsets. Often then, a pantry-man would emerge quietly from a side door and pass a tray to one of the resident footmen. On it would be 'a drop of port' or 'something stronger' for the seniors. Someone might then turn the gas lamps on the walls down a bit lower, and open the windows a bit more, while the younger servants danced the rest of the evening away until their feet were sore, and the Last Waltz was being played.

When the social evening ended, some of the older visiting servants were sometimes to be seen in the courtyard being 'handed up' into a pony trap or similar vehicle, by a coachman or groom who had 'borrowed' the conveyance for the evening. Others, if they lived quite a distance away, would walk or cycle to the nearest country railway station, stowing their bicycles in the guard's van when the last train of the evening appeared. Then the little train, having at least one of its compartments filled with bright-eyed but sleepy servants, would puff away to an echoey hoot in the night air.

The remainder of the revellers would journey all the way back on foot or by bicycle. Soon the quiet country roads and lanes leading away from the scene of jollity would ring to the sound of singing and laughter, as bands of tired but happy servants made their way homewards again – under the stars. The various 'big houses', dreaming in their landscaped grounds or parklands, would be all safely shuttered, bolted and barred for the night, except for one small well-guarded door at the back of each establishment. These doors, leading to the domestic quarters, would be merely locked, waiting for the revellers' return.

In the kitchen of each great house, probably sitting in the cook's chair and with his feet up by the kitchen fire, would be one of the footmen who had stayed on duty. On hearing three knocks and a whistle through the keyhole, or whatever was the password for that night, he would jump up to unlock the door and let them all in. The grooms, gardeners and chauffeur would have already disappeared into their rooms in outbuildings within the grounds. When everyone else was safely in the house, the footman would turn the giant keys, shoot the bolts, wedge the bars and hang the burglar bells. Then everyone would retire quietly to their own quarters where, in their own words, they would: 'sleep the sleep of the just.'

After an evening of 'learning to dance' in our Crawford Buildings home, the shiny surfaces of our records reflecting the gas lights and the fire light as they went round and round, Joan and I would be happily exhausted by bed time. Then we would snuggle under the bedclothes and listen from behind the door separating the two rooms, to the music still playing, softly now, as our parents continued to

4. Dancing to the gramophone.

dance. More often than not we would fall asleep with the gentle tones of 'Whispering Jack Smith' singing, so aptly: 'We're happy in our blue heaven'. But the happiness was not to last.

5

Ghosts and Shadows, Dust and Dreams

Our first spring in London had been filled with hope and excitement. It had also been bolstered by the money gift from the Maharaja.

I knew that my father spent a great deal of time looking for employment and that now and then he obtained a night's work at one or two places, especially at the Ranelagh Club, or wherever a special function had been arranged. Sometimes this involved the hired waiters being dressed up as 18th- or 19th-century English flunkeys in brocaded tail coats and breeches, white stockings, buckled shoes and with lacey frills at their cuffs and throat. Also, they had to wear white powdered wigs.

On our breakfast plates the following mornings my sister and I would find balloons, squeakers, paper streamers and silver masks which he had brought home for us.

Sometimes there would also be Japanese paper fans and petits fours – marzipan fruits and juicy grapes enclosed in brittle cases of boiled sugar. He also brought home the special menus of the many-coursed dinners, and I would polish up my reading skills while dreaming over the exotic contents of those – sometimes gravy-stained – pages.

I noticed that Father always seemed relieved at having found some job of work to do, however small or temporary, and that his dream of quickly becoming a headwaiter was rarely mentioned now. But he was never too pleased with the jobs where he had to wear a powdered wig while he was working because, he said, they were hot and uncomfortable.

One of his funny stories, much loved by us, was first told to us after one of the Ranelagh Club parties. Our father had apparently had experiences with flunkey costumes before. He reminded us that when at the age of sixteen he had been promoted to a third footman at Keele Hall in Staffordshire, they had measured him for two smart suits of livery. One was up to date and very suitable for 1918, the tailcoat having eight silver-crested buttons on the front, four on the back and four on the waistcoat. With the dress shirt he wore a stiff white upstanding collar and a white bow tie. When he was upstairs at the front of the house he also wore white cotton gloves.

At the same time they had provided him with a splendid suit of flunkey livery for use at banquets and balls. With it he was given a silver wig and a box of wig powder. He soon found out why the other footmen grumbled about it. The white powder fell down onto their costumes while they were working, and although it was brushed out before they finally went to sleep in the small hours, it nevertheless found its way onto the dark material of their ordinary liveries, where it lodged in the seams and necessitated a lot of extra valeting.

He had been told that footmen were expected to be handsome and elegant, if it was at all possible. At sixteen he was quite sure that his nose was too broad. It had been perfectly all right, he thought, back on the farm helping with the hay-making, leading horses, stone picking or scaring crows. But the other young footmen had begun teasing him about it. Very soon, every time he stood in the long dining room behind the chairs of titled people or assisted in clearing away the used silver or chinaware, while the butler carved and the head footmen and upper menservants served the following courses, he became convinced that everyone was staring at his nose.

The next time that one of the bands of gypsy women ventured on to the estate and called at the tradesmen's entrance with their baskets of handmade clothes pegs for sale, Father acquired one for himself and hid it in the lining-pocket of his tail coat. The clothes peg was made of two shaped pieces of whittled softwood, bound loosely at the top by a narrow strip of tin. Every night for a month, after the gas lights were turned off in the footmen's dormitory, and there was reassuring steady breathing or snoring coming from the other narrow beds, Father carefully attached the clothes peg to his nose and, with it poking up unseen into the air, went to sleep on his back.

The cure did not work. To make matters worse his nose became very tender. Young third footmen were not supposed to have noses which were so red and swollen that it looked as though they had been down in the wine cellars drinking all the port. Before long he realised that there had been nothing wrong with his nose anyway.

From our parents' fireside tales and bedtime stories in London, we learnt a lot about their past and, therefore, about ourselves. We developed a sense of 'continuity' and 'roots'. We also learnt from asking questions and they never left a query unanswered if they could help it. If they did not know the answers they would help us to look them up in the handsome set of children's encyclopaedias they had purchased one day from a doorstep salesman. It took them many months to pay off the debt but those volumes became a source of inspiration and entertainment for all four of us.

Our father, in particular, was a voracious reader. He had first discovered this joy when, as a young second footman at Lilleshall Hall in Shropshire, he had spent several months of one year helping his employer to catalogue his library. Officially, Father's part in the operation consisted of polishing the covers and spines of the leather-bound books, while a secretary–librarian did the actual cataloguing. But his employer, who was overseeing, noted Father's interest in the writings and told him he could borrow any of the beautiful volumes whenever he wanted to. In this way our father had entered a new world, opened up for him by the English classics.

He still had several Victorian bound editions of *Punch*, presented to him by one of his employers, and a set of old books bound in green leather which bore the title 'Old and New London' embossed on them in fading gold. As they had been published in the 19th century, the 'old' stories they contained were very old indeed. Father treated them reverently as though they were a treasure trove that he had discovered for himself. We referred to them as 'Father's green books'.

In his delving into the wordy chapters he somehow managed to pull out the best plums – the sorts of stories his little daughters could digest. He would then re-tell us the stories, using words of his own that we could understand. Soon afterwards he would take us for walks to visit the actual places where those fascinating events had happened. They were not the sort of happenings to be found in our history books. They were mostly not important enough for that. They were human stories about very human incidents. Our father's translations of them made the people seem so real to us, that we were given a vivid insight into the bygone life and times of our surroundings. The impact of these tales made me so keenly sensitive to the past, that there were times when I would walk through the Georgian Squares or wander along ancient highways, with the feeling that I was accompanied by the shadowy phantoms of people of long ago.

Whenever possible, at first, he tried to keep to stories about Old Marylebone, so that we did not 'wear out too much shoe-leather' or 'spend a fortune on penny bus fares'.

But Marylebone by itself provided us with a treasure trove of scenes from the past. Whenever we walked southwards along Baker Street, for instance, my eyes would automatically turn to the right a few moments before we came to the Selfridges' Food Hall – and I would practically see ghosts in Portman Square. There, under the trees of the railinged garden in the centre, I would see a vivid imaginary gathering of 18th-century chimney sweeps. They would have greenery on their hats and festooned around their necks, and be dancing and making merry beside long tables piled high with rich food, which was being served to them by elegant flunkeys. These hundreds of revelling chimney sweeps would be even easier to imagine if the date also happened to be the first of May.

The reason for this revelry was that, according to legend, a Mrs Montague had once lived in Portman Square – not always happily – for something tragic had occurred while she was there. A nephew of her husband, a child of four years of age who was much loved by her, had been stolen one day when out with his nurse. Kidnapped. A year of frantic searching had failed to find him. But one May day, when Mrs Montague had sent out for some sweeps to clean her chimneys, the first ones picked off the streets came in with two sooty little boys in tow – one of whom began yelling at the top of his voice so that a number of maids and menservants came running. The little chimney-sweep boy, in great agitation, claimed that he recognised his surroundings and wished to see Mrs Montague, his aunt.

The maids washed a clean space on his face so that his features showed through, while Mrs Montague, having been notified, hastened below stairs. During the emotional reunion that ensued, four footmen grabbed hold of the adult chimney sweeps, thinking they were the kidnappers. But the little boy shouted 'No!' He had been sold to them by the man and woman 'baby-snatchers' who stole him, and the sweeps had treated him reasonably well.

Mrs Montague was so grateful that, until she died in the year 1800, she gave a great feast every year on the first of May on the green space in front of her Portman Square house. All the chimney sweeps in London had an open invitation to it, and it became known as 'The Sweeps' Feast'.

Father's green books, or rather his interpretation of them, made us even more curious about our surroundings. As soon as we were old enough we used to go by ourselves around Marylebone, searching out the older places – the secluded backwaters and hidden courts. Some of the back courts still had pumps in them which drew up water from underground wells or springs. We were still very young when we first made one of these discoveries, for we found a pump that was situated almost on our own doorstep. It stood at the centre of an almost forgotten piece of London known as Freshwater Place. This hidden court was in Homer Street, lying between Crawford Buildings and the Marylebone Road. It was set back behind the other late Georgian and early Victorian houses in the street and could only be approached through a low archway, which had a spiked post set in the middle of the entrance. Our mother thought the post had probably been put there in olden days to prevent water carts making a nuisance of themselves by rumbling in and out all the time to draw water up through the pump.

When Joan and I wandered in through that deep archway for the first time, we found ourselves facing a broad rectangle of shaggy grass, like a village green. It was surrounded on three sides by old tumbledown two-storey cottages with small windows and very low doors. Cottagey flowers grew in pots on the windowsills, and the people who lived there seemed to be mainly late middle-aged or elderly. Some of the women wore shawls around their shoulders as they sat on chairs in their doorways to 'get the air'. Many of them knitted woollen socks on metal needles. *Click-click-click* went the knitting needles in the old women's hands as they talked or gossiped with each other. The old men sat with their newspapers, smoking white clay pipes, or pottering with the plants or with the sweet peas and passion flowers which had been trained on trellises up the cottage walls.

Sometimes the men took a 'constitutional' walk to the Beehive public house, which was to the right of the archway. The old women could often be seen on Fridays walking down Homer Street on their way to visit Mr Philips's grocer's shop at the corner. Their 'walking-out clothes' were nearly all in the fashion of Edwardian days: long black coats and skirts which came down to their laced or buttoned boots and wide-brimmed high-crowned black hats. Everyone was very polite and helpful to these old people, and they looked after themselves in the rented cottages until they died. Their clothes nearly always smelled of mothballs. Their homes smelled of oil lamps for there was no gas or electricity in them.

In Freshwater Place itself, a pathway of ancient uneven flagstones not only linked all the cottages together, but also crossed the grass in three places so that people could reach the pump in the middle without ever having to walk through the wet undergrowth. Father, after consulting his green books, was of the opinion that the cottages had been there in the early-19th or late-18th century, or even earlier. They had certainly been there, he said, when the site of Marylebone Station was a green stretch of orchard and cultivated land known as 'Jenkins's Botanic Gardens', and when the waste land around Lisson Grove was plagued by footpads and highwaymen. We found this especially exciting as there was not much crime in our district in the 1930s.

Just around the corner on the Marylebone Road was a very old public house called The Yorkshire Stingo. We learnt from the books that before Sir Robert Peel brought organised policing onto the London streets in 1829, The Yorkshire Stingo had been an assembly point for law-abiding citizens to form themselves into groups: checking that they had sufficient defences in the way of truncheons, and even guns, before setting out to traverse Lisson Grove on their way to St John's Wood.

There had been similar assembly points all over London, the most interesting, to our minds, being on the other side of Hyde Park in Knightsbridge. Tucked in close to a high wall where the park became Kensington Gardens was a notorious den of thieves, robbers, footpads and highwaymen. They congregated in an old inn and stables, which was known as 'The Half Way House'. So dangerous had it become for ordinary people to walk the journey between the Hyde Park Barracks and Kensington that a hand bell was rung outside the barracks at hourly intervals, to mark the spot where people wishing to find 'safety in numbers' could assemble into a group before setting out. On dark or foggy days, the barracks would often provide two or three mounted guards to accompany the frightened people.

Although our living room seemed full of books, our father still told us stories at night, often making up his own, which either has us rolling around with laughter in the little bed we shared, or else clutching the sheets in delicious terror. He regularly took us for long walks in Hyde Park, Regent's Park or Kensington Gardens, going on for miles it seemed, only stopping now and then when there was something that required us to stand still in order to observe it properly, such as Dingle Dell, in Hyde Park, with its rabbits and red squirrels, or the occasional small flock of sheep which grazed beneath the park trees within temporary enclosures of handmade wooden hurdles.

Sometimes, when we eventually got back to Speakers' Corner at Marble Arch again, he would actually stop of his own free will. This was usually to listen to Prince Monolulu, a large African man, very imposing to look at,

with a shiny black face, flashing white teeth and large rolling eyes. 'I gotta horse – I gotta horse'! he would shout to
the crowds from his portable pulpit, for he made his living
as a famous racing tipster. The red, white and blue feathers
which sprang up from a band around his forehead used
to tremble and shake as he got worked up with his patter.
What with the feathers and the leopard skin that he often
wore theatrically across his chest, he was exactly the way
that I thought an African prince should look. All the children were fascinated by him. He was the only black person
that most of us had ever seen outside of picture books.

Sometimes Father would take us on a marathon walk
to Green Park or St James's Park, often to meet his sister
there – our aunt, Alice. She worked as a nanny for some
titled people who lived in Belgravia. Sometimes when we
met her, she would have her children with her and be wearing her starchy blue-and-white uniform, complete with
a triangle of navy-blue 'nun's veiling' which floated out
from a starched white headdress, covering her dark curls
at the back.

She had blue eyes like Father and a similar broad smile.
Summer or winter her children wore gloves in the park,
and their high coach-built perambulator, when they were
small, had an ornate family crest enamelled on both sides
of it. Aunty Alice told us she spent up to an hour each day
polishing that pram and shining up the silvery handlebars
and wheel spokes. It was important for 'the good name
of the family' she said. The children, although somewhat
reserved at first, soon played with us as happily as any of

our less privileged friends nearer home. And if they ever noticed that we were wearing some of their excellent quality cast-off clothing, they had the good manners never to mention it.

Father would talk to us as we went along, explaining to us the nature mysteries of the grasses or the trees or anything else that took his fancy. Sometimes it was the architecture. 'Look upwards,' he would tell us, '... some of the most beautiful parts of London are up near the sky.' We really enjoyed his company for he was full of fun and ignited our imaginations.

Sometimes we would go by bus to Buckingham Palace and then walk down The Mall to Carlton House Terrace, which we knew was where our father had once worked and was one of his favourite places. In the early days the buses were great fun because they had brass-railed staircases attached to the outsides of the vehicles. Mother said they were a continuation of the methods used in the old stage-coaching days. You had to climb the curving stairs in the fresh air in order to reach the roofless upper deck, where you really had to hang on to your hat. The conductor kept his cardboard tickets strapped by elastic to a wooden board, and a little bell would go '*ting*' as he clipped our penny or tuppenny fares. All the fare prices and a list of destinations were printed on the ticket sides and they cost from a ha'penny to a shilling. We never witnessed a shilling fare being clipped, and I concluded that only travellers to the edge of the world would ever require one.

Carlton House Terrace was the place where our father had first 'fallen in love' with London. He told us quite early in life that just before he became a butler, in the Twenties, he had been employed as first footmen and valet to a Cheshire lord. The town house of this lord was in Carlton House Terrace and Father had accompanied his employer, travelling to London with him in a Rolls Royce whenever he stayed there.

The gracious architecture he saw all around him and the beauty of the adjacent parks had so enthralled him that he began to dream of one day living in London forever. He told us the reason that the roadway was extra-specially wide there was because so many people were expected to turn up to the grand balls, that it was essential in the old days for the carriages to be able to draw up several abreast outside. Inside, he said, there were so many 'fully draped' chandeliers, that the task of keeping them always sparkling clean was like 'painting the Forth Bridge'. This problem was made worse by the dense London fogs: which, despite the closely fitting and well-maintained windows and heavy doors, would still manage to seep into the lofty rooms, tarnishing the silver and leaving a dull film on the crystal droplets of the chandeliers. Many London footmen, he said, regarded the fogs as their number-one enemy because of all the extra work they caused.

Another of Father's funny stories had taken place behind the grand facade of the great house he showed us in Carlton House Terrace. In the spring of 1925 a visit- ing, rosy-faced lord had come to stay there as a house guest: making two lords to be looked after. The visiting lord had brought four of his own footmen with him, for whom extra accommodation had to be found in the basement sleeping-quarters of the male menservants. Two of the visiting footmen were always stationed behind their employer's chair at dinner.

Towards the end of the long meal they always had to be alert and ready to catch him, just before he slipped off his chair and under the dining table. They would then manoeuvre him into a standing position and with as much dignity as possible slide him, upright, out of the dining room on the slippery leather soles of his evening shoes.

While this nightly occurrence was taking place, the other guests – the gentlemen in evening dress and the ladies in their jewels and finery, some with tiaras on their upswept hair – would carry on eating their food and engaging in table conversation as though nothing was happening.

Outside the dining room door, hidden by a screen and guarded by the other two footmen, a canvas stretcher would be already prepared and waiting for him. The four menservants would lower him gently on to it and then carry him, by way of the servants' back stairs, up to his bedroom. There they would undress him and put him to bed. 'He was a good and thoughtful employer to them,' our father would say, explaining that the old lord always insisted that his footmen should leave a glass, a jug of water, and two decanters of whisky on his bedside table. Also on the table, within easy reach, should be a chamber pot. He was considerate enough of his servants that he did not want to pull the bell-rope at night and rouse them from their slumbers in order that they should see to his needs.

Father reckoned that in the old days there must have been tens of thousands of footmen employed in London alone. He was of the opinion that their original function had been the protection of their employers and their families, including the female servants, against the lawlessness that once prevailed. They were like personal soldiers, he said: a private army of helpful and protective men. In one of the large country houses, a small stately home, where he had once worked, one of the rota duties for the footmen had been to stay up all night guarding the house. Each long corridor would have its secret footman on guard. Hidden behind large screens, they would sit all night beside a small folding table on which had been placed two candles in candlesticks and a box of matches, a carafe of water and a glass, the footman's sandwiches or pork pie or whatever the cook had given him, a book or newspaper or *The Racing News* and a pack of cards for playing 'Patience'. Underneath the table, because the lavatories were miles away and he wasn't allowed to leave his post, would be a lidded enamel slop bucket. But the most important items would be on the table: a hand bell and whistle for summoning the aid of his colleagues should any intruders have made their way past the stable dogs, the locked and bolted doors, the bells and the closed and barred shutters. Also on the table would be a wooden truncheon, for protecting himself while waiting for help in overpowering the intruder if necessary.

When we were older, Father told us that many fine houses of the landed gentry had been doomed after the Great War. Their downfall, he said sadly, was due to crippling death duties, or even multiple death duties. These apparently had to be paid when the owner of the house and estate died: often as a direct result of the Great War. If this was followed by the death of another of the heirs next in line, or maybe even more – for many upper-class as well as ordinary families had been bereft of both fathers and sons in the heavy casualties – then the compounded taxes became so crippling that they simply couldn't be met. Although he did not disagree with the general idea of these taxes preventing estates being handed down whole from generation to generation, he saw that in the aftermath of the Great War they seemed like a one-sided tax on grief.

A tragedy like that had happened at one of the great houses where he had been employed. The lands had been sold to developers, the house had become an educational establishment, and the traditional life pattern of the family had disintegrated. It seemed to upset him very much. He retained feelings of great loyalty towards the various upper-class families who had employed him for more than sixteen years of his life. I never ever heard him say anything derogatory about any of them.

At the same time, our father was well aware that bad employers did exist – their names quickly spread around the servants' grapevine – just as there were good and bad servants. But the bad employers, he said, were more likely to be encountered either in those ranks of people who employed servants they could not really afford, or who for various reasons were so unused to employing servants that they didn't know how to treat them properly, or who had left the control of their staff in the hands of an unjust or tyrannical housekeeper or butler: which was not often or they soon wouldn't have any decent staff left.

Whenever Aunty Alice came to tea with us, which was twice a month on Thursdays, the three grown-ups would always eventually get around to the subject of private service and employers. It was at these times that we could not help but learn a great deal about the world of servants. It was also a world which employed at least someone from nearly every family we knew. When Father was reminiscing about his days with 'the real gentry' he would often return to the fact that a lot of hardship and unemployment had been caused in the countryside whenever any of the Big Houses 'went to the wall'. A lot of farm workers and country servants had come home from the Great War only to find that a great shock was in store for them. The mansion or manor which had presided over the district and their own family's sustenance and well-being for nigh on centuries, was either to be sold, pulled down, or just abandoned to crumble away into a ruin. This was because, after taxation, there was no money left to maintain what remained of the estate.

'We're going through a bloodless revolution in this country,' he would say to our mother and Aunty Alice: 'It's the beginning of the end for the old days and the old ways.' And they would nod their heads over their teacups and agree. Father still had three very well-cut suits which had been passed on to him during his days in private service, as well as trilby hats, shoes and gloves. He always looked very smart indeed whenever we went out. His shoes were consistently polished to the brightness of new conkers and, whenever we went walking in the parks, he always selected a choice flower for his buttonhole. Soon after we had arrived in London, one of the Crawford Buildings children had remarked to me: 'Your dad looks like a toff, don't he?'

Rather than walking the streets of Marylebone, our mother preferred the softer, less windy atmosphere of Regent's Park. She enjoyed things like boating on the tranquil lake, feeding the ducks with us, or simply sitting in a deckchair in the sunshine, shaded by a paper parasol, while we played in the daisy strewn grass. She too was always very well dressed for, like Father, she possessed many elegant garments that had been given to her when she was a lady's maid. Most of the lovely things were still in fashion and she, too, had a way of 'carrying off' good clothes.

As the summer of 1933 began to enfold us, I was still far too young to wonder why it was that our father had such a lot of time and energy to spend on children, instead of being at work. Or why our mother was sometimes very quiet indeed.

6

The Poor Man at his Gate

The elegant parts of London where our parents liked to take us for walks were, I found, vastly different to some of the poorer areas which existed. Another thing I noticed about the great city of nursery rhyme and fable was the way in which the rich and the poor often lived so close to each other. Just turning a corner could bring a big surprise. One girl I knew who was so poor that she had begun to fabricate a 'dream life' for herself would go around telling everyone she was a cousin of Shirley Temple: Doris lived in a slum, which stood within a stone's throw of a museum which housed some of the world's greatest art treasures.

When we were older my sister and I, along with various Homer Street children, regularly visited that museum, especially on rainy days. It was called 'The Wally's Collection'. At least that was how it was introduced to us by other boys and girls soon after we came to live in

Marylebone. 'Wanna come along wiv' us to see the Wally's Collection?' they asked us one day. We jumped at the chance. We had never seen a Wally and wondered what it was. Also we were curious to know what they collected.

All we found at Hertford House were slippery parquet floors, paintings, statues, furniture which was so uncomfortable that it really didn't need the notices saying things like 'Do Not Sit On This Chair' and lots of uniformed men on guard. There were no Wallies. But after the first few visits we stopped looking for them and just sorted out which paintings we would claim for ourselves – just as we mentally divided out between ourselves the wonderful showpiece cakes on display in the window of the Lyons Corner House at Marble Arch, which nobody but the wealthy could afford. In Hertford House none of us ever chose the paintings of dead fish or grapes. The boys preferred the action scenes, or the Laughing Cavalier by an artist called Frans Hals. The girls liked the romantic pictures of flowery swings and bowers, painted by Fragonard, Watteau and Boucher. On hearing the tortured pronunciations of those artists' names by the older boys and girls, followed by giggles and mumblings, the museum guards would come over to us and, with surprising kindness, tell us what the names really were.

By the time I was tall enough and erudite enough to read the words 'Wallace Collection' on the high nameboard outside, I was saddened to realise that the elusive Wallies did not exist outside of my imagination and that I would never have the thrill of being confronted by one.

But I was not too dismayed. In our search for them we had discovered instead the strange pleasure of entering another world by looking at paintings. We continued to visit Hertford House all through the 1930s, until Hitler put a stop to it.

But poor Doris, my friend, was a child who never managed to see those paintings at all. After we had enthusiastically described the collection to her, including the fact that there was no charge to go in, she took her little brother there. But they were apparently refused admission. Most probably they were dressed in very raggedy clothes and, possibly, looked none too clean either. Or maybe she had been followed there by some of the Moxon Street bullies from the other side of Baker Street. Whatever the reason, we all thought it was a shame: she couldn't help it that her family were so poor. Her father had eventually died from chest trouble after being gassed in the Great War, and her mother was on something called 'the Means Test'.

It was soon after this incident that Doris started her twilight secondary life of the cinema: sneaking in through the back doors without paying. In the cinema it was dark and smoky and nobody could see, or cared, what you wore. They had eyes for nothing but the dream life on the silver screen.

Another girl we knew who came from a very poor family who were also on the Means Test lived two landings below us in Crawford Buildings. But she was always clean and decently dressed, and her mother took the trouble to starch her clothes. Elsie lived with her parents and three brothers in an apartment just like ours, except that it had one extra little room. Mr and Mrs Grey slept in there while Elsie and her brothers slept in the other bedroom. A curtain strung across it on a wire gave her a measure of privacy.

Unlike Doris who was sallow-faced and lank-haired, Elsie was bonny looking because of her fair curly hair, wide blue eyes and fair complexion. If she had been a country girl she probably would have been chosen as Queen of the May each spring. Every night when she went to bed she put a picture of Clark Gable beneath her pillow. She even had it in a frame that she had purchased from Woolworths after saving up her errand money – instead of spending it on sweets like most normal children. She said she hoped the photo would make her dream of him. I used to think that this was a very strange thing to do considering she was surrounded all day by three brothers, not to mention all the other boys who lived in the buildings. I put it down to the fact that she was about three years older than me and therefore that much closer to joining the mysterious world of grown-ups, with all their strange ways.

But one day I came to realise why Elsie, too, needed her dreams to be as far away from reality as possible. Apparently her parents had been visited for years by 'the men from the Means Test'. They were nasty people by all accounts and very rude to Mrs Grey. Although her body was plump underneath her crossover flowered apron and her greying hair was carefully frizzed up with curling tongs so that she looked quite jolly, she was actually a tired and worried woman for most of the time. Whenever the Means Test men had been to see her she could always be seen afterwards standing on her doormat, dabbing at her eyes with a corner of her apron. But the difference between her and Doris's mother was that she still had spirit. She had no intention of abiding by a law which demanded disposing of all her family's saleable possessions in order to qualify for financial help.

As soon as she thought her tormentors were out of the way, she would peer over the iron railing that encircled the stair well and, rubbing her hands, knock on her neighbour's door to get her piano back. She apparently had an arrangement where, at these times, her old upright piano was quickly wheeled over her brass door sill and into her neighbour's apartment. Also her gramophone was hidden at the back of her coal oven, beside a fireless grate. Apparently if these things had been seen in her home she would have been ordered to sell them before she could receive the pittance of monetary assistance so grudgingly granted. 'My music is the only pleasure left to me' she would tell all her neighbours. 'If they take that away from me I might as well put me bleedin' head in the gas oven.'

Mr Grey and the two oldest sons were unable to find work. The youngest boy was still at school. Sometimes if you knocked at their door and they said 'Come in', which they always did because they were a very friendly family, the men would be sitting by the fire in their vests and trousers. That was because they had only one shirt each and their shirts were in the wash. They used to have the loveliest cups of tea; it was very strong and dark – Mazawattee tea – and they sweetened it with Nestle's condensed milk. Sometimes the men drank it out of their saucers because, they said, it got cooler more quickly that way. When I asked our mother if we could have condensed milk in our tea she said 'No,' and the first time she saw me drinking tea out of the saucer like Elsie's brothers, she was very cross. But she didn't stop us going to see the family. They were 'good people' she said, who had 'fallen on hard times'. She didn't know when she said that, that we were soon to fall on hard times ourselves.

When we first came to Marylebone I had been surprised by all the evidence of poverty, which had soon become apparent to me. At Queensberry House I had never dreamed that children could be hungry or have all sorts of things wrong with them through poor feeding. Also, what with the parcels of excellent-quality cast-off clothing arriving quite regularly from Aunty Alice's children – lovely garments fit for princesses, which I had always taken for granted, thinking that was the way all children were dressed – I was quite unprepared for the sight of a great many little boys and girls whose clothes were so thin and patched that they were almost falling into rags, and who shivered in the cold because their parents couldn't afford overcoats for them. The coats my sister and I wore at that time often had silk linings, and had matching muffs and cape collars and bonnets trimmed with real fur.

The gap between the wealthy and the impoverished was so wide and so marked that it was almost as if there were two distinctly different races of people living in London. I would learn later that a lot of good people were extremely worried about this and did what little they could to help. But the problem was so huge that it was almost insurmountable. Meanwhile, along with all the other children at St Mary's School and at the Paddington Chapel Sunday School, I happily, and with gusto, sang the third verse of one of our favourite hymns – 'All things bright and beautiful'. The words did not strike us in any way as strange: 'The rich man in his castle, The poor man at his gate, God made them high or lowly, And ordered their estate'. The bad times known as 'The Depression' were still going on and the results of poverty were there for all to see. After living in a well-ordered and maintained mansion, even if it was only below stairs, I noticed the shabbiness everywhere; the peeling paint on the shopfronts; broken house-windows plugged up with cardboard; tramps rifling through waste bins; women queuing outside bakers' shops early in the mornings with pillow cases in their hands, hoping to have them filled with stale bread for threepence. There were pitiful beggars, ex-soldiers and blind men standing by the gutters along all the main roads, and there were children in the early stages of consumption before they were noticed and taken away – spitting blood into their handkerchiefs. There were others with bandy legs from rickets or with crossed eyes that nobody could afford to have put right.

Our father, who had cherished such high hopes of getting himself a really good job in London, even of quickly becoming a headwaiter because of all his experience as a butler, had quickly found that waiter's jobs were unexpectedly hard to come by. Apparently there were lots of foreigners, especially Cypriots, living in London who were all looking for work, just like Father. He told us that the Cypriot men were all single, or had left their families in Cyprus, and were able and willing to work for far less money than anybody else. They were allowed to work in England, he said, because Cyprus was part of the British Empire. But in London, apparently, they would all sleep together, sometimes as many as ten to a room, and therefore they could afford to work for low wages and, consequently, get the jobs. Some of them were hairdressers, and some were something called 'pimps', but nearly all the rest, according to Father, wanted to be waiters. He didn't dislike the men themselves, but he did say things like: 'It's a fine thing when an Englishman can't get a job in his own country except as a blessed flunkey!' He had already explained to our mother that the reason he got precedence when it came to 'costume jobs' was that, in his opinion, English faces poking out from powdered wigs and lacy throat-ruffles, were less likely to look 'like organ-grinders' monkeys'.

Father was not a man normally given to insulting other people, but it was plain to see that his pride was being hurt in a great many ways. One of the things which really upset him whenever he managed to find temporary work was the fact that every morning he had to stand in line with other waiters to have his fingernails examined by foreign headwaiters. 'Jumped up Dagoes' he called them. And his humiliation was made worse at the end of every working evening, by having the front of his 'boiled-shirt', his dress shirt, scribbled on by the headwaiter's pencil to make sure he wore a clean fresh one the following morning. He was already a highly fastidious man by nature and, rightly or wrongly, he took exception to being scribbled on. He regarded it as an affront. Being without proper work made him angry. He had never had to go 'cap in hand' to anyone before, looking for work. He had never known anything but respect in his profession.

Eventually he obtained a part-time job in a place called the 'Holborn Restaurant' where, he said, the management were fair and decent. He would work for two or three weeks, and then they would lay him off for two or three weeks. They said that that was the only way they could be fair with everybody. I always knew when the three weeks had come to an end because he would come home looking so unhappy, and then he would tell our mother that he had been given his 'cards' again. I came to dread that sentence.

The time came when our parents found they had used up all their savings, despite the fact they had been very careful. There was nothing left in the Post Office book. Everything they had relied on seemed to have let them down. The Christmas of 1934 looked like being a very sad time for all of us. Our father had taken his place in the dole queue on the Old Marylebone Road, alongside hundreds of other unemployed men. But his last two amounts of money had been eaten up by three consecutive lots of doctor's bills at half a guinea a time. The terrible London fogs in November had affected our mother's chest, and she had acute bronchitis.

I already suspected that there was no Father Christmas, but that December our mother sadly explained to me there would be hardly any money for food, let alone Christmas presents or anything like that. She told me we would be given tangerines and apples to fill up our stockings, and that I must not tell Joan the truth but let her just think that Father Christmas was very poor that year.

'But we *will* have each other', she consoled me, suggesting 'wouldn't it be nice to have Daddy all to ourselves at Christmas for the first year ever, instead of him having to spend most of his time looking after other people'? And I agreed that it would. But I rather wished that we could have had our father at home and some presents as well. I didn't make a fuss however, because I was beginning to realise that our parents, like so many other grown-ups around us, now had great worries. I also realised why, at school, we were regularly asked if our fathers were working, and all those children, including me, who put up their hands for 'No' were given brown-paper carrier bags containing fruit, biscuits and sweets, and a few little toys, such as colouring books and crayons. These thoughtful gifts were apparently sent to the school by a group of ladies and gentlemen who lived in the adjacent Montague and Bryanston Squares.

There were only a few days to go until Christmas. School had broken up. Father was at home all day now. He played with us and did the washing for Mother, who was still weak after her illness. We seemed to be living on dinners of carrot and onion soup and pease-pudding flavoured with bacon bones, which he made while our mother rested. At other meals we had thick, tasty slabs of bread and dripping. When he took us out for his long walks he would give us each a paper bag filled with dry Quaker oats and sugar, which we found to be very pleasant. And when we washed it down with water from the drinking fountains it proved very filling too.

On the last Friday before Christmas we were startled by a loud *rat-a-tat-tat* on the door. I ran to open it. On the doorstep stood a man dressed in a dark cape, a peaked hat, a sack on his back and a big smile on his face. It was the postman. 'Sign here,' he said, handing Father a stump of blue indelible pencil. The receipt signed, he then handed over a registered envelope, fastened with red sealing wax. Our parents had apparently written to one of their private-service employers: the lady who lived in Trevor Square in Knightsbridge – the one who had offered to become my godmother if I was 'fostered out' when I was born. The letter our mother and father had sent to her, telling her of our present plight, was answered very pleasantly by her brother, a Mr Stanhope Joel, from an address in Park Lane. He said his sister was abroad, but would we do him the honour of accepting a small gift from himself? He hoped we would all have a happy Christmas and that Mother would soon be well and strong again. Inside the registered envelope were two large, crinkly, black–and–white five-pound notes. Ten pounds! A huge amount of money: almost a whole month's wages for an ordinary man. It meant that we could have a proper Christmas after all. Because of that gentleman's great kindness, we had one of our best ever.

There were hardly any shopping days left. Mother, who now had two little pink spots in her pallid cheeks, and eyes which shone as if they had dark candles glowing behind them, dressed herself up warmly in her black bouclé coat and tawny fox fur, and then the four of us set off excitedly towards Marble Arch and Oxford Street. The brightly lit shops, the coster-barrows piled high with Christmas fruit, holly and mistletoe, which stood at every corner, the sparkling decorations festooned across the wide thoroughfare and bedizening the lamp posts, the giant lit-up trees outside Selfridges, surely there could never have been such a festive atmosphere as there seemed to be on that crisply cold day in the West End of London.

Our parents spent carefully, taking care to put some of the money to one side for the next 'rainy day'. After we had been to the poulterer's and all the other necessary provisioners in Crawford Street, they also took a great deal of pleasure in getting together a cardboard box full of surprises for Mr and Mrs Grey and their family. All four of us went down to their apartment with the box.

'Come in,' the Greys called out. We entered and Father put the box down on the living-room table, telling them at the same time that it was a present from a Mr Stanhope Joel.

'Stanhope Joel!' Mr Grey exclaimed, running a hand over his thinning hair and then adjusting his round steel-rimmed spectacles so that he could stare at the box, 'Who's he when he's at home?'

But Mrs Grey quickly cleared her son, George, and his cigarette-card collection off the table, and signalled to our mother and father to open the box. Before their astonished eyes out came a chicken with feathers still on its neck. I had learnt that chicken was more expensive than other meat and was regarded by most ordinary people as a once-a-year luxury, at Christmas. It was followed by chipolata sausages and bacon, silver-wrapped tangerines, muscatels, dates, nuts, ginger wine, chocolate biscuits and a box of 50 cigarettes. Wrapped in a cloth was one of Mother's homemade plum puddings, prepared in October – and last of all came another box containing twelve red-and-gold Christmas crackers, or 'bon-bons' as we called them.

While Mrs Grey dabbed at her eyes with her apron, this time from happiness, our parents explained about our gift. Mr Grey seemed like a man who had never been given a present before and didn't know what to say. But I remember that his pale grey eyes were a bit moist behind his spectacles when we left. And as we walked away, leaving Mrs Grey waving to us in her doorway, I heard him say to her: 'Where's my razor strop? I think I'll have a good shave.'

On Christmas Day, after grace had been said, all four of our family were sitting around the dinner table. We girls had ginger beer to drink. Our parents had wine. Father raised a toast, holding aloft the glass of white wine he had just sipped and tasted for soundness. 'Here's to Stanhope Joel,' he said in a vibrant voice. 'Now he's what I call a *real* gentleman.' That was, in Father's view, the finest compliment that any man could pay to another.

7

Doorsteps and Copper-sticks

O ur father was still 'on the dole' for much of the time, while he was seeking that elusive 'permanent job' and it was early spring when our mother heard that there was a certain type of work available for women at the big houses in the Bryanston and Montague Squares. Somebody told her that the ladies who lived there were sometimes looking for women who would take in their personal laundry and hand-wash it at home. The ladies did not want to entrust their expensive underwear and delicate blouses to the proper laundries, in case it should be 'torn to shreds' by the machinery used there.

I remember accompanying Mother on several adventurous days as she went from door to door around those squares, lined with still, leafless trees. I held my fidgety sister's hand tightly as she rang doorbells and banged on door knockers, and then spoke to smart parlour maids when the heavy and impressive front doors were opened to her.

Sometimes those 'front servants' would look at her askance as she stood there on the broad doorsteps in her stylish black coat and chic forward-tilted little hat. Sometimes she had her fox fur wrapped around her shoulders if it was cold, for she was still not fully back to health. Underneath her smart outer clothing she wore Thermogene wadding across her chest, next to her skin. But as she stood on the marble-tiled doorsteps in the March breezes, enquiring whether the mistress of the house needed any laundry done, she did not look in any way at all like a washerwoman. Those parlour maids couldn't know, of course, that her clothes had been given to her when she, too, had been a servant. They didn't seem to know what to make of her and sometimes seemed slightly embarrassed.

At most places she was instructed to 'Wait there a moment', while the door was closed in her face. When the servant re-appeared, she would be told either: 'Thank you, but Madam doesn't require any washing done' or: 'Madam says will you kindly step into the hall and she will come down to see you.' Just to 'make sure' we would quickly run the soles of our shoes over the rim of the cast-iron shoe scrapers that were affixed to every entrance, just as the ancient link-light snuffers were still attached to most of the entrance railings. Seeing these railings close up for more or less the first time, I noticed that they were not as sooty as most surfaces in London, and presumed that the maids must regularly wash them.

Soon after we had followed our mother into the spacious and elegant hallways, invariably a bell would be heard ringing distantly. The mistress of the house would usually be already descending the stairs. As a rule, the mistress' posture was very erect and her hair carefully coiffured, and I would think I did not mind our mother doing washing for such queenly beings. Then, as if by magic, a starchily uniformed kitchen maid would appear from a side door into the hall and, at an instruction from her mistress, would take Joan and me downstairs to the kitchen, while Mother would disappear with the lady into a room on the other side of the hall.

Down in the basement kitchens it was rather like being back at Queensberry House again, except that everything had become very small – almost like Alice found when she was in Wonderland, but not so extreme. The ranges were not so long, the dressers not so high, the wooden plate-racks beside the sinks under the barred windows not so capacious, and the scrubbed tables, no longer being at my eye level, in no way resembled those vast flat wooden plains of my infancy. But most of those kitchens had a familiar-looking cook's chair beside the fire: they were like folding deckchairs but with thin carpet attached to the struts instead of canvas, and when everybody was very busy they could be folded up and put somewhere out of the way. Often, too, there would be a stiff-whiskered tabby cat sitting in the cook's chair, his whiskers showing that he was a good 'mouser', and that the larders would be clean.

In those kitchens I would relish again the expensive smells that were not usually found in ordinary homes – the smell of black pepper and the spice cupboards, the steam from the stock-pots, which were simmering their contents into rich reduced essences – a few bowlfuls of which would have greatly helped children like Doris. Casseroles bubbling in sherry-laced gravy, fish marinating in herby wine, the aroma of recently ground coffee and of cooling clove-stuck hams, the smell of vanilla pods and fluffy puddings steeped in liqueur sauces and the hot buttery smell of biscuits freshly taken from the black ovens. It was all so familiar and comforting. I didn't mind at all being back below stairs.

The cooks were kind to us, putting warm jam tarts or pieces of cake into our eager hands, while the maids would smile at us and rush forward to tuck starchy teacloths under our chins so we didn't spoil our clothes. A great many of the maids were fresh-faced Irish girls or young women. They talked 'twenty to the dozen' to each other in their caressing accents, saying what 'lovely little things' we were, and they hovered over us as if they were child-starved. I liked it, and Joan rewarded them with dimples.

Our mother soon managed to collect sufficient laundry orders from the squares and Gloucester Place for our bills to be promptly paid and for us to start eating proper food again. Also, most importantly of all, the extra money she earned for our family ensured that there would always be enough to pay our weekly rent of seven-and-sixpence for the apartment. Our mother's first priority was always that we should be able to 'keep a roof over our heads'.

It was fortunate for our family that St Mary's School took children into the 'Infants classes' from the age of three, because this meant that Joan could be looked after there for half-days, while our mother got on with her new laundry business. Joan was perfectly happy: Miss Bell was a motherly teacher as well as being efficient at making learning somehow seem like play. As we were still so young our mother collected us each midday, guiding us safely over the busy Seymour Place where there were as yet no traffic lights. After our dinner she would take me back to school again, only a short walk of almost two blocks. Joan would then be ready for a little sleep at home having spent a busy and happy morning playing shops with cardboard money, learning to count on a brightly beaded abacus, and learning how to hold a slate pencil so that she could 'write' on a little wooden-framed slate board which had a tiny sponge hanging from it by a string. Every infant was given one of these important looking slates to use, and any resulting marks made on it immediately took on the glamour of a framed picture. There was also waxy-smelling plasticine to be rolled into snakes and then coiled into baskets, shining squares of brightly coloured sticky paper that could be cut with little scissors into amazingly shaped animals to adorn the grey paper murals on the walls, crisp sheets of tissue paper that could be made into flowers for mothers, paintboxes and paper and pots of water, pots of clove-smelling paste, jam jars to be filled with buds and grasses from the parks, and fascinating 'sums' on the high black-board – on which Miss Bell's piece of chalk could also cleverly cut a round currant cake into four separate pieces. She would then rub them out, one by one, pretending that four hungry children had gobbled them up. Also, at eleven o'clock, Joan and all the other infants would have a mugful of warm milk each – a luxury that Miss Bell had managed to obtain for her infants, from the purses of the School Governors and their friends. So, every day at school Joan and I were happy. And when we came home now we found that every day smelled like wash day!

Apart from the four brown doors that were on each of the landings in Crawford Buildings, there was also a white-tiled passage leading off each landing, at right-angles. At the ends of these passages were two cold-water taps protruding over two large stone sinks. These were for communal use because there was no running water of any kind in the apartments. Men, women, and children took turns at taking empty china or enamel jugs out to the taps, filling them up, and then carrying them, full and heavy, back indoors again. 'The Taps' also fulfilled an important social function, for people would often spend a little time talking there with neighbours just as if they had met at a village pump or well.

Also, down each passageway were four open-topped flush lavatories: one for each family who lived on that landing. A few had rolls of crackly Bronco toilet paper hanging behind the doors, but most had a thick wad of neatly cut newspaper squares which had been pierced at one corner and threaded onto a loop of string, ready for hanging on a nail. Newspaper was not only softer than Bronco but it was also cheaper and quieter. We also found that the tabloid newspapers, such as the *Daily Mail*, the

Daily Sketch and the *Daily Mirror* were much softer than the broadsheets that Father sometimes brought home, like *The Evening Standard*, *The Evening News* or the evening *Star*. There was also a rubbish chute let into the floor of each landing, down which would rattle ashes and cinders and other household waste on its way to large containers in the basement which were emptied every few days by overalled workmen.

Another big door led into what was known as the wash house. There was one on every landing and they were all practically the same. Against the left-hand wall of ours stood a large enamelled bath with a brass plughole, four claw feet of iron, and a brass cold-water tap. Near the frosted window was a yellow stone sink with another cold-water tap and a wooden draining board beside it. The four women who lived on our landing all did their washing at that sink, taking with them their own scrubbing boards and brushes, with which they scrubbed clean, with yellow soap and soda, the dirtier parts of their washing: especially the loose collars which men attached to their shirts daily by means of collar-studs made of rolled gold or bone. Also, in the wash house was a fluted metal dolly-tub in which some types of washing were soaked overnight before being pounded up and down with a long-handled wooden plunger known as a dolly-stick, prior to boiling.

In the furthest corner stood a chimneyed 'wash copper' made of stone and brick. A metal-grated fire box and ash box was built into the brick bottom of the copper. In order to heat the water for the washing, or for baths, the women would light a fire below the copper, coaxing it up into a red furnace by using their hand bellows, or else by standing a tin tray against it to create a through-draught. Sometimes they used a sheet of newspaper instead of a tray, but it was a dangerous thing to do, said our mother. In the upper part of the copper was a deep, hollow basin actually made of copper. In shape, it was like a church font or a witch's cauldron. All the cotton and linen items were boiled clean in there, the whiteness ensured later by the insertion of a Reckitt's Blue bag in the rinsing water. People's coal or coke for the fire box stood beside the copper in buckets or scuttles, and care had to be taken that the clean laundry was not dirtied again by ash or coal as it was lifted out of the steam and bubbles with the wooden copper-stick. A heavy wooden lid went over the top of the font while the clothes were boiling there. Sometimes women also put their heavy flatirons on it as well, to hold it down. The force of the steam and the swelling of the washing used to lift the wooden lids right up into the air, and then all the soap suds would cascade down onto the stone floor, hissing loudly as they touched the red-hot firebox on the way.

Through looking at Father's green books we realised that these wash coppers everyone used were of exactly the same design as those used in the days of Dickens, and before. But they were extremely efficient. More modern were the white tiles all around the walls, on which the steam used to condense. When the women had finished their washing, they would wipe down the wet walls with their long-handled cotton mops, or with towels wrapped around the bristly ends of brooms.

When the wash had been lifted from the copper into buckets by use of the copper-stick, it was tipped into the sink for rinsing and starching, and the copper was emptied by means of a wooden-handled metal ladle – but not before the fire had gone out beneath. A lot of Robin Starch was used. It was believed that it kept linen and clothes cleaner longer. When ironed into flawless smoothness after being starched, the laundry certainly looked fresh and smart and made the women proud of their housewifery. As a skill, it was considered so important that housewifery was taught to us at school.

A mangle stood by one of the wash-house walls. All excess water was squeezed out between two wooden rollers, which were rotated by cog wheels and a turning handle. Most washing was put through several times, so that as much water as possible dribbled out into the slop-bucket below. Most underwear and anything that didn't show – such as woollen vests and combinations, petticoats, stays, bodices and nightclothes – usually had rubber or linen-backed tin buttons: which were unbreakable when the garment went through the mangle. Ordinary buttons of bone or mother-of-pearl always broke eventually and, on top of the regular weekly darning and mending, caused women a lot of extra sewing work. Long wooden racks were let down from the wash-house ceiling, on which the laundry was spread and then hoisted up again to dry. The heat from the still-glowing embers in the firebox would usually dry it all 'ready for ironing' by the following morning. It was finally ironed and 'finished off' in people's living rooms, where on other clothes lines close to the ceilings it was hung up to air.

People always apologised to visitors if they had washing or airing strung across a room. But it had to be done somewhere. And the living room where there was already spare heat rising up from the fire range, the gas lamps and, possibly, a gas oven as well, was the best place to do it. A great deal of 'show' had to be sacrificed for survival. People obtained their satisfaction and self-respect from their prowess at 'making do' or 'making ends meet', or by bringing up respectful and reasonably well-behaved families in difficult circumstances.

The ironing was done on living-room tables on top of several folded blankets and a clean flannelette ironing cloth. People's spare blankets were kept aired in this way. Every woman possessed two or three heavy metal flatirons and possibly also another one, small enough to manoeuvre around frills and sleeves. They were heated on the range or the stove, then picked up carefully with a thick iron-holder made of felt, after which they were rubbed, face down, in a tray full of salt before being used. The salt cleaned them and made the metal smooth. When ironed, the washing was folded carefully so that the heat still in it would be retained and help with the airing process. Every woman I knew had a horror of giving the members of her family either rheumatism, bronchitis or pneumonia through the laundry not being properly aired.

Even consumption was sometimes superstitiously blamed on this.

The wash houses were used on a rota system, both for washing days and bath nights. It was lovely to be bathed in there at the end of a wash day, with the atmosphere all warm and steamy from the fresh bath water bubbling up to heat in the copper, and the firebox reflections glowing red on the moist walls. And towards the end of every year the women would boil their homemade plum puddings in the copper ready for Christmas. The puddings were as round as cannon balls and tied up in squares of linen rag and the copper could cook six or seven of them at once. The wash house and wash days were certainly a most important part of everybody's life, even if fathers were inclined to be 'put out' by the weekly upheaval and the fact that they usually only had cold meat and pickles for their meals on wash days.

When our neighbours – Mrs O'Brien at number 66, Mrs Ripon at 65 and Mrs Barnes at 64 – learnt of our mother's endeavours to earn a little money, they arranged between themselves that she should be given priority to use the wash house on the extra three spare days of the week when it was nobody's rota day. It was very strange at first to see all the beautiful personal garments worn by the ladies in the squares being laundered in the communal wash house and then strung across our living room to air. Our mother seemed happy and relaxed as she stood with her back to the fire, ironing it all. Often, she would sing as she worked, or tell us stories while the iron alternately thudded down onto a trivet or smoothed over the garments with a soft soothing sound. Sometimes, she would crimp the frills of the blouses, using a very hot small iron over brown paper. The garment below would emerge with little ornamental ridges in its frills. We thought she was very clever, and she said crimping was becoming a 'lost art'.

Mother told us that laundering was a pleasantly easy thing for her to do because, when she herself had been a little girl and the orphanage had arranged for her to work in the laundry wing of a big house in Cheshire, she had worked so hard that everything that followed had become easy by comparison. She had a funny story to tell about those days. Her employers were 'hunting people' she said, and her main task during her first winter in 1919, had consisted of scrubbing out the mud from the riding breeches. Later she had been taught how to stretch them over wire cages ready for drying. Each cage, apparently, exactly fitted the personal rear dimensions of one or another of each of the two-dozen riding members of the family. There was one special cage for each person, and each one had a name tag attached to it so that it could be matched up to the name tapes inside the breeches. When all the cages were wearing the appropriate breeches, they were hooked onto a long wooden rack and hauled up to the high ceiling, there to shrink into the right shape as they dried. After this they all had chalk rubbed into them to make them smooth, soft, white and comfortable to wear when sitting on a horse. Our mother's dark eyes sparkled with mischievous glee when she told us that, although she never did meet any of her Cheshire employers face to face, she would have recognised their rear-ends anywhere!

The fine sewing Mother had been taught by the nuns at the orphanage, and later put to good use as a lady's maid, became invaluable again when she was able to make almost invisible repairs to the delicate silk, lace and chiffon of the laundry entrusted to her care. Three times a week, when the lovely garments were all clean, mended and crisply ironed, we would watch her fold them, very professionally, in tissue paper, and then pack them into the dress-shop boxes which her employers had themselves provided for that purpose. There would be a small slip of paper inside each box, itemising each garment in Mother's small, neat handwriting; with the price for laundering it alongside.

With our mother carrying the string-tied boxes Joan and I would accompany her back to the squares when afternoon school was over. Again, we would be asked to step into the various halls while the parlour maids took the box or boxes to their mistresses. Then they would come back with money in an envelope and the box re-filled with more soiled laundry. Sometimes a maid would also bring a message for us: Would we all go down to the kitchen below, where the cook would provide us with a cup of tea?

I did not realise at the time that this was often a polite ploy to enable the cook to give us titbits from the larder: cold mutton or the last of a ham on the bone, some chicken legs or a slab of cake. Sometimes they would give us a bowl of good beef or bacon dripping, turning it out onto a sheet of greaseproof paper so that all the rich jelly would be on the top. It seemed very strange at first, having watched our mother being queen of her own kitchen at Richmond, to see her now receiving charity from other cooks. But she always accepted it graciously, and people seemed to like her good manners and quiet ways.

I noticed that our rather tall father was beginning to voice his irritation at the lines of washing that seemed to be constantly strung across our living room. He had fixed up a washing line on the flat railinged roof. It ran from a nail in one of the chimney stacks, and across the small but high expanse, to the downpipe of the tank-house guttering. But every time our mother had hung the washing there it had quickly become covered with smuts and soot and had to be washed all over again. Eventually, despite being wiped with Scrubb's Cloudy Ammonia, the rope of the washing line itself became as black as pitch-tar and would immediately stain anything draped across it with a long straight black stripe. So in the end there was no recourse but to dry it indoors. Our mother did try to clear it away when Father was at home, but it was not always possible.

However, there were some mysterious pieces of laundry that Mother always did manage to swoop off the fireguard rail whenever Father's returning footsteps rang on the stone of our top landing. I had no idea what these small rectangles of quilted white linen were. They measured about eight-to-ten inches long by three inches wide and had two long cotton tapes stitched to each end. I knew that our mother always soaked them in a closed enamel bucket, filled with heavily salted water, before boiling them thoroughly in the copper. The only information I could ever elicit from her was that they were something that ladies used sometimes. Whatever they were, bundles of about two dozen or more of them, all clean, ironed, and folded in tissue, would be regularly carried in the dress-boxes with the other clean laundry to the various addresses of the ladies who lived in Gloucester Place and the Bryanston and Montague Squares.

I thought that now Mother was helping with the family finances, our father would be pleased. But he wasn't. He still played with us and told us stories, but sometimes he would become quiet for a very long time, just thinking his own thoughts and not telling anyone else what they were.

8

We Learnt About Hitler at the Mickey Mouse Club

It was through listening to grown-up conversations that I first became aware of a man called Oswald Mosley. It seemed that he and his black-shirted Fascists were beginning to play an important and unwanted part in the life of our Aunty Alice. Father didn't like it at all and was worried for his sister's safety when he found out that she had left her previous employers and was now nanny to the little daughter of one of Mosley's right-hand men. 'You must promise never to repeat anything you hear Aunty Alice say,' my mother warned me one day after she had found me sitting under the table, hidden by the long folds of the tablecloth, just listening. I kept my promise.

Our aunt now lived in another fine house, in a smart district on the other side of Hyde Park. She still came to see us every other week, drinking tea and playing cards with our parents, and talking about the upper-class world of the rich and the privileged. I liked most of all to hear about the children, but during this episode in my aunt's life, I also heard some very mysterious 'cloak and dagger' things as well. The man she worked for was a gentleman, there was no doubt of that, and he was titled too in a minor way, being an Honourable. The Honourable Ian Hope Dundas was his name. One day Aunty Alice accompanied his wife and their little girl to a children's ball at the Hyde Park Hotel, where the lady was introduced by the Master of Ceremonies to the assembled company as: The Honourable Mrs Dundas. Later that night, when the child was being undressed for bed, she was unnaturally quiet and solemn. When our aunt gently probed as to the reason, the little girl burst into tears and asked: 'Why did that man introduce my mummy as The Horrible Mrs Dundas?'

The Honourable Mr Dundas himself was, according to our aunt, 'a bit strange' and this strangeness was putting the child's life at risk and consequently hers as well. At least that was how it appeared to her. When she had first met him she was in the hall, ready to take the child into the park. Suddenly he came out of one of the ground floor rooms: 'Heil Hitler', he immediately greeted her, his right arm stretched stiffly upwards in the Nazi salute, and his heels almost clicking to attention. Aunty Alice found it quite difficult to cover her surprise. 'Well, what do you think, Nanny?' was his next utterance, 'What do you think of what I just did?'

Aunty Alice thought hard, and quickly. It was a good position that she held, one of the best in London from many points of view. 'I'm just a country girl, Sir', she said at last, 'brought up in the country, you know. I don't know much about politics, Sir.' It was obviously the right thing for her to have said, because she kept her job. But our father didn't like it at all when he realised her new employer was a Nazi sympathiser. And when she later told him she expected to be going soon to Germany where her employers had been invited on a holiday in order to attend a private wedding, at which Hitler would be one of the guests, Father liked it even less.

When Aunty Alice talked, she was always very detailed and explicit, in the way many nannies often were: 'he said' and 'they said' and 'I said' and so on. So it was easy to remember her remarks on things, practically word for word. It was also easy to see how the important nannies' grapevine worked and how some of the best-guarded secrets of society were passed from nanny to nanny as they sat in their tight 'magic-circles' in the parks or in Kensington Gardens, knitting or sewing and gossiping, while their charges breathed in the fresh air with each other in the middle of the circles. Each piece of gossip or information was then taken home by those nannies to their respective employers, to whom they often also acted as confidante. All this was apparently known about and accepted by many employers as a way of learning the high-society pieces of news that did not appear in *Tatler* or the newspapers. Also, the nannies considering themselves better than anyone else below stairs could be relied upon to keep the secrets safe from lesser mortals than themselves and their employers.

When I grew older, I used to think that there was more going on in Kensington Gardens than just Peter Pan blowing on his pipe, or Puck telling Oberon that he would 'put a girdle about the earth in 40 minutes'. It was not difficult to imagine all the nannies with little 'wings of Mercury' sprouting out of their velour hats or flowing head-dresses and from the heels of their sensible laced-up shoes.

It was through other nannies that our aunt first heard the stories coming back from Germany, about people who had been walking along the streets or sitting at outdoor cafes, discussing Hitler in a disapproving manner, and who had been overheard by secret police and immediately shot, falling dead at the feet of their companions. Father knew his sister was a chatterbox, and when he heard about this he became quite uneasy about her little holiday in Germany, where she would be taken into close proximity with Hitler himself. She also told our parents that a very strange sort of housemaid had come to work at the Dundas household. She performed her tasks properly during the day, but on her evenings off she would sit in her room in silence instead of going out as ordinary maids did. When the weather became too cold for her to sit up there she began to sit in a corner of the servants' hall, seemingly writing endless notes into a big notepad. Soon the other servants became curious: surely nobody could spend quite so much free time just writing letters home, or love letters?

And if they were love letters, why were there never any replies? Between themselves, 'just for a lark', they arranged that anyone who was passing her chair should peep over her shoulder to find out what she was writing: even taking her a cup of tea if necessary in order to distract her attention. They soon discovered that she was writing down every little thing that had happened in the Dundas establishment that day, both upstairs and below stairs. When she had finished she would put her notes into a big brown envelope and go straight out to the nearest post-box, even when it was pouring with rain, or a 'pea-souper' was making it impossible to 'see a hand in front of your face'. Our parents and aunt began to wonder if she was some sort of spy, but couldn't decide for whom she might be spying.

I soon gathered that there was an enormous hatred among ordinary people for Mosley, the handsome man I had once briefly glimpsed near Marble Arch during a parade of Blackshirts. Onlookers standing on the pavements were jeering and shaking their fists at the marching men. I learnt that it was not only that he was a fascist, similar to Hitler, but because he was trying to stir up trouble for the Jewish people here in England.

Every Saturday morning Joan and I and all our friends used to learn about Hitler at the Mickey Mouse Club. The Mickey Mouse Club was a three-penny film show just for children and took place at the Classic Cinema in Praed Street, just across the Edgware Road. There we saw all sorts of short films, mostly cartoons or funny films like *The Bowery Boys* or *Our Gang*, The Marx Brothers, Laurel and Hardy and Charlie Chaplin. There were adventure serials too, which always ended at a crucial moment. This 'brought the house down' with cries of outrage, orange peel being thrown up in the air and boys' Blakey boots being stamped, as we were forced to leave our heroes, Tom Mix and Flash Gordon, in dire peril for a whole week. The usherettes would shine their torches in our faces to 'shush' us and threaten to call the manager. And when the manager came he would mount the steps up on to the stage in front of the screen, and say through a microphone: 'No more films until you're all QUIET.'

5. At the cinema.

After this warning you could 'hear a pin drop'. Children stuffed handkerchiefs into their mouths trying not to giggle or went red in the face trying not to cough, and anyone who sneezed got thumped by their friends. But the appearance of the manager on stage was an understood ritual and all part of the fun. The Mickey Mouse Club was the place where children were expected to 'let off steam'. It was part of our weekly treat. Another part would be the manager and usherettes standing by the Pay Box later, handing out oranges or apples or other small gifts. These had been sent along for us by one or another of the numerous small groups of kindly people from the middle or upper classes, who raised money for this act of charity by holding bazaars and soirees, or even special dinner parties, so we were told.

When we left the cinema afterwards, having seen Jane Withers, Edith Fellowes or a very young Shirley Temple on the screen (all of whom had done the necessary and expected bit of tap-dancing in the middle of their adventures) the little girls of sooty Paddington and Marylebone would hold out their skirts and tap-dance all down the cinema front steps in imitation. And the boys, after watching legions of cowboys and Indians chasing each other across the American prairies, would get their cap-pistols out of their pockets and 'shoot up' all the golden balls outside the many Praed Street pawnbrokers shops.

But never, ever, did I see anyone imitating Hitler. Even though we saw him nearly every Saturday on the Gaumont British or Movietone News or the Pathe Gazette newsreels, as he ranted and raved and thumped his fist before thousands of regimented Germans while the clockwork armies of jack-booted soldiers goose-stepped past their Führer with arms extended in the Nazi salute. Noisy Herr Hitler with his hair quiff and bulging eyes looked funny, there could be no doubt about that, and his moustache looked as though his razorblade had slipped and shaved too much off one side and he had tried to level up the other side, and so on: always misjudging it, until there was only a comical little bit left in the middle. Also the newsreels themselves often belittled him, calling him 'Mr Shickelgruber' or 'The House-Painter'. We children would sometimes laugh then because we were led into it. But most of us, I suspect, found something to be wary of in this man who could, at one moment, be shaking hands with beautiful blond little Austrians, the boys with bibbed leather trousers and the girls in dirndl skirts and with flowers in their hair, and yet who could, at the same time, instigate the humiliation of venerable-looking old Jewish gentlemen, who were made to scrub the streets or be taken around on carts with insulting labels tied around their necks for everyone to jeer at.

We witnessed regular newsreels of Jewish shop windows being smashed and yellow stars and the word 'Juden' being scrawled like marks of condemnation over walls and doors. Yet the real seriousness behind it all went over our heads. We were too young to understand. Those newsreels were political and for grown-ups. But there was one we actually spoke of between ourselves afterwards. It had shown a nicely dressed Jewish-looking toddler in a snowy public park in either Germany or Austria. His eager little face beamed with smiles as some bigger children approached him as if to play. But instead of playing,

*6. We learnt about Hitler
at the Mickey Mouse Club.*

they pelted him unmercifully with large snowballs until he collapsed under the weight of them. A woman then rushed forward to rescue him and carried him away in her arms. But the part that affected us all was when we saw the little boy's face slowly crumple in puzzled surprise and hurt as he realised that his 'friends' were his enemies. We understood that.

Our aunty Alice said that in her employers' drawing room was a framed photograph of Mr and Mrs Dundas with joined hands, cutting their wedding cake with a funny sort of axe. When she described it to Father he thought it was probably a model of the Fascist insignia. Later on, our aunt found out that they were not only friends of Mosley, but of Mussolini, the Italian Dictator. We had seen newsreels of him too at the Mickey Mouse Club: he looked like a mixture between Nero in our history books, and the Italian ice-cream seller who stood by the Clarence Gate at Regent's Park – but without the mustachios and straw hat.

Sitting under our table I once heard something exciting. Our aunt was telling our parents that because Mosley had so many enemies in England, he apparently had to be very careful when he was going anywhere. He had a secret code, she said, which was used to warn the people at his destination of his imminent arrival: and that the secret code was: 'Uncle Tom Arriving'. From then on, the popular children's story about the old-time negro slaves in America, which was called *Uncle Tom's Cabin* became inextricably entwined in my mind with Oswald Mosley the Blackshirt and his secret code.

One day, much later, the Honourable Ian Dundas casually mentioned to our aunt that whenever she took the little girl out, two armed bodyguards would be constantly watching over them. Quite surprised, our aunt enquired: 'Are they men or women?' She was wondering if she knew them. 'They could be one or the other or both,' she was told mysteriously. 'It's better you shouldn't know who they are or you might accidentally smile at them when you're out and then any kidnappers would know who to deal with first, before dealing with you and then taking the child.' It was when our father heard about this that he finally put his foot down and said: 'You should get out of it, Alice. It's not the job for you.'

It was not long after this that strange things began happening at home. One evening Joan and I had eaten our supper and were ready for bed, but we were waiting up to say 'goodnight' to our father, who was in part-time work again at the Holborn Restaurant. But he was late. He had one evening a week free and this was it. It was also a Friday: pay day. Our mother had made everything look nice for his return, his slippers were by the fire, his supper was in the oven and she had arranged her hair prettily and dabbed at her nose with her powder puff.

She had just told us that we had better go to bed and not wait up for him any longer when he came in. His face was rather red and he had an evening newspaper under his arm. Placing his trilby hat, gloves and newspaper carefully on the sideboard, he suddenly announced in his best 'butler's voice', only rather louder: 'If I could get my hands on Mr Herr Hitler, I'd set him on a dish and carve his cheeks off!'

I looked at him hard. It was such a strange remark for him to make. Usually he said: 'Hello Mabs. Hello Kids.' And then he would kiss us all. But he didn't do any of that. 'Chris, your supper is ready' our mother said quietly as she helped him off with his overcoat after glancing at him with a look on her face I couldn't fathom. She lifted the savoury-smelling rabbit pie out of the range oven and set it upon the table where his place was laid. She seemed unduly anxious that he should get down to the business of eating. We had not even said 'Hello' properly to him yet. Also we had been hoping for a bedtime story before we said goodnight.

He didn't seem to want his supper. He went over to where the cutlery lay neatly in place and slid it all to the furthest end of the tablecloth. Then he went outside the front door again and picked up two brown-paper carrier bags which had, apparently, been waiting on the doorstep. He came back in and put these down upon the table, while our mother slipped the pie back into the oven to keep hot. 'Come and sit down,' he beckoned to my sister and me, sounding excited. He called our mother over as well, 'Come on, Mabs, come and sit down.'

Our mother didn't seem to be wanting to join in this new game, whatever it was, but Joan and I were full of anticipation because the next thing he said was: 'I've got presents for all of you.' Then he began emptying the contents of the carrier bags on to the table. 'One for you, one for you and one for you.' Small gifts were put in front of the three of us: flowers for Mother and comics for my sister and me. Back to Mother again with chocolates, then in front of us girls two celluloid Kewpie Dolls. They had pale-blue feathers stuck on their flat celluloid hair and around their bare tummies, the thick glue hidden by lots of sparkly stuff. We had always longed to possess one of those Kewpie Dolls that we had sometimes seen men selling from suitcases at street corners. But Mother had always said that they were rubbish and inflammable and that, with their fluffy Oxford- or Cambridge-blue feathers they were only intended for selling to the crowds on Boat Race Day.

Next on the table in front of our mother came a string of glass beads. They twinkled like Christmas tree decorations when Father turned them to catch the rays of the gas lamp. They looked really beautiful to my eyes, but Mother's face showed no response. Then Joan and I were each given a sherbet dab and a lucky-dip bag. The gifts were worth only coppers but enthralling to us, whose Saturday pennies would not extend to such luxuries but must be wisely spent on long-lasting sweets like satin cushions, lime juice nibs or Paregoric drops.

By the time it was our mother's turn for the next present – which was a set of two matching hat pins stuck through a piece of card in a presentation box – I was amazed to see that tears were sliding, very slowly, down her cheeks. It rather took the edge off our next present, which turned out to be a golden net bag each, full of chocolate money. I saw our father getting annoyed that our mother wasn't as happy and excited about his lovely surprises as my sister and I were. It wasn't an ordinary look of annoyance, such as he might have given to us if we had been naughty, it was directed at Mother and it was a hurt look, as if he had been a child and it was his mother who was rejecting his presents. Dimly I became aware that something was going on in our home which I didn't quite understand.

Father came to the end of the presents, barring one for himself which he placed on the table before him. It was a bottle of whisky. 'And now, something for Charles,' he said, using his working-name as he screwed up the blue tissue wrapping paper into a little ball. He then rubbed his hands as he added: 'Something for a hard week's work.'

By this time our mother had brushed away her tears and was endeavouring to smile. She went over to the fireplace and, once again, took the rabbit pie out of the oven. I remember that it had a pie-funnel shaped like a blackbird, and that the blackbird's head was sticking up through the middle of the pastry crust with steam coming out of its open yellow beak. She set the cutlery before him but he pushed it away. 'Bring me a glass, would you?' I had never heard him use this imperious tone with our mother before. But she did as he bid her.

'Have you any money for me, Chris?' she asked softly, as she brought him the glass.

'Don't bother me, woman,' he said, half-filling the glass with whisky. 'Just bring me some water.' Mother shooed my sister and me off to bed then. 'Take all your lovely presents with you,' she said in a smooth, small sort of voice. It was as if she wanted to placate our father and make him think we were all really happy as indeed Joan and I still were.

They both came into the bedroom to tuck us in and say goodnight, Mother smelling of Coty face powder and Father with a strange mixed smell of hair brilliantine and whisky. But he was jolly with us and gave us a big kiss each and a hug. Our mother bent over and kissed us both in an especially tender manner. The glass beads, which were now around her neck, tapped our cheeks as she did so. Then they both went back into the next room, closing the door quietly.

Our presents were at the bottom of our bed. Joan was soon asleep beside me, clutching her teddy bear in one arm and her feathery Kewpie Doll in the other. I removed it gently in case she lay on it and crushed it.

I was restless. It was partly through excitement at having an ordinary Friday turned into a Christmas Day. Also going through my mind was a puzzlement at our mother's strange attitude to our father's generosity. Through the closed door I heard their voices talking late into the evening. Eventually I fell asleep, still thinking about what a strange Friday it had been.

9

Scents and Sounds of Baker Street

It was just as well that Joan and I soon became familiar with the streets and squares of our part of Marylebone, because we frequently had to grope our way home from school or elsewhere through the thick and eerie London fogs. They began in November and came down with increasing regularity, often for days at a time, all through the winters.

The 'pea-soupers', as they were called, were dense and acrid and yellowy-green in colour, just like real pea soup. It was when one of these was down upon us that every dusty tree and every soot-blackened railing and lamp-post could be either a friend or a hazard, all depending on whether or not we knew that they were there. We would grasp each other's hands tightly and be filled with excitement as we haltingly made a precarious journey home through the blinding fog, trying not to trip or to bump into anything hard on the way. Even the solid iron streetlamps became mere faint and wispy shadows. They appeared to float, like long thin phantoms in the dirty yellow murkiness that had crept silently over the city and swamped it. The lamps were made visible only by a dull haloed blur of light which encircled the gas globes and extended for an inch or two into the suffocating air. Appearing faintly on high, at regular intervals, those dim lamps became beacons before our smarting eyes and helped to guide us towards home through an otherwise invisible world.

As soon as we were outside the big black door of St Mary's School we would pull our scarves up tightly over our noses and mouths so that we could breathe. We would already have taken our wooden rulers out of our satchels so that we could prod and search at the fronts and sides of us, holding them out like the white sticks of blind men: scraping and tapping them against walls and shop fronts, fire alarms and pillar boxes. Or else we would rattle them against the railings, using the echoes to steer us through a strangely dark and almost silent world. The normally busy streets of Marylebone were practically empty at those times, for nothing and nobody ventured out unless they didn't have a choice. There was no rumble or hum of traffic, no clip-clopping of horses' hooves or sing-song calls of the cart drivers. Also there was none of the usual high-pitched squeals of laughter from the other pupils just released from school with us. All we would be able to hear were muffled shouts and calls, barking, choking coughs and the tap-tapping of our own, or other children's rulers or sticks, as we bumped and stumbled along York Street

or Crawford Street, a few hesitating inches at a time. Even
the sparrows who usually crowded together in noisy lines
on the high ledges and rounded facade of St Mary's Church
opposite the school would have stopped their chattering
and stayed silent and hidden.

*7. Coming home from school through
a noon-day 'pea-souper' fog.*

Sometimes, when the fog was so thick and long last-
ing that it seemed we might go on forever in a midnight
world, we would glimpse the outlines of tar-burners on
metal wheels stationed at various cross-roads such as
Seymour Place, and we would hear that a dozen or more
of them were in use at Marble Arch and Oxford Circus

and places like Hyde Park Corner. These fog-days were the only times when the children of central London did not immediately set off to witness things they heard were going on, or were about to, in any streets that were reasonably nearby.

The blazing tar-burner at the Seymour Place crossroads was the one we had to pass on our way home from school. We saw that it did actually lift the fog upwards for a few feet – just enough to ensure that any hapless traveller still not home and crawling blindly forward at a snail's pace did not bump into any other ghostly traffic doing the same.

Our parents, after delving into Father's green books again, thought that the tar-burners we saw were a modern equivalent of the old 'link-lights', the flaming tar-torches of hemp-rope and burning pitch that Victorian street-boys used to carry, so that they could earn a few pennies by guiding people safely to their homes through the fogs: also that the link-light holders and snuffers that we saw attached to so many of the house railings in the Bryanston and Montague Squares had originally been placed there so that the footmen, who had lit the links, would have their hands free to safely help down the occupants of returning carriages and guide them up the steps and into the halls. They would also be used by grooms or coachmen to lead horses by the bridle around the corners to the stables and coach houses in the adjacent cobbled mews: possibly with two accompanying footmen now holding the link-lights and with carriage-dogs at their heels.

It was when the fogs were down that all that area around Baker Street seemed to take on a ghostly Victorian, or even Georgian, atmosphere: a feeling enhanced by the fact that most of the architecture in Marylebone dated to those periods. Baker Street itself was surfaced with old tar blocks and some of the smaller streets on either side were still cobbled. The sound of metal-rimmed cartwheels grinding slowly over the cobbled surfaces, when neither horse, cart or driver could be seen, was an eerie phenomenon that we shared absolutely with generations of Londoners long passed.

London in the Thirties seemed to be standing with one foot in modern times and the other still in the days of Queen Victoria. Yet the two eras were so closely enmeshed that the resulting situation seemed normal. Even our coinage – our pounds, shillings and pence – mostly had the profile of Queen Victoria on them. So many coins were minted during her long reign that they were still the most prevalent in any purse or pocketful of change. Relatively few coins bore the heads of Edward VII or George V. When we were given our Saturday pennies we would gaze upon them like misers gloating over gold before parting with them. On most of them was the profile of the older Queen, in veil and tiny crown. They were still thick and sturdy. But some pennies and other coins had been worn smooth and wafer-thin. These bore the likeness of a young and pretty queen, who wore her hair drawn up at the back into a loose chignon, with ribbons floating down from it. These coins had been minted not long after Victoria came to the throne. They were known affectionately to everyone in the Thirties as 'Bun Pennies' because of her hairstyle. By that time all but the most old fashioned of women had had their long tresses cut off, and what remained was either bobbed or shingled or burned into a frizz by being twisted around metal 'bobbins' and then plugged into the terminals of electric 'Permanent Wave' machines. Other women had their hair Marcel-Waved with tapers at the hairdressers. But the majority heated up their own iron tongs on their gas rings, or simply by sticking them into the burning coals like pokers, and curled the ends of their own hair at home. Because of this it was not uncommon for people's living rooms to smell not only of cooking, and washing–drying, but also of hot or burning hair. On Friday evenings there was, in the homes of most of our neighbours, the traditional smell of women's hair being shampooed with green soft-soap and then dried before the fire. Just as in Victorian days, the living rooms with their open coal fires and cosy hearths were the places where most working-class families did nearly everything during their daily domestic lives. Bedrooms were sparsely furnished and cold. The thinly curtained windows, linoleum floors and draughty fire grates, which only contained hot coals when anyone was ill, were not conducive to doing anything there but climbing as quickly as possible into bed.

The streets of London had a smell which was uniquely their own. In winter there was the eternal and all-pervading smell of soot and chimney smoke, which was all mixed up with the traffic fumes and the tarry smell of the coal sacks on the coal carts. Then there were the smells of roasted chestnuts sold hot from the griddle by kerbside vendors, of sizzling sausages splitting their sides in the iron frying pans of old watchmen sitting in wooden huts, all rosy-shadowed by the heat of their glowing braziers as they guarded any holes in the roads left by the 'navvies' as the road-diggers were called. There were waves of hot air coming up from the Underground stations smelling of arcing electricity and the rags of the beggar-men who gathered there for warmth. There was the clean, warm smell of wooden floors and mahogany counters which wafted through the open doors of the Woolworths stores. On damp days all that wood took on the smell of chewed pencils. From small grocery shops came the aromas of bacon, paraffin and vinegar, and of sawdust on the floors.

Bell Street and Church Street were redolent with a variety of scents – too numerous to separate one from the other – for that was where the stalls of the street market men stood permanently amid the bustling throngs of local Londoners out looking for bargains. But hanging over all was the smell of mothballs from the naphtha lights, the earthy smell of vegetables and the sweet tang of oranges, tangerines, pomegranates, Cox's orange pippins and other fruits. The savoury smells of the pie shops and jellied-eel parlours lining the pavements with their mashed potatoes, boiled onions and mushy peas all in the bowls with the hot eels were vying with the aroma of hot newspaper wrapped around crispy battered fish and chips fried in beef dripping. At the ends of the days came the smell of bruised fruit and vegetable throw-outs, rotting in the gutters.

In hot summers the road surfaces bubbled with melting pitch-tar. There was also a smell of old drains in the back streets and, rising from the churns waiting for collection outside cool, marble-tiled dairies, came the smell of souring milk. All summer long, especially outside the parks it seemed, road surfaces were constantly being resprayed with hot tar followed by the hot, oily machinery of the heavy steam rollers which ground the grit and gravel into new-smelling smoothness. The crisply ironed Sunday best or Whitsun-white dresses of most little girls smelled of starch and their white canvas sandals of freshly applied Blanco shoe whitener. Then there was the fresh, watery smell of the lakes in Regent's Park and the fountains and Serpentine in Hyde Park – so welcome after the hot and dusty streets. Whenever we were taken as a treat to the Thames Embankment, there would be the strange 'old' smell of the river, with its water-lapped steps and ancient river-gates, its long barges gliding downstream and its pleasure steamers puffing upstream under the wheeling, screeching gulls.

In streets nearer home the smell of homemade vanilla ice cream, kept under the shining round brass lids of the Italian ice-cream carts, could be detected by a child at 50 paces! On our walks with our parents they became adept at spying-out beforehand those beautiful yellow handcarts, with their flower-painted sides and striped awnings with brass barley-sugar rails, which were stationed at so many street corners. In our parents' efforts to avoid them we seemed to be constantly crossing and re-crossing the streets or taking short-cuts that were really long-cuts. We pulled at their coats and, in vain, pointed out that there was 'an ice-cream man down there' – just as if they had been blind.

One set of smells which never changed, summer or winter, came from the reeking wooden beer casks piled high on the horse-drawn brewers' drays. Then there was the combined aroma of hay and ammonia coming from the horse-droppings which bejewelled the streets in various stages from steaming plump newness to the flattened dry dust of decay. But most overpowering of all was the pungent stench of horses' urine which splashed down onto the roadways and then trickled into the gutters as the great beasts pulled their loads through the jostling streets.

As well as the motor traffic – mainly buses, lorries, taxis, and a very few private cars – there were still tens of thousands of horses on the roads of central London. They were mostly cart horses and dray horses and the streets of Marylebone echoed all day long with the slow '*ker-lip-ker-lop*' of their heavy hooves. Even the ever-growing hum of the motor traffic did not drown it out. Some horses pulled coal carts piled high with glistening black jute sacks, filled with hundredweights of coal and nutty slack. The drivers wore leather aprons, and flat leather hats with long leather flaps hanging down their backs to protect their shoulders as they carried the heavy sacks over to the pavement coal holes, or else humped them up many flights of steps to the lidded wooden coal bunkers which many people had in their living rooms. Certainly, everyone in Crawford Buildings had one, and so did the parents of those children we knew who lived in the terraced houses nearby, because they nearly all housed two families. One family would have the coal hole at the front, and the coals would come thundering down into their basement cellar under the pavement. The other family would have a coal bunker on their upstairs landing, and after a coal delivery mothers, like ours, would have to take a wet cloth and wipe every surface in the home to wash off the film of coal dust which would have settled. Usually it required more than one wiping and the water from the rinsed out cloth was, at the end, black as ink in the bowl.

Other horses pulled the ice wagons, which carried huge pieces of ice on their planked wooden floors – some of the pieces as big as chests of drawers. Generally, the ice was being delivered to the fishmongers' shops. We always tried to climb up behind the ice wagons so that we could grab hold of any of the cold and slippery slivers which looked like being wasted. These we would wrap in our handkerchiefs and then suck with as much relish as if they had been the proper water-ices sold by the 'Stop Me And Buy One' man on his navy-blue box-tricycle. Stolen fruits!

To be seen at some time during the day, in nearly every street, were the horse-pulled carriers' carts. They were hooded over on top by heavy canvas, supported on half-hoops of metal, and looked just like the covered wagons we saw at the Mickey Mouse Club film shows. In those cowboy films the wagons were usually chased 'hell for leather' across the prairies by howling bunches of Red Indians until, usually, one or more of the wheels dropped off. Nothing like that ever happened in Homer Street. Our covered wagons proceeded at a slow and steady pace, stopping only to make deliveries of sacks or parcels of goods to shops. The only deeds of courage or daring that happened were when we steeled ourselves to gently pat the huge heads of those horses as they stood with them bent down into feed-bags or nose-bags, while their masters made the deliveries.

The hay carts and straw carts always looked top-heavy, with their golden loads piled up on high until they were as tall as double-decker buses. There were a great number of these going around the streets and leaving behind them a trail of straw, dropped from the swaying loads. We used to search the gutters for any wisps of straw or hay which still had their ears of corn intact – they seemed to provide a mystic link with 'the real countryside' and were much prized, even to the point of being used for bartering. The reason there were so many hay carts was that all the horses in London had to be fed and housed properly.

I knew one place where cart horses slept. It was close to Marylebone Station. Joan and I stumbled upon it quite unexpectedly one day when exploring the side turnings along Lisson Grove. At the far side of a quiet cobbled yard with a drain in the middle and quite a lot of straw blown into the corners we saw an archway, and then two high, wide double doors set into a stone wall. Through an

open railinged grid over the doors came the clanging sound
of metal on metal. So we peeped in. To our amazement,
there on the right of a long stone stable with whitewashed
walls, were six conker-brown carthorses with long white
hair feathering over their broad hooves. On the other side
of the stable were bales of straw or hay. The horses stood
with their faces to the wall and their heavy collars hung
from big spike-nails knocked into those walls just above
their heads. Stripped of their harness and not dwarfed by
their carts the animals seemed enormous. Some of them
had their noses in feed-bags and were swishing their long
thick tails contentedly. One had its eyes closed, as if it
was sleeping standing up. As they were not wearing their
leather blinkers, we could see properly for the first time
how large and gentle their eyes were and marvel at the
length of their eyelashes. But when they moved their heads
towards us inquisitively, at the ends of their arched mus-
cular necks, we leapt away from them as if we had come
upon a stable full of prehistoric monsters.

At the far end of the narrow stable, away from the
straw, was a glowing forge where a leather-aproned man
was hammering at something that was sending out sparks.
Between him and the horses was a stone drinking trough,
just like the dozens that were in the streets outside. The
man at the forge turned around and shouted to us to 'clear
off'. A flurry of pigeons and sparrows flew up from the
bales of straw and onto the stable roof as we ran across the
cobbles. We emerged back into the busy and noisy street
with the sound of their flapping wings still in our ears.

When we told our friends of our discovery, they didn't believe us until they had been to see for themselves. Quite soon the horses and their stable were visited by scores of children, because the news of their discovery spread all over Paddington and Marylebone it seemed. By the time the stable had become almost as famous as Tutankhamun's tomb, the stable-men had taken to 'boxing' the ears of every child who came near.

I always felt very sorry for the brewery dray horses. The draymen, usually plump and rosy-cheeked from drinking beer, would sit perched up on their high wooden driving seats, in front of the piled-up mounds of wooden casks and barrels. They wore stout brown leather aprons tied outside their coats, and bowler hats on their heads, and often they cracked their whips and shouted across to any other draymen they passed in the street. If the other man should crack his whip back it was like watching brown lightning streaking back and forth across the sky. But the horses, usually two to a dray, often looked as if they could hardly pull the heavy loads. I once saw a dray-horse collapse in Crawford Street, just outside the Macready House Police Buildings. The poor thing must have just given up. Lying down there, so ungainly in the roadway, the sweating brown horse seemed even larger than those we had seen in the stable. He must have slipped out of the shafts and was, at first, rolling on his side near the gutter. Then his legs stopped thrashing and he lay still, with saliva running from his mouth and only his frightened brown eyes still moving.

The other horse had an imponderable look on his face. He seemed to be wondering why his mate was lying down there with his head on a kerbstone, instead of standing up in his familiar place between the shafts. Several policemen on their beats soon gathered round. They gently shooed us away as they took care of the situation, and the next thing I saw was the collapsed dray-horse lying in the back of a big open lorry and being taken away somewhere. I had no idea where the lorry was going but I felt instinctively that that it was somewhere not very nice. At that moment I didn't dare to think of the 'cats-meat men' who went around selling small skewered pieces of horse meat from wicker baskets, or of the smelly pet shop on the other side of Baker Street which had long strips of shiny dark horse-flesh hanging from ceiling hooks in its window – most of it covered in flies, and all of it dyed a horrible bottle green by law, so that humans would not be tempted to eat it.

❧

The Express Dairy used medium-sized, high-trotting horses with shining flanks and neat heads and feet to pull their milk floats along the thoroughfares. The floats had pneumatic tyres on their wheels instead of the metal-rimmed wheels that seemed such an intrinsic part of most horse-drawn vehicles. The milkman, who by then delivered the children's free milk to the school every day in special bottles which held a third of a pint, told us during one of his ten o'clock visits that the new rubber wheels had been introduced to make the early-morning milk rounds less noisy for sleeping people. When I asked him, politely, why they didn't also let the horses wear rubber horseshoes, he just looked cross and muttered something incomprehensible. So I never found out.

Some milk was hawked privately around the streets by men who drove beribboned ponies, pulling gaily painted traps. These backless wooden milk traps looked a bit like Queen Boadicea's war chariots (that were pictured in our history books) but without the long knives sticking out of the wheels. In the back of each milk trap were two or three glinting brass churns full of milk. These self-employed milkmen used hook-handled brass ladles to pour out precise measure of the foaming creamy liquid, and aproned women hurried out, or down into the streets, clutching their purses and china jugs, as soon as they heard the traditional sing-song call of 'Milk-o-lay-he-dee!' When not in use the measuring-ladles dangled from the lipped necks of the highly polished churns, and they made a lovely jangling sound whenever the trap was in transit.

My schoolteacher in the Junior school, the prim and strict Miss Carpenter who was still spinsterishly thin and angular in her middle years and wore corded pince-nez spectacles clipped to her fastidious nose, warned all her pupils that the milk sold from those little pony traps was not pure. She also, every Yuletide, explained the Christmas Story to us unflinchingly over her pince-nez, telling us that the Virgin Mary was not like other mothers because she was pure, without explaining what she meant. Pure milk and the virgin mother stayed mixed together in my mind for years.

❧

The happiest horse of all, at least we liked to think so, was the one who pulled the children's merry-go-round from street to street. For a small bundle of rags, or half-a-dozen empty jam jars, children were given a lovely wobbly and squeaky ride on the swaying wooden seats of the merry-go-round. It was fixed to a platform in the pretty red-and-yellow cart, and could only be reached by climbing up to it on a short ladder. The man who turned the big handle to make the seats go rumbling round and round wore a straw boater hat and had wide leather straps around his wrists. He also had several gold teeth. There were ordinary junk men too, who yelled out 'Rag-a-Bones' as they drove their carts slowly along the kerbsides, until they came to the most suitable lamp posts for tethering their steeds. The chosen lamp posts were often the nearest ones to the public houses where, as the men said, they could 'wet their whistles' and 'slake the dust' out of their 'froats'. These junk men were not so interesting to us because they only gave us money – one or two coppers to take back to our mothers in exchange for rags, bottles or bones.

Our father, having originally been a country boy, was very fond of horses and would stroke or slap the great cart horses in much the same way that Joan would cuddle every cat she saw sitting on a doorstep. Often Joan would bang on a door knocker so that the people inside would open it and the cat could slip in. She always ran away afterwards – not so much from fear of getting caught but, with lots of giggles, because she hoped the people would think the cat had given a gigantic leap and knocked on the door himself.

One day, sitting quietly at home, our father suddenly said, as if to himself: 'Well, if there's ever another war, at least they won't need to use horses this time.' In response to our 'What do you mean, Daddy?' he blinked as if in surprise that he had spoken out loud, and then told us that when he had been a young hall boy at Keele Hall during the Great War, he used to spend a lot of his free time in the stables where, apart from the horses, he also had the company of the young stable lads. On one of his visits there he had been surprised to see an artist setting up his easel in one of the courtyards. Then, for quite a few days afterwards he had watched the artist, whose name was Alfred Munnings, proceeding as if in great haste to paint the portraits of two of the favourite horses of the owner of Keele Hall. Apparently, those horses had been requisitioned by the government and were soon to be put into service on the Western Front. Our father had become quite upset when relating this story to us, and it was not long afterwards that I overheard something which possibly revived the painful memory for him even though it was not about horses.

Aunty Alice had come to tea, and Father was saying to her and Mother, that one of the waiters at the Holborn Restaurant had been telling him about having once 'done a season' at the Imperial Hotel in Torquay, down in Devon. I already knew about Torquay because, once a year, our aunt had to stitch up all the main nursery furniture into sacking so that it could be sent ahead to Torquay, where her employers always rented a villa for a month. Although nursery equipment could be hired in the town it was considered more hygienic, even though it caused more work, for the child's own things to be used. Apparently, the Holborn Restaurant waiter had been telling Father how, one day, when he had gone out for a breath of fresh sea air after coming off duty, he had walked along an old stone pier which sheltered the Torquay outer harbour. There he had seen long narrow strips of steel being loaded off the pier onto a large tramp steamer. He was told they were the town's old tram-lines. On examination of the white lettering on the bows, he saw that it was a German vessel, from Hamburg. One of the local 'old salts' who had been standing by, watching, had then remarked loudly in his Devonshire accent: 'They Germans will probbly be droppin' them tram-lines back on us one day – as BOMBS!' When the grown-ups realised I was listening, they changed the subject.

10

A Stranger called King Pin

The Christmas of 1936 had passed, and, with shocked talk of Edward VIII's – the new king – abdication on everybody's lips, the country shivered into January and a year of change. For my sister and me the school holiday of that fateful winter would be the last one when we would have our mother at home with us for most of the time. In retrospect it was also to be the last reasonably carefree time of our entire childhood.

As if with some premonition of this our mother had been especially loving to us during those weeks, leaving her household chores to accompany Father and us along the cold ringing pavements to the wintry parks, where dried twigs snapped under our feet as we increased our pace to keep warm and where ice cracked at the edges of the lakes, frost whitened the park benches and a low pale sun glinted through the icicles that hung from the black branches of the leafless trees. It seemed that almost as soon as we had returned to the warm, gaslit classrooms of St Mary's, with shining new pen nibs dipped into fresh, clean ink wells, and written the strange new date of 11–1–37 on the first pages of our excitingly unsullied new exercise books, our mother went out and got herself a proper job.

Apparently, one day, when delivering clean washing to a house in Montague Square, she had been asked again if she would care to go down below for a cup of tea with the cook. Over the teacups she had been informed that a position for a part-time cook–housekeeper was soon coming vacant at one of the mews houses nearby, and that the people, a Mr and Mrs Coburn, were known to be good employers.

Our mother had applied for and got the job. She told us that Mr Coburn was a tall, well-spoken gentleman with a clipped moustache, horn-rimmed spectacles and a quiet manner. In his well-cut, expensive-looking, pinstriped suit, he looked like a country gentleman, she said, up in town on business or to visit his club or the reading-room of the British Museum. She had been surprised to learn that he was a film director. His wife was a tall, fair, charming and elegant woman, said our mother, and they had one little boy called Richard, who was about a year younger than Joan. She finished up by saying that the house and kitchen had been modernised and would be easy to run and that it was a topsy-turvy establishment with the reception rooms on the ground floor, and the kitchen upstairs with the bedrooms and nursery. This was because it was partly built over stables and therefore was an odd shape.

She thought it would be fun to work in a kitchen that was not in a basement, and where light and air streamed in through large modern windows. Last, but not least, it was just a hundred yards or so from our school, and the kind Mrs Coburn had said that we could always call to see our mother if ever we needed her.

We soon discovered all these things for ourselves because, before long, we found ourselves quite regularly being invited to have tea with Richard in his wonderful cream-and-blue painted nursery, listening to tales of Noddy in Toyland and Mr Plod the policeman on Richard's smart cream Bakelite electric wireless, and playing with his expensive toys with him. He was fair-haired like his mother and quiet like his father. 'I like Mrs Elliott's cakes,' Richard said to us one day between munches, and we beamed with pride and pleasure. 'Oh, we have them *all* the time at home,' I said. 'Could I come to tea with *you* one day then, please?' he asked. 'Of course you can,' we answered grandly, 'come whenever you like.' But he never came.

Richard was a nice boy, with nice manners, but he seemed lonely. I was sorry for him. In some ways he reminded me of myself at Queensberry House, but in reverse. He really looked forward to our visits and was eager to know all about the 'other children' he saw in the streets, but was not allowed to play with. And just as we tried to give him as much information as we could on how 'poor children' lived their lives and amused themselves, it was through our visits to his home that Joan and

I were given our first London glimpses of how the rich lived. Richard Coburn became almost as much part of our lives as our friends in and around Homer Street, such as Elsie Grey, Ernie Willard, Kathleen Rock, Lola Petit, Freda Green, Mary Stamp, Mabel Walker, Ivy Brown and Florrie and Harry Fielding. Back at Crawford Buildings, our friends wanted to know all about him and the way he lived. Unlike ourselves they did not have access to the lives or homes of the rich or the 'upper' classes and so, rather like the nannies in the parks, we became the go-betweens.

❦

It was quite like old times to see our mother back in her stiffly starched white linen housecoat and apron, cooking expensive meals – *real* mushroom soup and *real* meringues – for other people. Only this time, unlike at Queensberry House, the saucepans bubbled away on the top of a four-legged electric stove of mottled grey enamel which heated up at the turn of a knob, and didn't have cinders to be riddled. Also, although our mother had no kitchen maids to help with preparations (the only other person employed in the house was a daily cleaning woman) she found that in that pretty buttercup-yellow and china-blue kitchen, with all sorts of modern equipment, including a refrigerator, cooking for one small family was a comparatively easy task.

When our father was not working he provided us with our midday meals. Soon it seemed perfectly normal to us to have our father at home and our mother at work for much of the time. He always made a great show of greeting us cheerily, usually dressed in one of the white-bibbed twill aprons he had worn sometimes in the butler's pantry or in the wine cellar of Queensberry House, and with his sleeves rolled up in business-like manner as if he was about to feed an army of generals. He became quite proud of his soups and omelettes, soused herrings, toad-in-the-holes, hotpots and bread-and-butter puddings, and to our delight he never bothered to wait for the once-a-year Shrove Tuesdays but gave us a special Pancake Day all of our own every Friday. He always tossed the pancakes in the traditional manner and as they flew up from the black iron frying pan towards the ceiling it was like watching a circus act, and we squealed with mischievous anticipation as they always nearly, but not quite, went a bit too far and threatened to miss the pan on the return journey.

We quickly learnt to compliment him on his latest culinary creations. It seemed to put him in a happy mood. The table was always spread with a good clean linen cloth and beautifully laid, with 'all the trimmings' and the bread-and-butter cut so paper-thin that you could almost see through it. If we squabbled or misbehaved at 'his table' he would rap us on our heads with a wooden spoon, ladle or fish slice, whatever he had in his hand, so that we quickly sat up to attention. And always, before meals, he said grace.

I slowly began to realise that our father did not usually do things by halves, and that he was just a little bit larger than life than most other children's fathers. I also began to notice that he did not always sit down to eat with us, saying that he would have his own meal later. At those times he would disappear at intervals into the bedroom and come back quite jolly. Sometimes he would then get his wooden ukulele down from its nail on the living-room wall and sing a few songs to us while we ate. Songs like: 'There ain't no sense sitting on the fence, all by yourself in the moonlight'. He also used to sing a gentle little song which began: 'If you believe in fairies, they say ...' He told us it was *our* song – Joan's and mine – because he had retrieved the crumpled manuscript of it from a wastepaper basket when he had been working for our 'Fairy Godmother', Mrs Walter at Trevor Square, before I was born. She had been writing it with Noël Coward for a Revue, but it was never used. So with his usual flair for making our lives colourful Father had kept it until we were old enough to have it sung to us or, later, to sing it ourselves.

When both our parents were working at the same time, our mother would somehow manage to 'nip home' to Crawford Buildings for just long enough to give us a simple meal and then take us back early to school – popping us into the playground with our skipping ropes and waving us goodbye as she raced around the corner and back to the mews, just in time to serve up luncheon for the Coburns. But if Mr and Mrs Coburn were expecting guests then she would not be able to get away, for she would have to serve at table also. On those days the key to our front door would be left under the door mat and Joan and I would let ourselves in to the empty rooms. It was not nice then because there would be no fire lit in the grate and I would have to heat up whatever had been left for us, usually lentil soup, on the big black gas stove. Also, the cutlery would be laid out on American oil cloth instead of a proper tablecloth, and there would be no comforting homely sound of the kettle singing on the hearth. Sometimes we would be invited in next door at number 66, where the pleasant Irish woman called Mrs O'Brien would make us a cup of tea while we played with little Patrick, her baby boy. She was to prove a very good friend to us before long. At teatime our father's cheery resonant voice and our mother's gentle presence would be back in the apartment, making it seem like home again. Then we would all have a very substantial 'high tea' beside a rosy fire, and all would seem well again with our small world.

As time went on our mother began to go out in the evenings occasionally, either to do dinner parties for Mr and Mrs Coburn or on a freelance basis for other people. This was only at those times when our father was without work, of course. She was asked back so regularly that before long she seemed to have built up a special clientele of dinner-party people. They mostly lived in districts like Knightsbridge, Belgravia and Mayfair. Sometimes if the weather was fine, Father, Joan and I and would accompany her to her destination, either by bus or by walking down Park Lane or across Hyde Park. She always set off quite early because she liked to have plenty of time to see that, in the house where she would be preparing and serving the dinner later that evening, the dining room was properly prepared. The table must be made to look as attractive as possible with flowers and candles, her lady's best canteen of cutlery checked to see if any utensils had become 'bloomed'– by seeping fogs or for any other reason – before being laid. The cut-glass crystal had to be rinsed and polished to ensure its best sparkling effect in the candle light, and the silver, the chafing dishes, the wine cooler and coffee pots, which would later appear upon the sideboard next to the inevitable salver of salted almonds, were checked to see they had been properly polished and with no traces of unbrushed-out plate powder still lurking in the crevices.

I knew all this because, in those places where she had become established, our father would go in to help with this prior preparation and, naturally, we would go with them – under threat of the direst punishment if we misbehaved. We never needed to be punished because, with the instinct of children for recognising the really important things in the lives of grown-ups, we knew that any money our mother managed to earn all became part of a bulwark between us and those sort of 'rainy days' that could bring Christmases with no presents or (our mother's greatest fear) that could take 'the roof from over our heads'.

The dinner-party ladies never failed to be charmed by our father. Also, most probably, they were intrigued to have the attentions of an ex-butler (to such a long list of distinguished people) focused upon their dining rooms at no extra cost. From his demeanour and bearing at these times he did not seem like a man who was unable to find permanent work and, consequently, was not very happy.

When he had done as much as he could to help our mother with the preparations, he would leave her at work and shepherd us back home and to bed. Sometimes we would walk back across the park again, with the sweet evening smell of the linden trees in our nostrils, all mixed up with the fresh watery smell coming from the quiet Serpentine. And when mauve shadows piled up under the trees, no winds stirred the leaves, and the moon was beginning to rise in the general direction of the Grosvenor Gate and Berkeley Square, then the park would seem like an enchanted island.

Our world was considerably enlarged by these visits, and we could never thereafter pass certain houses or mansion blocks without thinking of the interesting things we had observed behind their walls, or the idiosyncrasies of some of the people who lived within. In New Quebec Street there was the doctor's wife who had become so afraid of germs left behind by her husband's patients that she wouldn't turn any door knob without first covering it with her handkerchief. In Mount Street lived the elegant lady with shingled hair who modelled hats for *Vogue* magazine, and who always liked her cream to be made at home from butter and milk by means of a 'new-fangled' cream machine, of which we were sometimes allowed to pump the handle. In Chiltern Court at the junction of Baker Street and the Marylebone Road lived another doctor, whose daughter Jillian we sometimes played with in Regent's Park, supervised by her nurse, or met for pre-arranged picnics. Early in the evening of one of the dinner-parties at Jillian's home our father came across one of the doctor's medical books lying on the sideboard for some reason. The doctor was actually an eye surgeon and the book was all about diseases of the eye. Father's attention was caught by something in it and he subsequently browsed through quite a few pages. We had an awful time with him for about a fortnight afterwards because he was quite sure he detected the first symptoms of about twelve different eye diseases. When he had quite recovered from them all, he gave us a piece of advice. It was: 'Never read a doctor's medical book!' I filed the guidance in my brain alongside his other similar warning of: 'Never study your face in a magnifying mirror!'

I was always very impressed by the houses or apartments of those well-to-do people: whether they were of the traditional type that had rich furnishings, Turkish or Persian carpets on parquet floors, deep leather armchairs, well-lit oil paintings in gilt-finished swept frames and such things as antique writing bureaux, or whether they were modern and uncluttered, with clean angular lines to the low furniture, electric wall lights of Art Deco design, Venetian blinds, cream or white paint and a preponderance of chromium and glass. What few ornaments there were in those modern homes had sleek elongated lines – even the flower vases were tall and thin and were more likely to have twiggy things in them than burgeoning garden-flowers, and the impression of airy space was enhanced by long thin mirrors fixed flush to the walls.

But whether those homes were traditionally furnished, with much of the furniture looking like heirlooms, or whether they were so much like smart Hollywood film sets that I half expected to see Fred Astaire and Ginger Rogers come tap-dancing out of an adjoining room, they all had one thing in common and that was the cream-painted doors and woodwork.

That cream paint was, to me, symbolic of the huge difference in lifestyles between the rich and the poor – that, and the amount of light in the rooms. The poorer people I knew usually had dark flowery wallpaper, often varnished over to discourage bugs, with dark green or brown paintwork, dark linoleum and dark furniture, the whole dark effect completed by yellowy-brown stained ceilings and heavy lace curtains across the window panes. This darkness was evidence of a lost battle against soot, coal dust, gas lamps, smoky fires and the steam from washing and cooking as well as from the street-grimy hands of children who, unlike the children of the rich, had no quick way of washing them and lived constantly in the living rooms because they had no bedrooms or other retreats of their own.

Not that the women were not house-proud and clean – quite the opposite was true. Every single day they meticulously scrubbed their wooden-topped tables which, although usually hidden under a tablecloth, were also used as the surface for food preparation. They also got down on their hands and knees each day to scrub clean their coal-dusted linoleum. Daily also, they cleaned out their fireplaces and, after an application of Zebra lead-blacking, polished their ovens until they shone. Some, as if to prove the real efforts they made, even whitened their hearths with hearthstone. Twice a week they polished all their brass, and their wooden furniture and upright pianos shone like dark satin from frequent applications of wax polish and 'elbow grease'. But whenever they opened their windows, even for half an hour, so much soot and so many smuts would blow in that they would immediately have to take a wet cloth or duster to their china spotted dogs, leaping horses and framed sepia photographs of their relatives and, sometimes, ancestors. Many women had collections of knick-knacks, curly ornaments and sentimentally treasured gifts or souvenirs, which were usually china boots or little vases overprinted with gold lettering saying things like: 'A Present From Clacton' or 'Handsome Is As Handsome Does'. These required a lot of dusting, but they were never 'put away' into cupboards for they had sentimental value. The reason that only the rich had the light paint and the light rooms was that only the rich could afford to pay other people to do the cleaning and to keep it all constantly that way.

Sometimes, when our Aunty Alice came to tea with us, she brought her friend, Christine, with her. Christine, like our aunt, was a rosy-cheeked children's nanny to a society family. But Christine had a friend who had a friend who was friendly with the nanny who looked after the royal children, Princess Elizabeth and Princess Margaret Rose. In May of 1937 the Princesses' parents were to be crowned in Westminster Abbey as the 'officially reigning' King and

Queen. Everybody that I listened to was saying 'what a shame' it was that these two nice people, the former Duke of York and his wife, who had received no proper training for the part, were suddenly going to be thrust onto the throne with all its duties and heavy responsibilities of State and Empire: 'And him, poor chap, with a stammer as well,' was the sympathetic codicil added by many ordinary people who had heard about his speech difficulty. Many 'upper class' people felt the same way about it – at least that was the impression I received from our mother, who was now in a position to hear snippets of dinner table conversations from a variety of sources. Father, too, was hearing the same sort of remarks at his dining tables at the Ranelagh Club and the Holborn Restaurant. He had also recently been given a few evenings of work at the Trocadero, and the Grosvenor House Hotel in Park Lane.

Nobody, as far as I could gather, seemed to think that there was anything very romantic about Edward VIII abdicating so that he could marry Mrs Simpson. Most people thought it was an irresponsible and selfish thing for him to do. 'He was the one who, as Prince of Wales had been trained from his youth to do the job. He was the one who had lapped up all the adulation that had gone along with that expectation and so he was the one who should have gone through with it, and not left his poor brother "in the cart",' seemed to be the consensus of opinion of the ordinary 'man in the street'. Even the children I knew were of the same opinion and I heard reports that some of them had chalked rude words on the walls and steps of

Bryanston Court, where, so it was said, Mrs Simpson had lived with Mr Simpson.

At the Mickey Mouse Club the newsreels were preparing us to receive our new king, who would be crowned George VI, with film clips of him and his family at home – and pictures of him and his wife and the two little princesses were beginning to appear on articles like tea caddies and biscuit tins.

Along the most elevated branch of the nannies' grapevine and down through one of its tendrils to Aunty Alice's friend, Christine, came the rumour that the new King and Queen were worried about their untrained children's ability to sit perfectly still throughout the forthcoming long ceremony of Coronation. Then apparently the children's nanny had stepped in with a suggestion – which was accepted. So henceforth, every day, for ever-increasing lengths of time, she made them sit still on very hard chairs 'without moving a muscle'. They had started off with just two minutes at a time and it was hoped that, by the end of their training, they would be capable of sitting as still as statues for more than an hour. At least this is what Christine had said.

Because the princesses were then about eleven and nine years old – roughly two years older than my sister and me – we found ourselves identifying with them. So when we heard about their hard-chair training, Joan and I also wanted to be trained. Aunty Alice and Christine and our mother and father looked up from the baize-topped folding card table where they were playing cards when at first they heard our request about the training, and laughed. The idea seemed to amuse them. But then they changed their minds and thought it a good idea. Somebody said something about 'keeping them out of mischief for a while'. It certainly couldn't do any harm, our mother observed. And then Christine said that if we could manage to sit still for an hour by the time the Coronation came, she would give us sixpence each. And then Aunty Alice said the same. Such riches. They probably didn't think we could succeed. But we did.

By the day of the Coronation I could just about manage to sit still for a little over an hour, and wriggle-stitch Joan could manage it to just the bare second when the time was up. But of course we – lucky pair – didn't *have* to do it. On that May morning when those other two little girls were going through their great test, Joan and I, who had been given the day off school, were out in the streets looking at all the decorations, the flying flags and red, white and blue bunting festooning every street and lamp-post, and saw that even the cart horses had red, white and blue ribbons plaited into their manes and the same wrapped around the cart drivers' whips. We watched side streets being cordoned off by policemen, and long trestle tables being erected down the middles of them for the great feastings of ham rolls, sticky buns, jellies, strong tea and beer, that were to come later. In some streets even peoples' pianos were being rolled out onto the pavements and the barrel-organ man, with a patriotic cockade on his battered top hat, was having a field day as he played the song that everyone had learnt at school: 'Here's a Health Unto His Majesty' over and over again. And then when we walked with our parents to Marble Arch and were fortunate enough to secure a place at the front of the thronging crowds, we had a good view of the new King and Queen and the princesses, all wearing their long robes of Coronation as they passed.

We hugged to ourselves the secret that we too had been trained for the great day, at the same time thinking ourselves lucky that unlike the princesses and the restricted life that was by all accounts ahead of them we could still jump about and do cartwheels and get dirty and play with all sorts and manner of children, and on top of that we still had what promised to be a jolly street party to look forward to, as well as the sixpences from Aunty Alice and Christine.

❧❧

Several months had passed since the Coronation before I began to realise that our father did not drink in the same way that other men did. I had never ever seen him go into a public house as quite a number of men in Crawford Buildings did – every Friday night without fail, some of them. Some fathers sent their children out with the big china jugs off their washstands to buy quarts of beer for them from the jug-and-bottle hatches of The Beehive or The Grapes. The fathers would then drink this at home, giving the mothers a glassful or two if they wanted it.

Sometimes the mothers went down for the beer, occasionally with more than one jug to be filled. But more usually the men would 'pop out for a quick one' by themselves on Friday or Saturday nights, and come home for their suppers, merry but not drunk. Our next door neighbour Mr O'Brien, was like this. He had his drink but didn't get drunk.

The O'Briens were a really nice couple in their late twenties. She had a lovely Irish face with dark hair, high cheekbones and an expression similar to the angels in the stained-glass windows at church. He was not as tall as she was and looked quite like the crooner called Bing Crosby, whose picture I had seen in still photographs outside the Blue Hall cinema on the Edgware Road. It was a delight to take their son, Patrick, for walks around the block in his smart grey hooded pushchair with chromium mudguards.

Our mother often went into number 66, to share a cup of tea with Mrs O'Brien and of course Joan and I went too. As usual we would listen to their conversations. A lot of adult talk I fully understood, but some of it was still incomprehensible to me. Like when Mother told Mrs O'Brien that our father had been coming home late from the Grosvenor House Hotel one night after a long and arduous term of duty, when he was accosted outside the Lyons Corner House at Marble Arch by two 'street women'! Apparently they had said to him: 'We haven't eaten for two days Guv', so you can have either of us for ten bob.' When Father had protested that he hadn't got ten bob, in order to get rid of them, they had put the price right down to 'half a dollar' which was half a crown, or two shillings and sixpence. Father still refused, and increased his walking pace. They had clung on to the lapels of his dark grey Melton overcoat and cried: 'Oh, come on sir, you can have the BOTH of us for half a dollar.' Father had then stopped and explained to them gently that, sorry for them though he was, he was nevertheless a very tired waiter who had just come off duty, and would not have been able to take advantage of their kind offer even if they had paid him. Whereupon they had turned on him with verbal abuse to the effect that they had mistaken him for a toff, whereas he was nothing but a horse-dropping.

Another conversation that didn't make sense was when Mrs O'Brien told our mother that she didn't sleep with her husband in the bedroom, but slept each night on the 'put-you-up' bed-settee in the living room instead. She was scared of having any more babies, she said, because she had piles. I thought she meant piles of children and couldn't understand it, because she only had Patrick.

Mr O'Brien was a gentle fair-haired Irishman. He always dressed nicely in a three-piece suit, and went off early each morning with a ledger under his arm to some mysterious job somewhere. Whatever it was it was regular work and you could tell from their home that his wife was in receipt of regular wages. This was partly because everything in their living room had been hire-purchased, new, in sets, and everything matched everything else. Another strange thing in that world of brown paint and brown furniture that we lived in was that nearly everything in the O'Briens' living room was of a delicate shade of blue. Mrs O'Brien liked it that way. She said it was the colour of the Virgin Mary. They were staunch Roman Catholics.

As the orphanage where our mother had spent the greater part of her childhood had been run by Catholic nuns she and our neighbour often talked about nuns, and subjects like that. My sister and I knew very little of the Roman Catholic religion because we were Church of England, as was our school. On Sunday afternoons we became Methodists as we went to Sunday School at Paddington Chapel which was on the Marylebone Road just at the end of Homer Street. We could see its rooftops from our living-room window, next to Queen Charlotte's Lying-in Hospital. Many women had their babies there, and hanging suspended over the pavement outside like a tradesman's signboard or a barber's striped pole was a giant, painted wooden stork, with a bonny baby in a napkin hammock swinging from his beak. It was about ten feet high and hung out over the highway by an equal distance. No woman looking for that maternity hospital in a hurry could have missed it.

Our father 'didn't hold with' the Catholic Religion. He had been brought up very strictly as a Wesleyan Methodist. He often told us that one of his ancestors had been very friendly with the Wesley brothers, and that they had all galloped around the country on their evangelical horses, spreading the 'Good News' from the gospel. But although he spoke of these historical things, he very rarely went to Chapel himself. Only at Harvest Festival times. He liked looking at the wheat sheaves and plaited loaves and all the vegetables and flowers.

One rainy afternoon our mother was upset. Father was speaking in a loud voice and refusing to eat his midday meal, even though it was by then about three o'clock. He smelled of whisky again. I was returning from the taps on the landing, trying not to slop water from the over-full enamel jug. Joan was playing outside our front door, throwing her ball up the stone steps leading to the flat roof and letting it bounce lazily down again, taking care it didn't roll through the iron bannister rails and fall down into the dark, echoing stairwell, storeys deep. Suddenly our front door opened and I saw Father come out of our living room and step on to the stone landing. He stood still a moment and then took two strides forward yelling 'I'm King Pin!' and leapt over the bannisters. He was still yelling like a Red Indian as he disappeared, feet first, down the stairwell. There was a thud, and then all was silent. I put down the water jug and cried out: 'Mummy, come quickly!' On tiptoe I peeped over the bannisters. Joan, letting her ball roll into a corner, tried to look down through the bannister spaces – her brown eyes quite as round as they had ever been at the Mickey Mouse Club.

Far down below I saw the people who lived in the four corners of the dark basement depths rush out of their doors, as if to discover what had come noisily down into their previously little-used part of the stairwell. They moved simultaneously to the centre of the well, like dark patterns in a turned kaleidoscope. Then they stooped down over the prone figure of our father. Four men carried his limp body back up to us, cursing under their breaths as they manoeuvred his dead-weight along the five landings and up the six flights of steps to our front door. They laid him out before our mother and us, with his head resting on our front door mat, and his feet resting on Mr and Mrs O'Brien's front door mat. 'Chris! Oh Chris!' Mother almost shrieked as she knelt beside his motionless form. 'Speak to me!'

But he didn't speak. Or move. Damp strands of dark hair wove waxy patterns across his pallid forehead. His features were still, his blue eyes hidden by his closed eyelids, as if in peaceful sleep. 'Somebody ought to go and get a doctor,' said one of the men, looking worried.

'Dear God! It's too late for a doctor,' cried Mrs O'Brien, 'somebody had better be fetching him a priest.' At the word 'doctor', I thought I had seen a tremor run along Father's long slim body. At the word 'priest', one blue Wesleyan eye opened and Father came back from the dead.

By this time a little crowd of other neighbours had gathered round. To sympathetic murmurs of: 'Come on old man,' 'Steady there' and 'Easy does it,' our father did some amazing contortions in front of that encouraging audience, as he struggled to rise to his feet. With the assistance of our mother, and Mrs O'Brien and the basement dwellers, he would get part way up and then, like a new-born colt, his long legs would straddle out from under him and down he would go again. Then all of a sudden he was on his feet properly, looking as pleased and proud as any butterfly just emerged from a chrysalis. Somebody said that he shouldn't really have been moved, another said that he must have broken his fall somehow, or he wouldn't have survived. It seemed to me that everyone there except Joan and me, and our mother, after I had whispered the truth to her, was taking it for granted that our father had simply *fallen* over the bannisters, somehow. Some instinct told me to keep quiet about what my sister and I had seen, and Joan seemed to have been struck dumb by it all anyway. Father was, miraculously, quite unhurt, and his quick descent from the top of Crawford Buildings to the bottom seemed to have sobered him up. Standing erect now and with head high, he smoothed back his hair with his hands. Then he bowed from the waist to his rescuers and, with an elegant flourish of his right hand and forearm, swept off a non-existent top hat. 'You are all gentlemen, sirs,' he said, 'and I thank you.' Then 'King Pin' followed our mother indoors to eat the meal that she had been trying to 'get into him' for hours – and we girls skipped in after them, thankful to see everyone happy again and proud that we had not betrayed our father's secret.

But it was a secret we would not be able to keep much longer. The 'King Pin', alias Dr Jekyll part of our father, would soon be taken over, at intervals, by a terrifying Mr Hyde. Many times in the past he had said to 'always remember, you nippers, that you come from good stock.' I already knew from our mother's activities that 'good stock' was the basis of a good soup. Fairly soon I began to realise that he was not talking about soup but possibly trying to tell us that if we were lucky, we too might grow up to have nine lives just like he had. The time was fast approaching when, one way or another, we were going to need all nine of them plus all the love, for the three of us, that our mother had to give.

'All the world's a stage,' said Shakespeare, 'and all the men and women merely players.' We were not aware in that fast fading summer of 1937 that the first act of our childhood was over, nor that the second act was about to reveal some horrible new twists in the tale. For meanwhile, standing in the wings awaiting his cue, was Hitler. Yet before the second curtain came down, we were going to learn some unexpected things about the nature and power of love. And that, ultimately, is what this true story is all about.

11

A Fog to Remember

Just before Empire Day in May of 1938, when I was ten years old and my sister nearly eight, we were issued with gas masks. After collecting them from the Marylebone Town Hall we had climbed up onto one of the stone statues of lions, outside the high entrance doors, to try on the peculiar-looking contraptions. There we had sat with several of our school friends on the lions' backs, all wearing our new gas masks, and falling about with laughter as the smelly black rubber at the sides of our faces snorted and burped and made rude noises, like a row of whoopee cushions, as we purposely breathed very heavily in and out. The sun was shining brightly on the busy Marylebone Road. Many passing grown-ups, when they saw us having such fun on the lions, smiled or waved at us as they walked by. Some even paused a moment to watch us. Nobody told us off for misbehaving, which was quite unusual.

Against a background of impending crisis in Europe and big black headlines on the news boards of all the newspaper sellers, a smaller and more secret struggle was taking place in our own home. Our high apartment in Homer Street, up with the sooty sparrows and the smoking chimney pots, had become the scene of many hair-raising, or even spine-chilling incidents. In the end I think that even our sensible mother was beginning to wonder whether our two rooms were haunted by a malevolent spirit – whether, in fact, our father had become possessed by some evil entity which had decided to dwell with us.

My sister and I were sometimes, for safety, put to sleep at night on a single mattress in the enamel bath which stood on its four claw legs in the communal wash house. We took turns in sleeping at the uncomfortable end, underneath the brass cold-water tap. Even though our mother plugged it up with a cork at such times to ensure it didn't drip on us, we nevertheless always had the feeling that it might!

Sometimes, when we slept in the bath, the remains of some other family's wash-day fire would still be glowing in the firebox under the brick copper. After she had kissed us goodnight, our mother would turn the big iron key in the door lock and then go back to our rooms at the end of the stone landing to face our father alone. We would then watch the fire-glow glistening on the damp walls, straining our ears for sounds we had come to dread. Still wondering, helplessly, about all the things we knew might be happening between our parents, we would eventually fall asleep. But it was not easy.

The first inkling that all was not well had come one Sunday in the previous winter of 1937, just as we were about to sit down to our midday meal. As far as we could tell it was going to be a very ordinary London day for the time of year, being cold and foggy and nearly as dark as night. Since late on Saturday evening the fog had been wreathing around the buildings. Now it was like a thick greeny-yellow blanket smothering most of the great sooty city. The Marylebone streets below our windows were silent. The fog pressed in so close to the cold windowpanes that everything had disappeared from view.

It seemed so warm and cosy in our living room compared to the inhospitable world outside. I knew that all the motor buses would have been withdrawn, the taxi cabs would not have ventured out, and down there in the murk lots of people would be helplessly lost – tripping and stumbling blindly against kerbstones and bumping into lamp posts as they tried to find their way home from churches and chapels. As Joan and I finished laying the table, and the shining cutlery was all set out in proper fashion on the best starched white damask cloth, reflecting the gaslights and the rosy glow of the fire, I thought again of how safe and secure we all seemed in our little nest, marooned together on high.

Mother lifted the roast beef and Yorkshire pudding out of the polished range oven on the right of the fire and after putting them onto the big blue-and-white oval meat dish she carried them to the table. There she set them down beside the gravy boat and the lidded dishes of hot vegetables. We knew they would be followed later by the traditional Sunday pudding of apple pie and custard. Our father came over to the table. He had been drinking during the previous week. His face was very pale, and his eyes were red-rimmed. But now, at last, he seemed to be getting over it. I said a little prayer of thanks behind my closed eyes and prayer-positioned hands as he started, very shakily, to say grace before the meal: 'For what we are about to receive may the Lord make us truly thankful. *Amen.*'

'*Amen,*' we all repeated after him and then everyone sat down, ready for the meal to begin. Everyone, that is, except Father. Nothing seemed wrong. He was just a bit slow, I thought, at picking up the carving knife and fork and starting to carve the joint – that was all. I took no notice of him until I heard him say, in a quiet voice: 'I'm going to do away with us all. You girls first, then your mother, then me.' I looked across at him in startled amazement and saw that he was holding a gun: a revolver.

I can't recall what our mother said or did, but I can still clearly remember Joan and myself squealing: 'NO Daddy DON'T!' in very high voices, and ducking under the table – my heart beating as fast as a bird while we crouched within the encircling folds of the long tablecloth. I also remember the awful feeling of dread as we waited for him to 'do away with us' while we were down there. Strangely too, although I was only nine years old, it bothered me that I was going to die in such an undignified manner. I saw Joan looking at me in the shadows with big frightened eyes. Her full lips had disappeared into a tense white line and her little face was as pale as the tablecloth. Her fear so affected me that I put my arms around her. After which my mind became a total blank.

The following day I learnt that our father had picked up the gun in the house of Mr and Mrs Coburn where he had gone to meet our mother from work one evening after a dinner party, and arriving too early, while the guests were still in the dining room in fact, had seen the gun while passing the open drawing room.

When our Aunty Alice came to see us the following Thursday, our mother related all this to her, including the interesting thing her employers had said to her when she later returned the gun to them. Apparently, it was Mr Coburn's old army revolver and Father had looked for the bullets and loaded it. But had he fired it, Mr Coburn said, his hand would have been blown off because there was something wrong with the mechanism. Mr Coburn had also, it seemed, been most concerned for the welfare of Mother and Joan and me, and didn't know what to do for the best. In the end he decided not to take the matter further because of the stigma that would fall on us if there was a prosecution. But he had asked her to consider whether it might be better for her, and us, to leave such a dangerous husband.

'It's all because of Chris' sunstroke, you know,' said Aunty Alice after she had listened to the whole story: 'You know, Mabel,' she said, 'he was such a kind boy. It must have been the sunstroke.'

I then heard for the first time one of the really old family stories from the days when our father had been a boy, and Aunty Alice a little girl: with their six or seven other brothers and sisters they had all lived together in Shropshire at the place called Allport Farm. It seemed that in the August of 1911, when our father was just nine years old, he had been sent into the fields of a neighbouring farmer to help the men gather in the harvest. It was apparently one of the hottest days ever recorded in England. The temperature was climbing up to the top of the blistering nineties. Just before noon, all the men and boys had sat down in the shade of a hedge-bottom to eat and drink. When Father had finished his billy-can of cold tea he was still thirsty. One of the men, for a joke, offered him a drink of the beer he had brought with him in a brown stone jar. It was a strong brew known as 'Harvest Special'. Just a few mouthfuls had such a comical effect on the young boy that the other men let him drink some of their own beer too. It was all done in good fun, but before long he was sick and feeling poorly. They then laid him in the shade, under the widest hedge-bottom, to sleep it off, while they went back to work on the far side of the shimmering cornfield. The sun began to drop from its noon position and was soon shining down from the other side of the hedge, full onto Father's sleeping form.

When the men returned they found him collapsed with sunstroke. Hurriedly they lifted a field gate from its hinges and four men carried him on it through the shady lanes to his home. Another man ran across the fields to the village in the opposite direction, in order to fetch the doctor. When he arrived in his pony trap he found our father so ill that he quickly transported him to his own home, where he could receive proper nursing, and straw was laid thickly in front of the house to muffle the sounds of cartwheels, horses' hooves, hobnailed boots, and the occasional carriages or anything else that could disturb him.

The story ended with Father slowly getting better, and then being warned by the doctor that, because his sunstroke had been so nearly fatal for him, he must never again in his life stay out in the hot sun. Also, that, when he grew up, he must never touch alcohol, or he might get 'brainstorms'. It was mainly because of this that, as soon as he was fourteen and all the 'big houses' were short of footmen because of the Great War, his mother had seized the opportunity to put him into private service rather than risk him working on the land.

After first listening to the sunstroke story I immediately began to wonder why, if that was what a lot of sunshine could do to you, so many grown-ups were taking up the fast-growing summer fashion of sunbathing, and why the banks of the Serpentine were so heady with the fragrance of sun-tan oil all through the summer months. Didn't people know of the danger they were in?

Soon afterwards I heard our mother tell Aunty Alice that Doctor Armstrong, our family physician, had now diagnosed his problem as dipsomania or alcoholism. That, apparently, meant that Father could never again with safety touch even one little drop of alcohol. That he must forget the desire to be like other men, refreshing himself with a glass of beer after a hard day of work because, by some quirk of nature, he had become one of those people who would never be able to control their drinking. That just one little drink would assuredly set things off again. Even after an abstention of many months.

Aunty Alice didn't like to admit to the possibility that there could be alcoholism in her family, because of the shame that was attached to the word. She preferred to think that it was all because of his sunstroke – at least that was the impression I got. Our mother also didn't seem to know what to think. I knew she was getting all mixed up with her thoughts, because she had begun to talk to me about some of her feelings. Slowly I was becoming her confidante. She could not understand how a man who professed to love her could keep gambling with their love. She was referring to his repeated attempts to prove to himself, and others, that he really could have just one drink and leave it at that. It always ended in disaster and with me and my sister having to sleep in the bath again.

In between the times when I was afraid of him or even hated him, and those other times when he was his old normal self and I loved him, there were moments when I experienced an insight quite beyond my years and realised what secret shame he himself must be suffering, as he became aware that something incomprehensible was happening to him. I also felt a great hurt for him inside me when I noticed that the proud man who was my father was no longer respected by some of the people who knew him.

Meanwhile, neither my mother or sister or I ever lost hope. He still had the kind of smile that made you feel warm and important, and performed little kindnesses or 'surprises' that few other men would even have thought of. Whenever he came to the end of a drinking bout and was looking ill, or even wept, he would ask us to forgive him: promising it would never happen again. We always forgave him. And we always believed his promise. After the incident with the gun, I really believed that the realisation of what he had nearly done would cure him by giving him as big a shock as it had given us. I didn't much care for sitting under a table waiting to be shot.

Ever since the time when Father had jumped over the bannisters shouting, 'I'm King Pin,' I began to notice that he seemed to be known by several names. Whenever he drank, the frequent yell of 'I'm King Pin' would let the neighbours know that his 'other self' was in residence at number 67. I once heard two of them agreeing that he was a 'Doctor Jekyll and Mr Hyde' although they called him Mr Elliott to his face. To our mother and aunt he was Chris, to us he was 'Daddy', to Mr Barnes the Yorkshireman who lived opposite us at number 64, he was sometimes 'that drunken sot'. At work where, apparently, he was so popular with the guests or diners that their enquiries as to his whereabouts after the many times he was sacked for turning up drunk always ensured that after a decent interval he was taken back on again, he was known either as 'Charles' or, especially to visiting Americans at the Grosvenor House Hotel, as 'Jeeves'.

Every morning when he was sober, which was still the greater part of the time, he would bring us all biscuits and tea in bed saying: 'Here comes Charles with the tea,' as he carried in the tray. Or if Joan or I woke in the night with cramp or 'growing pains', he would get out of bed and 'rub it better' saying: 'Doctor Elliott will soon cure this.' And he did cure it, too. What he couldn't cure was our uncertainty as to whether our normal loving father would be coming home to tea, or supper, each day, or whether a monster who, behind his red face, tumbled hair, bared teeth and red rolling eyes looked vaguely like Father, would be lurching noisily around our domain – and smashing some of it.

Whenever he got drunk and roared his way home, arms flailing, fingers gesticulating, and voice raised to a pitch five times above the accepted noise level so that people could still hear him even with their doors tightly shut, our problem became one that was extremely difficult to keep secret, or to ourselves alone. I frequently felt that I could have done without having such a well-known and famous father. Psychologically it was very mind stretching, because we all loved him and were proud and ashamed all at the same time.

After each one of Father's periodical Doctor Jekyll and Mr Hyde impersonations, it took ages to get the family finances back in order. Because of the sheer dramatic scale of them they required a lot of money. As he had none, Father ran up credit by having his drinks put 'on the slate' in various pubs in Marylebone, and sometimes beyond. His wages or dole were sometimes 'in hock' for months ahead. He always chose the nicer types of public house, like The Yorkshire Stingo on the Marylebone Road, or The Wellington in Crawford Street. The ordinary spittoons and sawdust type of places were not at all to his taste. Also, apparently, he was very generous to every stranger he met, when well into one of his drinking bouts.

'He was drinking and throwing his money round like a lord,' our poor mother would sometimes be told by neighbours, or others who had happened to witness the scene. It was one of the few things that could make her really angry. Sometimes she would cry bitter tears. It sickened her to think that he was distributing drinks around with the same sort of largesse as some of the gentry and the other privileged people they had once worked for, while she was having a struggle to bring up her children properly and make ends meet. Often it meant that our mother had to take in washing again or do sewing for people or do extra dinner parties, as well as work for Mr and Mrs Coburn and look after us all. She once told me she could never understand why publicans and tobacconists kept giving him credit. It made her either angry or despairing, depending upon the size of the debts she had to repay. Yet at the same time I think she secretly knew that, because he was so very likeable when he was sober, other people couldn't resist him or withdraw their support any more than she could herself.

On top of ordinary debts Father would pawn things, and then more money was needed in order to reclaim our possessions. The pawning was often the first and only

warning that he was 'off again'. As time went on I began
to think of myself as our mother's protector. Sometimes
I even wished that I had been born a boy so that I could
have protected her better. Sometimes I felt much older
than I really was. There were days on end when our home
life was like trying to live, eat and sleep on a brightly-
lit theatre stage during a non-stop Victorian melodrama.
When our mother cried out or wept it not only frightened
and saddened me, but I felt that as the eldest child I had to
sort it out somehow and I didn't know how to.

The reason our father pawned things when he badly
needed to drink was because that was the most usual way
for working-class people to obtain money quickly. The
traditional pawnbroker's sign of three golden balls suspended from outside wall brackets were a familiar sight in
the streets. They hung out quite a way over the pavements.
The brightly lit fronts of the premises were usually in
main streets. Electric lights shone down closely on ladies'
unredeemed wedding rings or engagement rings, making
them sparkle as if they had recently adorned the hands of
duchesses instead of the probably work-coarsened hands
of women who had once been full of romantic dreams,
but were now worried to death about things like rent or
doctors' bills, or children's boots or how to get a proper
meal on the table. Or even, as with our own mother, about
their husbands' drinking, or gambling or inability to find
permanent work. So there, at the sides or rears of the pawn
shops, usually in dingy back streets or alleyways, were
dark doorways where people wanting either to pawn or

redeem their possessions went inside. When they paid back the money they had received on pawned items, plus the interest, it was called 'redeeming the pledge'.

Behind the metal-barred windows of the pawnbrokers' shops there were also men's silver or gold pocket watches, fob chains, cufflinks, silver cigarette cases which had probably been wedding gifts, dressing table sets, and hat boxes or collar boxes made of leather. Bundled against the glass in less prominent windows were shirts, blankets, boots and shoes and piles of yellowing linen. In 'oddments' windows were violins, piano-accordions, banjos and ukuleles and other such popular instruments. Gazing into such windows made me feel sad. Our own mother, somehow, had rarely failed to get enough money together in order to redeem our things. But even she had been unable to save the presents that the Maharaja's children had given to Joan and me so long before. My silver bangle and Joan's silver necklace had actually been pawned by her in desperation, along with her own engagement ring and Father's 21st-birthday wristwatch from the Cheshire lord, during the awful time just before the mid-1930s when we had no money and nowhere to turn. By the time the situation had eased, the date on the redemption ticket had long run out and we never saw our treasured things again. Mother used to grumble that, had she known the pawnbroker would eventually be able to claim them and sell them, she would have demanded a decent price for them.

In Praed Street, the road leading from Paddington Station to the Edgware Road, there were so many pawn shops that it was known locally as 'the street of golden balls'. The pawn shop our father most frequently used was in a quiet street beside Dorset Square. It was not far from our home, being halfway between the Marylebone Station and the Regent's Park end of Baker Street, but there were many times when it felt to me like a trek from the outskirts of the city.

As soon as I was old enough, it became one of my 'jobs' to take the green pledge ticket and the necessary money to this pawn shop, in order to retrieve the item that Father most frequently took. Our mother was too ashamed to collect it herself, because it was not something that could be hidden in a handbag, or a shopping bag, or even under a coat.

'Hello. Come for your gramophone, have you?' the pawnbroker would ask affably as he turned to take the familiar black-cased instrument down from one of the deep shelves behind him. He knew me well. His eyes always twinkled when he spoke to me – possibly at the sight, once more, of the thunderous scowl of disapproval I always put on my freckled face just for him.

Then I would have the job I hated: of carrying the heavy machine across the Marylebone Road, down York Street to Seymour Place, and then to Homer Street. All the way I would have to keep changing it from one hand to another because its weight seemed to increase as the journey pro-gressed. I blushed madly if anyone looked at me. I felt sure that anyone seeing a young schoolgirl lopsidedly carry-ing a heavy gramophone along those busy thoroughfares would know for certain that she was not about to join the buskers or the street musicians, but that she must have come straight from the pawn shop. I found it irksome and strange that something which was so commonplace and often a necessary way of life for many people should at the same time be considered so shameful. Pawning was thought of as a disgrace in much the same way that children with nits in their hair, or fleas, or bug bites were scorned for something they couldn't help. Or like the shame suffered by the poor children whose mothers gave them bits of old rag for wiping their noses instead of properly hemmed handkerchiefs. All too often they were the butts of jibes or taunts from other, more fortunate, children. Just as I was, now and then, for having been seen coming home from the pawn shop or having a drunken father.

When at last I got the gramophone home again, we would always immediately play it to ensure that it was still all right. And later in the day when our father came home from wherever he had been, he would say, sincerely, how pleased he was to see it again, and how sorry he was that he had taken it away from us, and how it would never happen again. And, believing him, our eyes would shine and we would hug him with happiness and relief that everything was so normal and pleasant again. After which he would do something for my sister and me that he had done dozens of times before: 'I fancy an egg for my tea,' he would say. 'Where's my egg-laying record?'

Quickly we would hunt through the pile of gramophone records on the end of the dresser for the green-labelled one called: 'The Happy Fellow'. We would set it up ready to be played and then our father would place a folded linen table napkin over the small pit beside the turntable, which was a common feature with most gramophones. Then he would start up the music. It was a whistled tune, and he would whistle along with it to get the 'magic' working properly. The piece would be brought to an end by a recorded cockerel shrilling out a loud '*Cock-a-doodle-doo*!' There would be an expectant silence, apart from the repetitive '*click*' of the polished steel needle running around the deep grooves at the centre of the record. Then would come the muffled sound of Father's hand groping in the pit below the folded napkin, to see if the gramophone could still lay eggs. Sure enough, to our never-ending delight and surprise, it always could. Our mother would stand beside him, smiling, as he brought his well-manicured hand up from the bottom of the pit and there, nestling in his palm, would be a beautiful brown egg.

The other items which made regular trips to the pawn shop included Mother's best underwear. It had been passed on to her by her kind and glamourous employer, Mrs Coburn, the film director's wife. To our mother it was much more than mere clothing. The pure silk and lace of the gossamer-light petticoats, French-knickers, camisoles and cami-knickers all seemed to symbolise to her the femininity she struggled so hard to retain during her long and arduous hours at various employments. They represented the part of her that had once been Miss Mabel Hartley – proud and good-looking and full of romantic dreams.

Those delicate garments she wore only for special occasions. At other times she kept them wrapped in tissue paper at the back of the chest of drawers. She might well have become used to them being pawned, as it happened so often. But she never did. So I would often sit beside her on our parents' bed, trying to comfort her – not knowing quite what words I could say that would stop her shoulders heaving and her eyes and nose becoming swollen and red behind her scented handkerchief. Even when I once told her that Joan and I loved her so much that we would never, ever, leave her it did not seem to help. All she could keep saying between her sobs was that our father didn't love her. It was as if that was the most important thing in the world to her, and I remember tears of hurt and bewilderment coming into my eyes as I tightened skinny arms around her in a kind of despair.

12

Patriotism, School and Empire

Opposite the brown-bricked Georgian edifice of St Mary's School in Wyndham Place, Marylebone was St Mary's Church. Its creamy stones gleamed white in the sunlight and, to me, it looked like a tall wedding cake with its six rotunda pillars supporting a rounded first layer with another high round tier sitting on top of that, like a decoration.

If the trees of Bryanston Square had not grown so tall it would have been possible to stand on the church steps and look southward, straight down Great Cumberland Place to Marble Arch. To the east of the church, just two crossings away, was Baker Street, and just around the corner in the other direction was our home. Inside the church, up on the flat, pale-blue ceiling, were dozens of painted gold stars which looked very calm and heavenly. I liked to gaze up at them during church services. This was especially so after we had filed over to the church from the school on the chilly mornings of every 11 November, which was Remembrance Day. This sad day always drew us closer to our strict school teachers, for when we sang the hymn: 'O God, Our Help in Ages Past', especially the lines: 'Time like an ever-rolling stream, Bears all its sons away', our teachers could not hide their grief from us. Miss Carpenter's cheeks would glisten with silent tears, and some of the men teachers would remove their spectacles and wipe them with their handkerchiefs, and then cough.

As we came to the fateful moment when the church bell above us ceased its tolling of eleven ponderous chimes, I knew that the whole of London – indeed the whole of Great Britain, so we had been informed, would come to a complete standstill. As the last vibrations of the tolling vanished in the air and were followed, immediately, by the booming sound of big guns being fired off in Hyde Park, all work everywhere – whether in shops, factories or offices or on farms, or wherever – would cease absolutely. Grown-ups and children alike would stand up to attention for two full minutes, with their heads bowed in respectful silence. They were all remembering those who died in the Great War. In London, as elsewhere, all traffic would simultaneously come to a halt. Motor engines were turned off and cart horses tightly reined as drivers bowed their heads in general respect for the fallen. All men, everywhere, removed their hats or caps. Even the policemen on traffic duty, as well as all those on their beats, stood to attention bareheaded.

Nobody would have dreamed of breaking this code of social honour. Indeed, almost the only sounds to be heard in London during those reverent two minutes were the cooing of pigeons and the chattering of the sparrows. Their innocent happiness, audible for 120 seconds as never again at any other time during the year, sounded almost disrespectful and out of place, as they sat watching from the thousands of soot-blackened ledges in the city.

❦❧

The school had a fine scholastic record. Mr Oliver, the headmaster, was tall and thin under his high-domed forehead and brown curly hair. He wore a brown tweed suit with leather elbows and buttons. Hidden slightly behind a studious and gentlemanly manner was a man who was as keen and quick as his springy cane.

Every day, he would lead all the children in the prayers and hymn-singing at morning assembly. Afterwards, the whole school would recite the multiplication tables in sing-song fashion and all but a rare few children would be dreading the moment when the 'tables' would come to an end. For it was then that Mr Oliver would point his cane at random individuals along the rows, expecting his pupils to give correct answers to his quickly fired questions: 'What is seven times eight? Nine times six? Eight nines?'

We knew that those children who gave wrong answers would have to stand up in shame on wooden chairs at the side of the long room. When he had questioned children from all the rows he would start again at the beginning and we would all begin to curl our toes up in our boots or shoes with the tension. We feared what might be coming to us if we had neglected our learning. The ritual was repeated three times. Anyone standing on a chair who was unfortunate enough to give a third wrong answer had to go forward at the end to receive a stroke of the cane. The ordeal of the tables lasted for about half an hour every morning, after which the assembly was dismissed. Our sighs of relief and the rubbing of caned hands were sounds usually lost in the stamping of feet on the wooden floor as we marched in single file back to our respective places in our classrooms, while music such as Elgar's 'Pomp And Circumstance' was played on the piano by one or other of the teachers.

When our teachers also had eventually seated themselves at their high individual desks and let their gaze sweep over the 35 or so children seated before them, such a hush came over the classrooms that you could hear the gas lamps softly hissing and popping at the ends of their long overhead brackets. Nobody even dared cough or shuffle their feet. Mr Oliver ran St Mary's like the captain of a convict ship. He was strict and authoritarian but he was also fair and just – and he cared greatly about his pupils' futures. Mutinous children were periodically supressed by the judicious use of 'the cane' and our respect for him was very real indeed. Many boys and girls, boys in particular, who in some cases had started off with very few home advantages had, through his high standards and dedication, ended up in very comfortable positions in the world. For several months before children sat for their scholarships, Mr Oliver would keep them behind at school at least twice a week while he personally coached them in their weakest subjects, and in the understanding of examination papers – particularly the intelligence tests.

I was not overly fond of school. I merely tolerated it, except for minute parts like Friday afternoons, when we were allowed to take our own books to school and read them sitting two to a desk under the gas lamps while the teachers marked exercise books. Yet even Friday afternoons could be spoiled by the boys. They nearly all had a catapult hidden on them somewhere and whenever Miss Carpenter left the room they would try them out in class. They used them mainly to flick pellets or wads of blotting paper which had been dunked in the inkwells. The wooden floor was almost navy blue with ink stains. I was thankful my hair was not in long ringlets or plaits, like a lot of girls, because the boys liked nothing better than to gently take hold of the long hair of any girls sitting in front of them and gleefully dip the ends into their inkwells.

Miss Carpenter kept order by use of a ruler across the knuckles. There was no psychology used other than the spreading of the certain knowledge that 'Crime begets immediate punishment', and apart from Friday afternoons the discipline was of a very superior order. It was all quite fair. We knew where we stood. There was no resentment.

Boys were punished more than girls. It seemed to be accepted by most grown-ups that boys, on the whole, had

a definite leaning towards bad behaviour or even wickedness. If anyone had questioned that fact they would have
been laughed at. The worst boy in my class was Jimmy
Harris. He didn't seem to know when he had gone too
far. One day Miss Carpenter leaned forward in her desk
and shouted at him: 'You'll swing from the neck one of
these days, Jimmy Harris, you see if you don't!' Nobody
thought it a strange remark. We just turned around in
our desks to look at his bright-red face and ears below
his short, straight haircut, and above his doomed neck.
'Nipping things in the bud' was what adults called their
strict disciplining of boys.

A part of school I really hated came on Thursday afternoons, when the girls had sewing lessons while the boys
were taught carpentry. It seemed to me that most of the
sunniest and hottest afternoons of my life were reserv-
ing themselves for those sewing times, making my hands
warm and moist, the cotton thread limp and easily knotted and the needle so sticky that I could hardly push it
through the harsh unbleached calico that we learnt on.
From this unbeautiful material we were taught to fashion
such items as pen-wipers, needle-cases, comb-cases and
some strange, small, triangular wall-hanging receptacles,
which Miss Carpenter referred to as 'hair-tidies'.

I would not have dared to ask her why we were making these objects, but she told us anyway. She said they
were for storing ladies' hair-combings and the loose hair
retrieved from their brushes. Apparently when she was
a girl at the turn of the century all the mothers would

collect their loose hairs and roll them into fat sausage shapes which they called 'rats'. These they used as bulkers, she said, to pad out their upswept hair. The fact that most of our 1930s mothers had short, bobbed, crimped, Marcel-Waved or shingled hair seemed not to bother Miss Carpenter – we had to make them just the same, as presents for our mothers, and then have to answer their gentle enquiries as to what exactly it was that they were.

We also had to make that horrid material into knickers which our mothers were then expected to buy. We all used to worry in case we were forced to wear them, as they cost 3/6d. Three shillings and sixpence was a lot of money.

Having tried those knickers on at school, we knew that because of the pattern they would be garments of real torture, both physical and mental. The elastic-threaded legs were long enough to hang down below the average length of a dress, but the body was so short between the waist and crotch that nobody could sit down in them without acute discomfort. My mother paid for mine without too much complaint and then, sensibly, used them as a polishing cloth. Pulled up over the end of a fat mop they brought up a lovely shine on the linoleum.

At intervals during our sewing struggles with French seams, felling, back-stitching, feathering and smocking, Miss Carpenter's voice would drift over the rows of bowed heads, telling us: 'Needlework is a gentle and womanly occupation. Do not *wrestle* with your work, as though you were in prison sewing mailbags. Sweep your needles up and around, taking them through the air in graceful arches. Practice making yourselves into pretty pictures for your husbands one day to look at.'

Arithmetic lessons were another bane to me. All our workings-out had to be written neatly in the margins of our exercise books so that Miss Carpenter could see which way our minds were functioning. The scratchy steel nibs of our pens were forever making splatters and blots all over the paper. I had a fateful compulsion to ignore the horrible arithmetic and just concentrate on the blots. Joined up with a few lines and maybe an extension here and there, they could be turned into all sorts of interesting silhouette pictures. Those blots became migrating birds, spiders on webs, elephants, steam trains, camel caravans, the great pyramids of Giza. All the world was there in those navy-blue smudges, I thought, just waiting to be brought to life – by me. But Miss Carpenter did not like illustrated arithmetic books, especially when they had the sums all wrong.

What with the blue ink stains which constantly coated my fingers, and the frequent bright-red marks across my stinging knuckles from her punishing ruler, my hands were often a very patriotic red white and blue, and I feared I had no hopes at all of ever becoming one of Mr Oliver's scholarship children, and having my name painted on the end wall of the building in gold letters along with all the other winners of honours for the school since the previous century.

Two of the most enjoyable days of our school year, times when even the boys behaved themselves without correction, were St George's Day on 23 April, and Empire Day on 24 May. These were the two spring days of every year when we knew that many places would be bright with flags and bunting and there would be a holiday feeling in the air.

All we school children had been well versed in the belief that London was the most important city in the world – the place from which was governed the greatest and best-run Empire that the world had known for a very long time. There was a lot of poverty and a lot of wealth in London, and in both cases it showed. But in everybody, rich or poor, there seemed to be an inbuilt sense of pride in being British – and it was real.

On St George's Day we learnt that there was a further refinement to our great good fortune in having been born British and that was in being born English. England was the 'Merrie England' of our Anglo-Saxon and Norman forebears. Those people who had their roots in England were proud of their separate identity – just as the Scottish, Welsh and Irish took pleasure in being what they were. The Scots, we were told, were intrepid explorers and fine administrators. The Irish were courageous soldiers and fearless fighters. The Welsh were bards and poets, but also invincible when their deeply passionate natures were aroused. As for Merrie England, we learnt that 'Merrie' was a very old word, meaning 'good, fair and wholesome', and we were expected to live up to that label. 'English and proud of it' was a well-known saying. 'British is Best' was another. Always boosting our sense of identity was George our patron saint. Backing him up was the fact that both our recent kings had been christened George, and a great number of little boys were also called George. Our most graceful buildings were Georgian and often, when people saw something they liked, they would exclaim: 'By George!'

At school on St George's Day we were regaled with legendary tales of how he slew the evil dragon with his shining sword. Somehow it was instilled into us all that to be English was to be the inheritor of a sacred trust. To be English was to be honourable and just, and noble and true. 'St George and Merrie England Forever' was the cry on 23 April, and all the boys, especially those called George, sat tall in their desks.

Every year on 24 May, Empire Day, the streets and the school were suffused with a holiday spirit. My sister and I would get up early on those mornings feeling perfectly happy to be going to school, for we knew it would be an enjoyable sort of day. Even before the sound of the tolling bell in the turret above the school building had begun to echo over the rooftops, we would have scampered out into the streets carrying our Union Jacks. Many of the shops in Crawford Street would have British flags suspended from their hanging trade signs, or be displaying them in their windows, and most of the cart horses we passed would have red, white and blue ribbons plaited into their manes. Lots of the grown-ups we skipped past on the way, would be wearing patriotic rosettes.

We would arrive at school to find red, white and blue paper garlands festooned around the walls of the class-rooms and corridors and an atmosphere like Christmas pervading the entire building, making the teachers smile. Empty jam jars, which were waiting to receive our flags, would be standing on the window ledges and on the teach-ers' high desks and on the tops of the wooden stationery cupboards. By the time that approximately 32 to 38 boys and girls per class, all wearing red, white or blue jumpers or dresses, were seated at their desks and the same number of flags had been deposited in the jam jars – standing stiffly like bunches of gaudy flowers – each classroom would be looking truly festive.

After the register had been called and the morning assembly hymns and multiplication tables were over and done with, then the rest of the day would be devoted to the glorification of the British Image, including, of course, the reasons why we should try to live up to it. This included the telling and hearing of marvellously uplifting examples of courage, dedication, stoicism and vocation all wrapped up in tales of the hardy or long-suffering men and women who had made hazardous journeys overseas to serve in all sorts of outposts of the British Empire. These would be mixed up with fascinating stories about the lifestyles of those exotic faraway children our adopted cousins: who lived all over the world in our great Empire, and who were black, white, brown or yellow.

But first of all, because it was a special day, we would each be given a fruit drop from Miss Carpenter's round tin. Then out from the back of a cupboard would come a long pole, around which was furled a large map of the world. Printed on shiny cotton-backed oilcloth, the map had a special exciting smell all of its own. It was carefully unrolled and hung on the wall. Miss Carpenter would tell us: 'Everything you see which is coloured pink on this map is part of our Empire. As you can see the pink shaded portions extend over every part of the globe.' Then would come the sentences we enjoyed most: 'As you know the sun rises in the East and sets in the West. As the planet revolves the sunshine creeps across country after country until it comes back again to the beginning. So extensive and so widely scattered is our British Empire that during every minute of every hour of every day, the sun is bound to be shining on some part of it, however small. It is because of this fact that we call it "The Empire on which the sun never sets".'

Then she would instruct us to copy into our exercise books the names of all the countries, islands, mandates, federations and dependencies which constituted our Empire and Commonwealth links, and which she had already chalked upon the blackboard. Apart from the really big places like India, Canada and Australia, the Union of South Africa and the Dominion of New Zealand, there were also about 40 more other places on the map coloured pink – important places like Burma and Ceylon in the Far East, the Kenya Colony, Nigeria, Uganda, Rhodesia and Tanganyika Territory in Africa – the list seemed endless. There were also about twenty or more groups of small islands, like the Bahamas and the West Indies, to be neatly written down.

When we had all copied the list to Miss Carpenter's satisfaction she would then give us examples of some other instances in which, she said, Great Britain was 'A leader of the world'. We were told that our country had many of the finest museums, libraries, art galleries and universities on the face of the earth – *plus* the greatest number of inventors and men of science, medicine, engineering and literature. We, as a nation, were clever, we were the great innovators and initiators – even the Industrial Revolution had begun here on our own small island. Because of this the entire world had taken a giant leap forward into another age.

We were also brave, Miss Carpenter said. Our people, our British explorers, traders, missionaries, sailors, soldiers, teachers, nurses and doctors, engineers, administrators, and many more, had gone forth to all corners of the world in the great adventure of tending to the British Empire. In the earlier days they had frequently to venture into uncharted territories, at great personal risk. But they had taken with them new knowledge and methods and laid at the feet of relatively backward peoples the gifts of European Enlightenment. The missionaries, in particular, had offered the principles of Christianity in places where before there had often been barbarism, superstition, witchcraft and continual tribal warring. In some places, we were told, there had even been cannibalism, and in others the practice of widow-burning. While listening to Miss Carpenter at these times, London seemed to me a very safe place by comparison. Yet I could see the light of adventure shining in the eyes of the boys.

It was during these Empire Day types of lessons that we eventually came to believe that, by having been born British, we certainly had something to live up to – and a great challenge lay before us if we were ever to match the shining example set by our forebears. But even though the task might have seemed a trifle daunting to some children, there was little evidence of it. Judging from the faces around me and their chatter afterwards, most children seemed to get a good feeling from identifying with heroes.

It was also very carefully explained to us that although, like the rest of the world throughout the centuries, we had for a while been misguided enough to engage in the practice of slave trading and owning, we had also been the first country in the world to see the wrongness of it. Miss Carpenter would go to great lengths to ensure our proper understanding of 'that wicked trade', informing us that on the west coast of Africa, the place where most of the slaves were purchased, the foul trade had not been started by ourselves but had already been established for centuries before we got there. 'Those poor creatures,' she would tell us, 'were not captured by us, but sold to us by slave traders who were either North African or, even worse, their own people.' It was left to an Englishman, she said, to break the spell. This had come about through the stoic efforts of William Wilberforce, the eloquent son of a merchant of Hull who even as a grammar-school boy in the 18th century had written to the papers condemning 'the odious traffic in human flesh'.

The story ended triumphantly when, in 1807, after unremitting struggle and in failing health, Wilberforce saw the abolition of slave trading within the British Dominions become law. But on a sadder note we learnt how he had died in London in 1833, just nine years after our school was built, just four years before Queen Victoria came to the throne and just as the bill for the total abolition of slavery and the emancipation of slaves was being passed in Parliament. 'Great Britain, again, was the leader of the world, in something good,' Miss Carpenter would beam – and we all thrilled with pride.

On Empire Day we learnt even more about the great armies of our men who patrolled and protected the Empire from other, greedy and less noble, eyes. Through responsible force and administration, we had become the great peacemakers, we were told: 'Even the tribes of India which had been massacring each other for centuries had become more peaceful and united under British rule.' To India in particular we had taken railways, a common language, modern medicine, education and law – so many things which had helped that ancient country become prominent in our modern world of the 1930s.

We also learnt that we had the greatest and most invincible navy ever to sail the seas. 'Jack Tar', the name used for British seamen, was respected throughout the world: for our navy had finally swept piracy from the high seas for the first time in history, making the oceans free and safe, at last, for all the other nations of the world to use.

There seemed to be so many things for us to be proud of. But the most important, the real message that came over to us was that God, in His wisdom, had given us a part to play in aiding the evolution of the world. That it was our sacred duty to carry out His intentions with honour and to the best of our abilities, no matter how small our part might turn out to be. It was a tall order, but it gave us the seeds of self-respect and something to live up to. Especially the boys. It gave them a pride in themselves and a certain feeling of responsibility for their actions. At least, that was how it seemed to me.

Meanwhile, we were told, we should take pride in and never forget the fact, that without resorting to any oppressive regimes, it had been simply by the enormous efforts and sacrifices made by our own British forebears, our relatives and our ancestors, that so much had already been accomplished towards the evolution of the world's great family. I think that all the children of St Mary's School, even the poorest of us, went home on those Empire Days with our heads held high.

'During the Great War,' said Miss Carpenter, 'countless brave men from the Dominions and Empire took up arms and came overseas to help us – their Mother Country. We should be eternally grateful to them,' she told us. Then she added, in an almost sad sort of way: 'Should Great Britain ever find herself in such trouble again, I pray to God that those loyal friends would once more rally to our aid.'

13

City Enterprise

On days when poor weather or some other reason prevented us from going out to play, Joan and I would usually read or draw, or play with the toy sweetshop that our mother had made for us out of large cardboard boxes. Its sturdy walls and shelves had been glued together with Seccotine and then wallpapered. Ten matching glass fishpaste jars contained lentils, sago, pearl barley, split peas and suchlike things, which we weighed out on small tin scales. Our mother had made lots of toy cardboard money and homemade paper bags, and had then drawn miniature advertisements which she pasted up all over the 'outside' walls. She made three of these shops during our London childhood, for their life span was about two years. Each one was called 'Orchard Stores' and we played with them until they literally fell apart.

But sometimes I did not feel like playing with anything and would just curl up comfortably on the old blue-covered ottoman chest in front of our living-room window and gaze out through the wet panes at the ever-busy rows of chimney pots which stretched before my view. Out there in the sooty London rain some chimneys seemed to glower like cannibal kings under the sawtoothed metal crowns of their Victorian cowlings. Others leaned matily together in groups, as if for support. Tall and stately mediaeval chimneys looked down their noses at square-set Victorian brick chimneystacks, so caked with soot that they were as grimy as the little chimney-sweep boys who had been forced to climb up the insides of them with brushes and scrapers not so very long before. Soldierly rows of newish chimneys stood erect as guardsmen on a few of the rooftops, but I knew that their uniforms of red pottery or yellow stone would not stay bright up there for long. Soon they, like all the others, would begin to resemble lines of dirty, battle-grimed troops.

London being such an ancient city, and its buildings having been huddled together mostly undisturbed for so many decades, or even centuries, meant that the chimney pots above accurately reflected the various historical groupings of the buildings below. There they sat, like landmarks, but mostly unseen, except from the higher windows such as ours. Happily puffing away, they lived in a world of their own. But for one child, at least, they provided a magic kingdom where imagination could transcend the bounds of reality.

As buildings were not often pulled down, it was easy to soon acquire a feeling of having roots. There was a sense of continuity coming from their bricks and stones. Those soot-rimmed buildings which I sometimes tried to imagine brightly clean and new, as they had once been, had all been witness to so many things and to times which had gone, that the streets had a definite atmosphere. It was almost as if the captured images of past happenings had been soaked up by the walls and possibly could be released, like ghosts, if only one knew the secret key.

Most of the larger Marylebone houses, especially in the Georgian-built Bryanston and Montague Squares, had wooden notices attached to their area railings bearing the words: 'No Hawkers or Circulars'. Many of the notices looked as if they had been there for a hundred years, at least. But they were still needed as protection against the many types of street hawkers who went around knocking on doors, trying to sell anything from glass beads to satin garters. Yet the muffin man was apparently exempt from this prohibition. Every afternoon at teatime he would walk around the squares and along Gloucester Place, ringing his wooden-handled brass bell and shouting 'muffin man, muffin man' on a long drawn out note. On top of his head, supported by a coiled circle of twisted white cloth, he carried a long wooden tray piled high with freshly baked, plump and yeasty muffins. A white cloth covered by a green baize cloth protected the muffins from the elements, and the man wore a long white-bibbed apron over his coat. On wet days he rang his bell with one hand and held a broad black umbrella over his muffins with the other. It made a very funny picture.

Sometimes the maidservants coming up the area steps in answer to his handbell and call would bring him up a cup of hot tea or even, if his muffins were all sold, invite him down into the kitchen for a hotter drink straight from the pot, and beside the fire. All the maids I ever came into contact with were always very friendly with the regular tradesmen. And the tradesmen, like the nannies in the parks, often carried newsy gossip from house to house. Sometimes they married the maids.

There were only a few muffin men in Marylebone. The other types of street-people were much more prevalent. As well as the chimney sweeps, of course, there were the lamplighters to be seen mornings and evenings, or at any other time of the day if there was a fog. Navy-blue uniformed, they carried their long-hooked poles around the streets on their shoulders like lances, and used them to switch the flinted mechanisms of the gas lamps off and on. Periodically, when the gas jets needed attention, they would appear on the scene carrying pointed ladders on their shoulders instead of poles. Often, they rode bicycles at the same time and wobbled lopsidedly along the streets like funny circus acts. Their bicycles were then propped against the lamp posts, their ladders propped against the lamp post bracket arms, and up they would climb: usually surrounded by a small circle of watching children. There wasn't much we could actually see, but it was all 'part of life'.

There was quite an assortment of other people who earned their living out 'on the streets', and they all added to our entertainment. The knife grinder sat by the kerbsides on a bicycle-shaped contraption which had a grindstone set up at the handlebars end. As he pedalled madly the bicycle stayed still but the grindstone, which revolved at speed, sent out showers of sparks, like Guy Fawkes sparklers, as it honed steel-bladed dinner knives to near-lethal sharpness. The knife grinder was also very popular in the squares, where rattling trayfuls of kitchen knives were carried up the area steps by the kitchen maids. It was so much quicker than laboriously 'stropping' them all on a 'steel'.

The tinker-men not only had barrows or small horse-drawn carts full of iron or tin pots and pans for sale, but they would mend peoples' own kettles and saucepans in the street. They used either screw-in metal patches or solder. Many customers brought out their tin or enamel saucepans which had holes burned right through the bottoms. Poorer people often could not afford to replace them, even after the bottoms had worn eggshell-thin. Enamel saucepans in particular were notorious for 'catching' or burning the food, and wire or metal scrapers soon scraped the bottoms away along with the burned parts.

There was only one Indian 'Taffy' man. He sold sweets which were forbidden by many parents and which were therefore made much more interesting. He had skin the lovely colour of vanilla fudge and soft brown eyes like chocolate buttons. He dressed theatrically in a cummer-bunded white satin tunic and wore a high bejewelled turban. Looking at him, I used to wonder whether the visiting Maharaja at Queensberry House, whom I never actually saw, had looked something like the Marylebone Taffy man

– only without the tray of dingy-looking pulled-sugar strips of toffee held against his chest by leather shoulder straps. 'You buy my Indian Taffy,' he would say in a rather high voice: 'Very good for you.' We felt sorry that we were not allowed to even taste the mysterious Eastern sweets of this pleasant man. I often wished I could have afforded to buy a halfpenny-worth from him which I could have thrown away when he wasn't looking, just to save his feelings and give him a proper dignity to go with his appearance.

The chair mender sat by the kerb on a smart wooden chair of his own, while he mended other people's broken ones. His glue bubbled in a heavy iron pot above a paraffin burner. He also used seagrass, raffia, pieces of leather, tin tacks, screws and nails: always giving his customers' chairs a quick free polish with some special secret oil from a bottle, after they had been mended. Even the tattiest old kitchen chairs could be rejuvenated by the chair mender. The thin-faced umbrella mender always wore either a long, black, tattered overcoat or else a threadbare black cloth mackintosh, depending on the weather. On his head was rammed a greeny-black bowler hat a size too big and his bony wrists protruded from cuffs that were frayed at the edges. He seemed to match the black umbrellas with which he was always surrounded. From a distance, as he sat on a stool beside his wooden pushcart with the broken brollies beside him – either flapping in the breeze or lying in distorted angles – he looked like an old scarecrow surrounded by dead or dying crows. Nearly all the street-people had carts or hand-carts of one kind or another, some of them homemade, and these men nearly all gave 'service with a smile' as they worked all through the hours of daylight in their hard struggle to earn an honest living.

The most prevalent and possibly poorest of all were the street musicians. We got to know nearly all of them in our district because they all had their unofficial territory which they jealously guarded. 'Git art of it!' they would yell at any interloper who might be trying to sneak in on part of one of 'their' streets. There seemed to be a great number of Irish street singers, many with fine, sweet, tenor voices. Quite often they would be accompanied by a fresh-faced but pale young wife, who usually wore a shawl draped over her shoulders. Sometimes the wives carried shawl-wrapped babies and other small children played around their skirts. I once saw one of these thin and small, but usually beautiful children traipsing quietly along behind her parents on the gutter-side of the cold winter pavement, with blue-mottled bare little feet. I ran all the way up to our apartment to beg our mother for something the freezing infant could wear on her feet. Mother gave me a pair of Father's well-darned old woollen socks, saying they would be 'better than nothing'. When I gave them to the street-singer's wife she said 'God bless you,' and put them in her skirt pocket. I was surprised and disappointed that she didn't immediately put them on the feet of the little girl, and when I told our mother she shook her head and looked cross, but didn't say anything.

People would throw down pennies and halfpennies to street musicians from upper windows, and the money was usually wrapped in a twist of newspaper so that it wouldn't roll away or go down a drain. There were fiddle players, concertina players, men playing tunes on brass cornets, tin whistles, banjos and Jews' harps. One day I even saw a man standing at the corner of Seymour Place playing a buzzy sort of tune on a comb-and-paper. I thought he must have been terribly poor, for the pawn shops had plenty of cheap second-hand musical instruments for sale.

Once a week the barrel-organ man visited our part of Marylebone. Groups of children would dance in the street to the happy tinkling music which was churned out for us by the turning of a handle. Even gentle Mary Stamp, who had a club foot, would join in. Her brother Freddy was a Homer Street bully, but Mary, so pale and thin and other-worldly, seemed like an almost invisible person for most of the time. She hardly ever spoke to anyone. The barrel-organ looked like an old upright piano, mounted on wheels, and with two handles at one end, by which its jolly red-nosed owner would push it through the streets. Mary called it 'the piano on the wheelbarrow'. The man would turn the handle very slowly when tunes like 'Daisy, Daisy' began to play so that she could join in. And if Freddy Stamp was around, he would stand with his thumbs in his braces, as if daring anyone to make fun of his sister's heavy boot with the four-inch sole, as she limped around the dancing circle with us.

Most children that Joan and I knew, including ourselves, were given between a penny and threepence pocket money every Saturday, so it was rather necessary that we should earn a bit more for ourselves by our own efforts. The easiest way was to knock on peoples' doors and ask: 'Do you want any errands run, please?' Each errand, to the grocer, tobacconist, chip shop or whatever, earned us a halfpenny, and they soon mounted up.

Another way was by selling firewood. Using Joan's wooden scooter we would collect wooden vegetable crates from the backs of Cooper's or Sainsbury's on the Edgware Road. After hauling two or three at a time back to Homer Street, we would prop them between the roadway and the kerb and jump on them until they were smashed up. Then, after tying the bundles together with twine we hawked them around people's doors and sold them. At a penny a bundle, or two for three-halfpence, they were cheaper than the sticks sold in the grocers' shops.

One year we saved enough money not only to take ourselves to the Regent's Park Zoo, but also to buy an elephant ride. Most of our entertainments, though, were either free or self-made. Among the free offerings were the South Kensington museums, which were within easy walking distance across Hyde Park. The favourite with most of us was the Science Museum, where there was lots of fun to be had with the knobs and buttons of the working-models in the children's department. We also thrilled to the sight of James Watt's original steam engine. The slow, ponderous motion of the huge wooden beam seemed somehow awesome, because it was man and nature working together in harness.

The only other things I knew which could evoke a similar feeling, even in the girls, were the steam trains in Paddington Station. The gleaming black metal of the engines, the red-hot fires, stoked by sweating and coal-blackened stokers when they were 'getting up steam', the water pumping in from above and dribbling onto the tracks, the hissings and rumblings, the echoing shrieks of the air-blasted whistles and finally, the belching clouds of white steam thinning into wispy water vapour up near the soot-black glass canopy of the vaulted station roof. All these things seemed linked in with the deep dark forces of elemental power that were locked in nature itself. And something in us stirred and responded. Especially in the boys. They nearly all wanted to be engine drivers when they grew up – either here or in the Empire.

Baker Street had a special place in the hearts of my sister and me for, in the summer of 1938, that was where we found riches. Not lost ones, the sort Sherlock Holmes would have tracked down. These riches were self-made with a little help from dozens of navvies with picks and shovels and pneumatic drills. The upper end of Baker Street, on either side of Marylebone Circus, had for as long as we could remember been surfaced with oblong wooden blocks coated with tar. They had a wonderful soft feel to the feet, although some grown-ups complained that they were slippery in the rain. During hot summers the tar bubbled up between those wooden bricks with a wonderful smell that reminded us it was the summer holidays and school was closed. We liked them.

But one chilly morning we found that groups of navvies were there, digging up the blocks and throwing them to the sides of the road where they lay in deposed little heaps, waiting to be carted away. It didn't take Joan and me long to obtain two hessian sacks from a Crawford Street greengrocer and run back to our stricken friends. For three days we worked like beavers, carrying sackfuls of old Baker Street around the squares and up and down the many steps of the Seymour Buildings and the Crawford Buildings, knocking on doors. We sold tar logs by the quarter-dozen over people's doorsteps, until we were aching so much that we had to be put into a hot bath in mid-week.

We were told later that the tar logs lit quickly and burned with a unique blue-and-orange flame. One of the cooks in the squares said they made the fur of her kitchen cat smell 'all medicinal', and an old lady in the Seymour Buildings was convinced that the smell of the burning pitch-tar did her cough good. Everyone had been eager for more. We had no trouble at all in selling them, only in carrying them, for they were heavy. By the time the lorries arrived on the third day to take away all the dug-up logs, the men found that they had nearly all been spirited away by children who, like Joan and me, recognised a good opportunity when they saw it.

By the time Baker Street was all used up, we were worn out but rich. After counting up the heaps of sixpences, shillings, florins and half crowns we had collected, we excitedly told our mother to sit down and then tipped all that shining silver money into her lap. It was one of the greatest memories of our childhood. The look on her face when she received that gift from her two young daughters was like a moment of glory.

❧

The chairman of the junior branch of the local Primrose League was Ernie Willard's father. They lived below us at number 63. Mr Willard was always very pleasant to me. Frequently, on my way home from school after I had been climbing up all the stairs of Crawford Buildings lost in a daydream, I had opened his front door and been halfway across his living room before realising I was in the wrong home. Once, happily surprised at the lovely smell of tinned salmon and pineapple chunks that were laid out in glass dishes beside the bread and butter, I had hungrily sat down to tea before it struck me that it was Ernie Willard's parents and not my own who were looking at me, with some surprise, across the tablecloth.

Mr Willard was tall, wiry and energetic. Even after tramping the streets all day as an insurance salesman and collector, he could still bound around the wooden floor of St Mary's Hall in Crawford Street, supervising dozens of us children in lively team games. I couldn't understand why he was called a chairman, because he rarely sat down. He once took us all – about 50 of us – to the Albert Hall where, the girls all wearing white-and-yellow dresses and the boys wearing white shirts and yellow armbands, we all sang: 'Three cheers for the red white and blue'. It was a public performance and all the Primrose Leagues of central London were there. All the children were seated around the balcony and each was given a flag of either red, white or blue, which we raised up and waggled in the air when the appropriate word was sung.

It was a good job the weather was fine because all 50 of us had walked there, in two yellow-and-white crocodiles, across Hyde Park and through Kensington Gardens. The girls were led by gentle, bespectacled Mrs Willard, who had somehow transformed herself into a sort of warrior queen for the occasion, while the boys were led bouncily by the chairman. All the rich children in the park with their white-aproned nurses, stared at us as in two long chattering lines we wound our way under the sweet-smelling trees and over the sparkling Serpentine, via the bridge, towards the exotic outlines of the Albert Memorial and the Albert Hall. Afterwards we walked back the same way and then straight into the Lyons Corner House at Marble Arch, where we were fed on jelly, sausage rolls, sticky buns and Tizer.

We also had the Band of Hope for our entertainment. This was a 'temperance society' for working-class children, which had been started in the north of England in the days when Charles Dickens was writing his stories. Their aim was to instil in us a knowledge, awareness and hatred of the evils of drink. Also to get us to 'sign the pledge': which amounted to writing our names on a printed form which promised we would never let alcohol pass our lips. The meetings were held in the wide Drill Hall underneath Paddington Chapel, which stood on the corner of the Marylebone Road between Homer Street and Harcourt Street, and only a stone's throw from the famous old tavern called 'The Yorkshire Stingo'.

'Wanna join the Band of 'ope and Glory?' a bunch of Homer Street children had asked us one murky November afternoon: 'It'll cost ya a ha'penny fer the collection plate, but there's a lovely concert an' a Christmas party in free weeks' time.' We joined!

The meetings were held on Saturday afternoons, and we found that they also provided a wonderful source of joy in the shape of what were called 'Magic Lantern Shows'. The gas lights around the basement walls would be turned down so low that they popped and flickered, and a not-unpleasant smell of London gas escaped into the room. The Magic Lantern itself smelled of lamp oil and hot metal and was set up on a baize-topped folding card-table at the back of the hall. On a low platform in front of our rows of wooden chairs stood a big white screen. The usual hubbub of coughs, sneezes, chair-scraping and cries of 'Stop yer kickin'', quietened down at last when the Magic Lantern, having been lit, was ready to be worked.

First of all a long beam of yellow light travelled down the darkened gangway between the chairs, and a myriad of dust particles, disturbed by the stamping of boys' boots, rose up from the wooden floor and sparkled momentarily like distant stars as they passed through the lantern's golden rays. Often then, usually at the last moment before the treat in store for us was finally revealed, a black wavering shadow like a giant goblin would lurch across the screen as someone or other dashed wildly back from the 'lavvies' and crossed the beam of light. Finally, in the hush, we would hear the first glass slide *'click'* into position. Sometimes the projected image would be upside down and then the silence would be lost again, and a sound like the howling of disappointed wolves would fill the air until the matter was put right.

Quite suddenly, to the cries of 'oo-oh' and 'aa-ah' and 'cripes', larger-than-life picture-images from something called 'The Rake's Progress' would fill the screen. In sequence, we would witness the disintegration of a loving family-man into a drunken monster. Then even worse things followed: Images of gross depravity in Georgian days, as seen through the eyes of an artist called 'Hogarth', Mothers being ruined in gin-palaces with babies falling from their naked breasts, and the frightening of innocent children by grown-ups who had been made hideously ugly by drink. It made us all sit pop-eyed on the edge of our chairs.

Then other pictures of the consequences of 'the demon drink' would slip shockingly onto the screen: rolling-eyed fathers chained to walls in a terrible place called Bedlam, the youngest children of the family in the burial ground through injury or neglect, mothers in the workhouse, sons running thieves' kitchens and daughters with painted faces and very low necklines, smiling at men on shadowy street corners (for some mysterious reason which wasn't properly explained to us).

All the children present were both chilled and thrilled with vicarious horror. After the first visit I took one of the Band of Hope forms home to our father in case he felt like signing the pledge, explaining to him all we had seen. But as, after reading it, he went out and got drunk, I didn't bother him with it again. I decided to enjoy the shows for what they were, like all the other children. None of them seemed to associate what we saw with reality. It was picture-book stuff, a better sort of Grimms' Fairy Tales even though it might have given nightmares to a few.

After the shows we all sang jolly Temperance songs. Finally, an adult standing by the door would give us all a fruit drop as we filed out. By and large the Band of Hope was well worth every halfpenny we put on the collection plates. And when Christmas came around we enjoyed the promised party and concert with a merriment which quite drowned out the noise issuing from The Yorkshire Stingo.

Almost every Sunday afternoon of our London childhood was spent at the Paddington Chapel Sunday School. Down in the same basement Drill Hall, where we enjoyed so many Magic Lantern shows, bran-tub bazaars, concert parties and tea parties at other times, we now drew religious pictures with wax crayons, sang rousing songs (like 'Jesus wants me for a sunbeam' and 'I'm H.A.P.P.Y') and listened to stories about the man called Jesus who especially loved little children, like us, and who would watch over us.

Jesus' representative at our Sunday School was sandy-haired, middle-aged, owl-spectacled Mr Green who, with his bicycle clips in the pocket of his Norfolk jacket and a big ever-ready smile always waiting to break out under his ginger toothbrush-moustache, was a person much liked and respected by all the children. It was he who organised the Sunday School outing each summer, which took us out of London for a few hours and into what we thought of as the real countryside. On those glorious days the chara-bancs took us to places like Box Hill, in Surrey. Big moon daisies grew wild in the fields there among buttercups, cornflowers and poppies. Butterflies, in all the delicate colours of water-ices, fluttered about in their hundreds in the sweet-smelling air, and fragile dog-roses shone like pink stars on the dark and brambly edges of mysterious woods. It was such a wonderful experience that, even as the chara-bancs brought us back to the big city again through the evening shadows – all clutching fast-wilting bunches of wild flowers and pretty grasses – we could hardly believe that it had all been true. But on that day each year when we returned again to the countryside, and found once more the golden fields and a deep silence that was broken only by the humming of bees and the chirruping of crickets we would know that it had not been a dream.

When we went there in the summer of 1938 we had no idea that it would be for the last time, or that the world we lived in was soon to be turned upside down.

14

In Sickness and in Health

Our Aunty Alice had been concerned about finding the right moment to leave the employment of
the Honourable Ian Dundas: the man who, she said, was
Oswald Mosley's closest aide, and who had greeted her
with a fascist salute when she first became the nanny to
his little girl.

The moment for looking elsewhere came when her
employers announced that they were going to Italy for
several months as guests of the Italian dictator Mussolini.
On their return she handed in her notice – sorry though
she was to leave little Melissa, of whom she had grown
very fond. Our father was much relieved. And when she
became nanny to the grandchildren of Viscount Falkland
instead he was overjoyed: 'A good old family,' he said.

But through her friends and the servants' grapevine
our aunt was still in touch with much of what Dundas and
Mosley and their Nazi-sympathiser associates were doing

or saying. On one of her afternoons off I heard her discussing it all with our parents, across the card table they had pulled beside the fire. They were talking in low voices: Aunty Alice, in fact, was using her spread cards as a sort of fan, from behind which she was speaking with her head bent forwards and sideways. So of course my ears pricked up.

What I made out was that Mosley had been saying something like: the Jews had swept down on Germany like a pack of vultures when the country was weakened after the Great War, buying up and taking over businesses and enslaving the German people.

Our parents, with the memory of their first London employer Mrs Walter and her brother Stanhope Joel still fresh in their minds as shining examples of Jewish kindness, bristled at this. Father said: 'More terrible propaganda,' and Mother said 'Where is it all going to end?'

It seemed to me, too, an awful thing to have said about the Jews. The only Jewish person I knew was meek and mild Mr Jacobs, the tailor. His little shop was on the ground floor of Crawford Buildings opposite the Macready House police buildings. He was such a quiet and gentle man. He would never have enslaved anyone, I thought. He also worked extremely hard and could be seen bent over his sewing machine at the back of his shop, long after the shop itself was shut. He had once made a most beautiful set of coat, bonnet and leggings for Joan when she had come out of hospital after having scarlet fever and had charged our mother only for the cost of the materials used.

The political talk that seemed to be arising in so many adult conversations, and which I vaguely realised carried some sort of ominous significance even for children, was all very difficult to understand. Mostly I would just register what was being said and then carry on with the things I did understand.

I remembered back to that springtime when my sister, bright red in face and body with the scarlet fever, had been taken away in a stridently ringing ambulance to a place called Orchard River Fever Hospital which, so I was told, was 'out in the country.' I later learnt the hospital was in Dartford and was used for epidemics of scarlet fever and diphtheria.

A large crowd of children and adults had gathered around the entrance of Crawford Buildings to watch Joan's little form being carried on a stretcher to the white L.C.C. ambulance. 'Don't go too near' was a whisper which seemed to sweep around the assembled people as mothers drew back their children from over-close inspection, and other grown-ups held handkerchiefs to their noses for fear of catching the fever themselves. Joan had a very high temperature. She had been convinced that the bedroom walls were falling down on top of her. After the ambulance left some people from the health authorities came and took all our bedclothes and mattresses away to be fumigated and left something called 'a sulphur cone' burning in the bedroom. Mother was instructed to put all other linen and clothing into the fire oven bundle by bundle, so that the heat would sterilise it, and to wash every surface in the home with carbolic soap.

Our parents were extremely worried while Joan was in hospital and spent all their spare money buying little presents to send to her. After an inoculation in my arm I was kept away from school for three weeks. I could hardly believe my good fortune. But soon, to my surprise, I found I missed the company of my sister and was glad when she finally came home.

The most common diseases or illnesses that children seemed to be prone to included diphtheria, measles, whooping cough, mumps, rickets, ringworm, impetigo and tuberculosis or 'consumption' as it was known. Grown-ups seemed to be stricken mostly with dropsy, goitre, lameness, rheumatism, bronchitis and consumption. There was a lot of bronchitis – invariably made worse, or even fatal, by the fogs. Also, almost every man and a great many women smoked cigarettes. It was normal and very fashionable to smoke.

The bronchitis in women was made even worse, not only by the smoke and soot which was everywhere but by the common practice of riddling the cinders after a fire went out, in order to acquire a bulk of coke-like material for bolstering up the next fire. The cinder dust made the women almost choke with coughing even while they were doing it. But it didn't stop them. Financially they couldn't afford not to do it.

The roughest type of men constantly cleared their throats and spat into the fire. In the street they would spit into the gutters or onto the pavements, or elsewhere. Some of the big houses had wooden notice boards fixed to their railings saying 'No Spitting' to stop these men spitting down into their basement areas. It was because of this habit that many public houses had spittoons in the bars and sawdust on the floors, and some of the motor buses had notices pasted up which threatened fines of five pounds for this offence. I sometimes wondered whether, when all those expectorations had dried up and turned to dust, it would be other people's fate to breathe them in. I wondered the same thing about the horse dung in the roadways. After it had been flattened by motor-car tyres and ground-up by the metal-rimmed cart wheels it very quickly flew about the streets as yellow dust – even when, in summer, the sprinklers of water carts had tried to swill the messy ordure into the gutters and down the drains. Some people said you could get consumption from it and several elderly people had told me that the grooms and ostlers of their young days had been very suscepti-ble to that dreaded lung-wasting disease. They thought it was caused by something in the horse dung itself. Others believed that people went down with lung trouble if they became too thin.

The most common afflictions of childhood, apart from diseases, seemed to be tongue-tie, stammer, crossed eyes and the bandiness caused by rickets. Quite a large propor-tion of the children we knew had their lives made difficult by these sorts of troubles. Presumably nothing much could be done to help them or it would already have been done. But there was a sort of health-consciousness blowing in the wind, and the idea was going around via magazines and lecturers who visited the school now and then that a bright new future was coming to us all. One of the signs of this was that free milk started to be delivered to the schools to stop any more children getting rickets. We were told that it was something called 'pasteurised' which meant that no germs could live in it. We all had to do paintings to illustrate this and most of us painted great big hairy germs crawling out of the milk bottles and running away. 'Germs' were new to us.

Everyone was very careful indeed about draughts and chills and about linen or clothing being properly aired. People would pull their underclothes into the bed with them in the mornings in order to warm them up, before getting dressed in the chilly bedrooms. Chills were feared because people 'caught their deaths' from them, it was said. In summer the great fear was of catching diphtheria. 'Hold your breath when you go near any drains,' we were told. And all children believed that if you swallowed an orange pip you would get appendicitis.

If anyone still caught a chill after all the precautions, they were given a hot mustard footbath (one tablespoonful of English mustard to a bowl) and put to bed with either hot water bottles or oven-heated bricks wrapped in pieces of old blanket. Then they were given a cup of hot tea with at least two teaspoonfuls of whisky in it. Even children were dosed in this way, only in their case there was less whisky and more sugar. For coughs we were given a mixture of vinegar, sugar and melted butter to swallow. Our chests were rubbed with camphorated oil or wintergreen ointment. Some children we knew told us that they had to submit to having goose grease put upon their chests, which was then covered with brown paper and ironed with their mother's hot flatiron until it had all melted into the skin. They said when the used brown paper was thrown on the fire afterwards it would crackle and bang as it burned, and their mothers would count the number of bangs to tell how many days the cough would last.

We were warned to keep away from children with impetigo scabs on their faces, or who had shaved heads or purple ointment on their scalps, for this meant they had ringworm. The greatest continual warning given to us, though, was to keep well away from any children who might have incipient consumption. That was the really dreaded disease and we were taught, by parents and neighbours, to be wary of any children we met who had very bright eyes, over-rosy cheeks and a transparent look about them, especially if they had a persistent cough or if their handkerchiefs had blood spots on them. Children unfortunate enough to cough up blood were taken away to places called sanatoriums and not seen again for what seemed like years. Some we never saw again.

Women got a lot of painful whitlows on their fingers, which they had to put poultices on. Most working-class women did a regular amount of scrubbing, and the whitlows were said to be caused by the scrubbing-brush bristles going under their finger nails or simply piercing the skin of their hands. Thorns, boils, splinters, festers, or anything else under the skin which shouldn't be there was 'drawn out' by the use of these poultices. O dreaded treatment! All children feared them. Poultices were sometimes made of linseed, but large breadcrumbs were more often used. About three cupfuls of crumbs were put into the centre of a large square of old linen, which was then folded over to form a 'bandage' of many thicknesses. Our father usually did our poulticing to spare our mother's anguish. Holding the ends of the 'bandage' he would lower the bread-filled centre into a bowl of near-boiling water. When the bread was fully soaked he would lift the poultice up and wring the surplus water out of it by twisting the dry ends. How terrified we would be, watching the steam rise to the ceiling when he did this. It meant the moment was imminent when the burning-hot pad would be slapped on to the offending part – arm, chest, finger, foot or whatever and held down on the 'bad' place. Quickly our mother would then wrap a piece of green oiled-silk around the entire poultice to keep the heat in. The method was drastic and painful, but it invariably worked. The main care required was in getting the heat just right – enough to cure, but not to scald.

Bandages were made from old clean sheets which had been torn up and then rolled into strips for use when necessary. Afterwards they were boiled clean again in the copper for re-use, if possible. It took a long time for sheets to become fit for bandages because when they became thin they were usually split down the centre and then turned 'sides to middle' and sewn up again. Thus the thin parts would now be on the outsides. They were also patched and darned. Sometimes the cotton or linen sheets were used until they were so thin that they would actually rip and come to pieces when people turned over in their beds or tugged too hard at the bedclothes. It was a really ghastly feeling when a sheet ripped or gave way softly under the pressure of one's feet and the prickly wool of the blanket, felt through the hole, was an all-night reminder that when morning came a non-too-pleased mother would be confronted with yet more mending.

Quite a few older people used ear trumpets when their hearing began to fail. Rich and elderly invalids, accompanied by nurses or paid companions, could be seen being wheeled around the parks in wickerwork bath chairs. Often they were pushed along beside the flower beds in long, triangular, three-wheel conveyances, each of which had a knob-handled steering lever at the front. They also had collapsible hoods and clip-on mackintosh covers, like babies' perambulators. We all thought these looked like great fun, and would often walk along beside them regaling the occupants with our chatter about childish things. Far from being annoyed, the old people's eyes would light up, and their wrinkles crease into smiles as they asked us about our homes and schools. There was a great camaraderie and understanding between elderly people and children. Maybe it was a sort of brotherhood of the disadvantaged. Whatever it was we had time for each other.

Old people would often rummage under their shawls or in their pockets for bags of bullseyes or Paregoric drops, which they kept there specially for offering around to any children they met on their outings. Most old people stayed in their own homes until they died, and lots of children would visit them there – usually with parents' admonitions ringing in their ears that they mustn't make a nuisance of themselves or tire the old folks out. What we usually did was tidy up their piles of newspapers or fill up their coal scuttles from their coal bunkers.

Sometimes they had a good fire going and would ask us to get down on the hearth and make a bit of toast for them. This they would often then dip in their cups of tea or mugs of Oxo. We ran errands for them for things like 'a bit of shin beef and some pot vegetables.' Or we would take their 'thruppences' to the baker's shop late on Saturday afternoons and, laying their straw carrying-bags up on the counter, ask for 'three-pennyworth of stale bread and cakes, please.' The bags would be filled to the tops with a jumble of all sorts of food that would otherwise have gone really stale during the weekend. When we took this bounty back and displayed it all on big meat dishes for our elderly friends to exclaim at, we felt like Robin Hood. When we left they would usually give us a few sweets as a reward. Sometimes the sweets had been kept in their chests of drawers and would taste faintly of moth balls.

Every now and then a black, glass-sided and silver-ornamented hearse, pulled by two black-plumed horses, would pull up outside Crawford Buildings, and we would know that an old friend had died.

❦

Flies were a great nuisance. They would settle on the steaming piles of horse dung in the streets and then fly up onto the raw carcasses of meat which hung from hooks outside every butcher's shop. And no matter how high people's windows were, they still flew indoors if they could. Most homes that I went into had fly papers hanging down from the living-room or kitchen ceilings. Even the kitchens of the wealthy in the squares had to use these ugly things. They were long sticky strips of brownish paper which had been coated with a mixture of arsenic and sugar. Sometimes the 'News of the World' reported cases where wives had tried to kill their husbands by sweetening their tea with fly paper scrapings. The flies loved the papers. They would greedily guzzle the sticky stuff and then find they couldn't walk or fly away because their feet were stuck. So they died there in their dozens, with all their friends. A fly paper crowded with dead flies was an object to keep one's eyes averted from, when having a meal. But, 'better dead flies than dead people' was the common-sense attitude which prevailed.

Most families had either a mesh-sided meat-safe, which was a portable cupboard that was to be stood in a draught or a cool place, or else mesh-covered domes which were placed over food in their larders. Even the wealthy people with gas refrigerators often still used these things for the meat, so that the air could circulate around it. Milk was protected by beaded lace covers on the jugs, and during thundery weather it had to be stood in bowls of cold water to stop it from 'turning'.

My sister and I, like most children whose parents managed somehow to afford it, were dosed every day with a spoonful of black treacle, a spoonful of Parrish's Iron Tonic Food, a spoonful of cod liver oil and malt. Every spring we were put on a week's course of sulphur tablets, which were supposed to cleanse our blood and prevent spots, pimples and boils. The list of home-cures and preventive measures was so long it could have filled a small book. People with constipation drank senna-pod tea. The senna looked like dry brown pea pods and were brewed up in the tea pot. Some people didn't bother to wait for constipation but just slipped a tiny bit of senna pod into every pot of tea they made. It was one of the hazards to be watched out for when invited to 'have a cup'.

Fresh air and hiking had become very popular among young adults. Every spring, summer and autumn weekend, hordes of them set off on the Green Line buses, steam trains and tube trains, bound for the sleepy villages, country lanes, orchards and cornfields of nearby places like Hertfordshire, Surrey and Kent. They all wore clothes very different from the usual neat and tidy work-day apparel. Women wore either thick skirts or knee length shorts with short sleeved jumpers or blouses, and cardigans. The men wore all sorts of trousers, either baggy grey flannels, plus-fours or long khaki shorts topped by open-necked shirts with silk scarves tucked into the openings and V-necked woolly pullovers. They all wore lace-up shoes and ankle-socks or knee-socks. A surprising number wore very French-looking berets, both men and women.

Some of the men wore trilby hats or caps. Some carried walking sticks. Both boys and girls had small canvas haversacks strapped to their backs. It was very strange, although commonplace, to see young men and women that we knew through the week as shop assistants, clerks, hairdressers and so forth venture out every Sunday in such carefree groups and wearing such un-city-like clothes.

The tube station walls were lined with colourful posters of people hiking in really idyllic countryside, which, they implied, could be reached for the outlay of a few coppers. One of the most popular songs began: 'I'm happy when I'm hiking, off the beaten track – I'm happy when I'm hiking, with my knapsack on my back'. I really looked forward to going hiking one day when I was grown-up. But due to our father's sickness, for which there seemed no cure, there were times when I wondered if I would live long enough.

15

A Time For Change

In the middle of a clear and frosty night towards the end of February 1939, just a few days before my eleventh birthday something shocking happened. The moon was new and the sky was filled with sparkling stars. Against this background rose the tall silhouetted shape of the clock tower which stood sentinel over the Marylebone railway station. The silver rails beneath would have been lying quiet in the starlight for it was long past midnight. No smoke issued from the plantation of chimney pots which stretched, just below eye level, between the station clock and the high windows of our two roomed apartment, for most of the neighbourhood fires would have been banked-down for the night leaving the chimney pots to cool as they slept, in their sooty rows, on the rooftops .

Our sixth floor bedroom, lying just under the roof of the ancient Crawford Buildings, was one of the highest in Marylebone. I still shared a bed with my little sister and her two teddy bears. Most nights we fell asleep to the sound of the night breezes of London gently rattling the cowlings of the chimney pots just above us, and we did not wake until morning when sparrows began hopping and chirruping on the smoke-blackened window ledges.

On that February night we had fallen asleep much as usual. Earlier that evening our father had been drinking, but not enough, as yet, to worry us. We had been relieved that it had not turned into one of those 'bad' nights when our mother would have to take us along the outside passage in our nightclothes and put us to sleep in the old bath beside the brick copper in the communal wash house. It was scary lying behind the locked door, watching out for the occasional drips from the brass cold-water tap at the end of the bath, and wondering what was happening to our mother.

But that evening had been quite pleasant. Our father had been in a playful mood and had even told us one of his special olden-days stories that we so loved to hear. This one had recalled his youth when he had been an aspiring third footman not all that many years older than ourselves, and it had been both touching and funny.

We had been asleep for about five hours when my peaceful dreaming was broken by the sound of the bedroom door crashing back against the wash stand, and the roar which was coming from our father's wide-open mouth as he raged into the room. The glass juddered as he opened the sash window wide. Then he lurched over to us and, almost falling on us, wrenched off all our top bedcovers including the sheet, and hurled then into a heap in the corner.

The rush of cold air onto our warm bodies plus the loud noise startled us into sudden and full awakeness. Our father was shouting that he was going to throw us both out of the window: 'You bloody kids lost me my proper butler's job that I'd worked so bloody hard for,' he was bawling, 'and have cost me thousands of bloody pounds more since then.'

When our father was sober his manners were impeccable and he never swore. What was more, he made it obvious that he loved us. And we loved him too. But now our ears rang with his curses. From the look on his bright-red face and the way his eyes were glaring at us until they were nearly popping out, he seemed to have gone raving mad. There were even flecks of foam at the sides of his mouth.

Joan and I screamed in unison and clung tightly to the nearest thing at hand which was the bottom sheet. It quickly parted company from the underblanket and flock mattress beneath and was dragged across the linoleum floor as he pulled us both, still screaming, towards the open window. Our mother, who had staggered into the room holding her face as though she had been struck by quite a heavy blow, now also screamed at the top of her voice and tried to pull us out of his clutches. But he was stronger than she was. He was winning. 'Daddy, Oh DADDY STOP!' I managed to gasp out as, twice, I saw our mother nearly fall backwards out of the window herself during her struggles to keep us inside. And Joan, considering she was only a skinny eight year old, was fighting him like a wild cat, clawing at him with her one free hand and her thin legs flailing as she tried to kick him off with her bare feet.

There was a hammering on our front door and then Mr and Mrs O'Brien, our closest neighbours, burst into the living room and rushed into the bedroom with cries of 'Dear God' and 'Oh Dear Lord!' followed closely by two other neighbours who helped Mr O'Brien overpower our father and sit on him. Then some other people closed the window and pushed a wardrobe in front of it while our distraught mother comforted us, and Mrs O'Brien ran all the way to Harewood Row beside Marylebone Station to fetch Dr Armstrong.

༝༝

Within less than a week our mother had found us other accommodation. The family was not splitting up. Father was so truly sorry afterwards for what he had done that, despite the awfulness of it, none of us really wanted to leave him. We were quite sure that the knowledge of what he had nearly done would help him to keep his promise, this time, to never drink again.

Our new home was the bottom half of a house at number five Shouldham Street, which was just around the corner from Crawford Buildings and Homer Street. The rent was half a guinea a week, which was quite a lot of money for a family like ours to have to find. But it was worth it for the house was nice, a real step up in the world for us. Made of those mellow dusty brown bricks which seemed so much a part of central London, it was third from the end of a Georgian terrace that stood opposite the smart new Seymour Hall, which had only recently been built. The house itself was narrow, four storeys high with tall graceful windows and a well-built basement floor, which had an area enclosed by railings in front. Our part of the house, being so close to the ground, made my sister and me feel much safer. 'If Daddy wants to throw us out of the window here,' said Joan with a brave sort of grin which showed her dimples off to perfection, 'he'll have to throw us up in the air instead of downwards.'

A glass door in the street-level hall separated the two flats from each other. For the very first time in our lives all four of us had complete privacy. The top flat was inhabited by a childless business couple. We saw little of them, but whenever the coalman tumbled our coal down through the hole in the pavement and into our cellar he would then carry three sackfuls upstairs to the coal bunker on their landing, so they must have been at home sometimes. Our two bedrooms, sandwiched between their living quarters and ours, provided good insulation from noise.

We were still living only a few minutes' walk from both Hyde Park and Regent's Park and the house was in a really nice road. From a few paces to the left of our front door we could look down Crawford Street and past our school to the busy traffic of Baker Street. If we looked to the right there was the corner of Bryanston Place and a district of very exclusive flats where only wealthy people lived. Just around the corner were the Montague and Bryanston Squares, in which, especially when the muffin man went by ringing his hand bell, or the lamplighter was seen at dusk, using his long pole to light up all the gas lamps, it was easy to imagine that time in Marylebone had stopped and the giant wheels of a hansom cab might come grinding over the cobbles at any moment.

Once Father had recovered he was soon back at work again. He was still employed on a sort of rota system, spreading his undoubted abilities as a waiter between his old favourites: the Ranelagh Club, the Holborn Restaurant, the Trocadero and the Grosvenor House Hotel. Whenever any of them sacked him for turning up drunk he would give them a rest and then, in time, apply to one of the others. He was always re-engaged. Despite the fact he had become disenchanted with the conditions of life he had to endure as a London waiter he still could not help but do the job well – when he did it. Even though our father was no longer a butler in private service I was quite sure, knowing him, that wherever he reported for work as a waiter, he would do his level best to 'out-Jeeve Jeeves'.

Once we had moved I began to notice the ways in which other people moved house. Provided that the rent of the new place could be afforded it seemed that it was a relatively easy thing to do. None of the people we knew thought it necessary to own the homes they lived in. Even the rich ones, as far as I could gather, merely leased their properties or even rented them, like ordinary working-class families. It was as if poor people paid their rents weekly while the rich paid monthly or yearly, or for several years at a time. And that, I was told, was because most better-off people could plan ahead financially whereas poorer people could not. The Marylebone streets always had a great many houses displaying wooden notices saying 'To Be Let'. Even more houses had cardboard signs in the windows indicating that there were 'Rooms To Rent – Cheap'.

When people moved house it was often because the children of the family were growing older and the parents wanted somewhere with an extra bedroom so that the boys and girls could sleep apart. Sometimes it was because one of the children, having reached the age of fourteen, had started work. As a reward for tipping out their weekly wages onto the living-room table each Friday night they were handed back the traditional half-a-crown pocket money just to spend on themselves. The remaining money helped to pay for a better standard of living for the whole family, and this often included a move.

Most people did not move very far away, just into the next street or around the corner as a rule. They would carry most of their belongings to the new address by hand, sometimes borrowing a neighbour's perambulator for the smaller things and the boxes. Pieces of furniture which had wheels, like armchairs and bed steads were often wheeled through the streets, one by one. Sometimes families would hire a long handcart or wheelbarrow for a whole Sunday from one of the weekly traders. Only the really big or heavy things, like mahogany wardrobes and marble-topped washstands, were transported at the last moment in the back of a carrier's lorry.

Frequently we would hear that a family had done a 'moonlight flit'. This usually meant that because they were in debt for the rent, they had quietly arranged for the removal of their belongings elsewhere during the preceding days and had then themselves disappeared in the middle of the night. Presumably to somewhere a little further away than usual, so that they could start afresh without debts. Even so they could not have ventured too far, because their children would come back to play with us in Homer Street or Shouldham Street. Street loyalties were very strong.

I was there when our mother spoke to Mrs O'Brien about her working plans for raising the money to meet the extra rent required at Shouldham Street. Also when she confided to her the big hopes she had that the better surroundings of our new home would make Father so happy that he would at last manage to give up drinking. She said that she could 'well understand' that after spending seventeen years, almost the greater part of his entire life, working in private service and living in the spacious surroundings of his upper-class employers, his subsequent five years of confinement in our two small Crawford Buildings rooms must have seemed like a term of imprisonment to him. Especially, Mother went on, as he had found it so difficult to obtain employment at first and was trapped at home looking after children while she went out to work. 'And him such a restless soul, too,' said Mrs O'Brien, shaking her head in sympathy.

At Shouldham Street there was soon pretty new wall-paper on all the walls and an exciting smell of new paint everywhere from our parents' shared efforts at decorating. The extra space that was all around us seemed wonderful and strange. Father said it was 'a big relief', and made us laugh by remarking that he now understood how ladies must feel when they took their corsets off at night. He also said, quite out of the blue and with a look on his face that was a mixture between gentle and honest, that in such splendid new surroundings we would all witness 'A New Man' emerging, where the other one had been. I personally did not want Father to become a new man. I liked him the way he was. I just didn't want him to drink any more.

Somehow he must have forgotten that we now lived in a comparative palace, because not long afterwards he slipped into one of the worst drinking bouts we had ever witnessed. And then, when he seemed to be 'coming out of it', something happened that we had never seen before. He was sitting at the living-room table trying to eat the light meal that our mother had placed before him and complaining of feeling strange, when suddenly the knife and fork fell from his trembling hands, and with his eyes nearly jumping out of his head towards what he saw he let out a truly scalp-tingling howl of terror. 'It's COMING at me!' he shrieked. His forearms were crossed in front of his face and his eyes were staring out over the top of them. 'LOOK it's coming through the wall!'

I followed his horrified gaze to the inside wall which joined us to the basement next door, just as I heard Joan's chair crash backwards. 'What's coming through the wall, Daddy?' she squeaked, already having leapt as quick as lightning to the door and, with her hand on the knob, preparing to flee altogether. 'It's a blasted great SHIP,' Father shouted out. 'LOOK, it's the Queen Mary.' His voice became a gurgling sort of screech: 'Aargh it's coming right at me.' Then his chair, too, crashed backwards onto the linoleum as he pulled himself to his feet.

I looked again at the wall. All I could see were the peaceful white daisies on the yellow wallpaper. Not a ship in sight. I had never before seen a grown-up being afraid of something which was invisible to everybody else and felt very sorry for him as well as being scared myself of this strange phenomenon. 'But the Queen Mary couldn't get into our living room,' I began quietly telling him – trying to calm him down with logic. Then my mother pulled me out of his way as he lurched across the room with his arms thrashing at the empty air yelling 'GO AWAY' to the apparition.

He went to hit it but lost his balance and put his fist through a glass-panelled door instead. Then I had to run to the Edgware Road to summon a taxi to take him to St Mary's Hospital in Praed Street, with his arm swaddled in bloodied towels and then pushed into a brown-paper carrier bag. Although he could only get one arm into his coat jacket, he insisted on wearing it, and his trilby hat. Our mother, too, had her best coat and hat on – they didn't often travel by taxi. Climbing into the leathery-smelling interior Father waved his remaining good arm in lordly fashion to the driver and said: 'Hasten to the hospital, my good fellow.' Then he carried on having the terrifying visions, and that was how I saw him and our mother drive away.

Many thoughts filled my mind as I waited for their return. Among them was a story I had often heard our mother tell, of the days when she and our father were courting when, not yet twenty, she was a lady's maid at a grand country mansion and he a handsome young first footman to a lord at another great country house some fifteen miles away. With the trousers of his smart tweed suit carefully fastened at the ankles with bicycle clips, he would pedal his push-bike all through the country lanes to visit her in the evenings when they had a few hours off. Whenever her employers were away they would stroll through the shadowed shrubberies and around the velvety lawns until they came to their favourite secluded spot by the lakeside willows. It was there, our mother would tell us with dark eyes shining, that our father liked to pull all the hairpins one by one out of the heavy coil of dark hair she wore at the nape of her neck. 'I would shake it all out until it fell to my waist,' she would say softly, 'and he would tell me how beautiful I was.' Once he had told her that in the moonlight she was 'like a pale, proud, princess, dressed in a shining cloak of sable'. And many times, in the moonlight, they had waltzed together on the lawn beside the lake to music that only they could hear.

'Just one drink to celebrate our new home. That's all I ever intended,' Father later wept. He was truly downcast.

'It will never happen again,' he promised. Our mother did not trust his promises any more. Nevertheless, she seemed happier than I had seen her for a long time. Her home was a never-ending delight to her, and she made spruce new covers and curtains for every room. She and Father now had a bedroom to themselves for the first time since we children had been born. In that spring of 1939, our father was 36 years old and our mother was 33.

Times were changing. First of all, I began to realise that life was beginning to offer me other things to think about – things far removed from the small and worrying world of our own family concerns. Earlier in the year Mr Oliver, the headmaster of St Mary's School, had decided that I was worth coaching for a scholarship. Consequently I had lots of homework to do. I also had something to dream about. There were other interesting things happening, too, which seemed to be promising adventure – maybe even getting away from home for a while. People were beginning to talk about something called 'evacuation'. It was a totally new word in my vocabulary and apparently it meant that arrangements were being made for most of the London schoolchildren to be taken away to the countryside if there was a war.

16

Elephants in The Sky

The summer of 1939 turned out to be the strangest of our childhood, up till then. Some very peculiar things were happening in Marylebone and, apparently, all over London. There were barrage balloons in the sky. Trenches were being dug for air-raid shelters in Hyde Park – right on the spot behind Marble Arch where Joan and me and our friends usually played rounders. And somebody kept on testing out the new air-raid siren on the roof of the police buildings at the end of Shouldham Street – just a few doors away from us. The first time it happened we were eating breakfast by the open window. It really made us jump. Joan's Post Toasties flew up off her spoon and came down all over the tablecloth.

As St Mary's School was only a sparrow's flight over the chimney pots from Hyde Park, I had, for months, been listening to the sounds of school with one ear and to the sounds of artillery practising in the park with the other. All sorts of weird changes were taking place. Even the grown-ups seemed to be altering into slightly different people and everywhere there was a feeling of tension. Many children however, had been growing ever more excited since that time, earlier in the year, when it had first begun to filter through to us that if there was a war between Great Britain and Germany, we would all be 'evacuated' to the country for a lovely holiday. The prospect of 'war' did not seem to mean anything. The only word that mattered to us was 'holiday'.

Joan and I were already without much hope of an ordinary holiday and it was becoming clear to us that there probably would not even be any short trips away from home during the six weeks of school closure before the autumn term began. Vaguely I wondered whether this was because of the unsettled conditions all around us, or simply because there was even less money than usual to spare for such things.

We were not alone in this deprivation. Quite a few of our friends had never been outside of London at all, apart from the Sunday School outings. The years of the Depression had really left their mark and most people we knew still had to take the greatest care of their 'pounds, shillings and pence', or whatever little money they had. And yet we were fairly unique, because we should have had some money. I knew that with both our parents going out to work we could have been better off than we were. But because our father so frequently wasted the family income on drink we were often reduced to quite shaming poverty.

One Saturday in the late spring of that year when our father had been temporarily out of work again and was at home, supposedly looking after us while our mother was at work, he had taken the money that Mother had left out for him to buy the midday meal and spent it on beer. Joan and I had just come back from playing in Regent's Park. One look at him told me the worst. He already looked ill, even though he had only been drinking for a morning.

I knew that we must run immediately to Mrs Coburn's mews house and warn our mother that he was 'off again'. Then she could quickly finish her duties and hurry home. The hope was, as always, that she could stop him going any further by coaxing him to eat something. If she failed this time, as she usually did, I knew that – now he had taken a drink again even after a reasonably long abstinence – he would be under some sort of compulsion to keep on drinking until the bout had run its full, agonising, course. Something would go into the pawn shop that afternoon for certain and by nightfall, or earlier, he would be shouting out that he was 'King Pin' and our mother would be trying to soothe him. Then would follow the fearful and dreaded several days when, despite anything anyone could do, he would gradually turn into that wild-eyed madman who could hardly be recognised as the kind and loving father who told us bedtime stories and tried so hard to show us the beauty and interest that was in the world.

By now I had a black hatred for that 'other father', who seemed to me to be gradually killing off the real one. I didn't want him to materialise. I decided that before going for

Mother I would cut some bread and cheese and implore him to eat it. There was just a chance he might. He now seemed to badly want me to respect him when he was drunk, even to the point of expecting me to stand up when he spoke to me and call him 'Sir'. He never baited Joan in this way – only me – and when I sided with our mother against him he would say that I was 'as hard as nails' and call me a 'little bitch'.

I went to the larder, deciding at the same time that I would also butter some bread for Joan and me to eat, even if it should entail eating it as we ran down Crawford Street towards Baker Street to fetch Mother if my plan failed and he was not interested in getting into my good books by eating what I put before him.

It was then that I saw that the bread crock was empty and the larder bare. Except for jars of split peas and lentils and things like that which he had not bothered to prepare. I then remembered that Mother's wages had recently been used up, mainly for clearing the debts left by Father's pre- vious drinking bout. She was only buying fresh food as and when we needed it. My own hunger lit up my anger and I scowled across the unlaid table to where Father was standing by the empty fireplace. He put his glass of beer on the mantelshelf and looked at me with pleading eyes: 'Don't let your mother know you've had nothing to eat.' There was a mixture of sadness, shame and hopelessness on his face as he uttered those so obviously silly words. At that moment my anger towards him melted a little and I felt sorrow for him. It was a feeling that actually hurt physically in the wishbone space between my ribs.

Then he said: 'I don't want your mother to come home and find you girls have had nothing to eat. Take a bowl from the dresser cupboard and then go to Bryanston Square and ask any of the cooks there if they could let you have some old dripping or a few bacon bones. Tell them your father's out of work and there's no money in the house. Maybe they'll then give you something to eat as well – something proper.' His speech was already slurred as he spoke.

'No, Daddy, I won't,' I actually stamped my foot and my sorrow turned to hot rage that he should even think of turning us into beggar-children – worse off, even, than the children of the street singers. They at least had only to carry their father's hats round to people in the street and their fathers had actually done something for the money – and they were there to back them up.

But he insisted. He even fetched the bowl. 'Please,' he said, 'there's nothing wrong in it.' Then he went on to tell how, when he was a boy living in the Shropshire country-side, children often went with bowls to the cooks of the Big Houses. How they often came back with bowlfuls of rich fruit cake and other pleasant things. Even later on, he said, when he himself had become a footman, and then a butler, 'even then they used to come.' Under his dark brows his blue eyes, made moist by the beer, seemed to shine as he recalled those memories of the long-ago days when he had been young and full of the joys of living or else had arrived at a position where he felt himself to be a person of some importance. Sometimes it even seemed to me that he missed the peace of the countryside where he had grown-up and the graciousness of those ancient country establishments where he had been taught the arts of a profession that was not only dying but was no longer available to him anyway.

Then Father began to talk of a brainwave that had just occurred to him and attention was brought sharply back to the matter in hand – the begging. 'Try speaking to the kitchen maids in an Irish voice if you can, Enid,' he was saying. 'Lots of them have come over from Ireland, you know. Try making them think you're a little Irish girl, so that they take to you.'

His enthusiasm was growing and I knew he was quite sure we were going to do his bidding. There was a feeling of numbness creeping all over my body. It was caused by fear. Then I became aware of something else: a sort of insistent little bell ringing somewhere within my consciousness. I sensed that beyond my fear, some part of me was rising to the challenge of it all. And then thoughts began to occur – if I could actually carry out Father's crazy idea then subsequently he would feel obliged to eat some of the food I, hopefully, returned home with. And once food had passed his lips and gone down into his tummy the spell would be broken and his compulsion to carry on drinking would vanish.

I decided that any challenge, however distasteful, or however little chance it had of success, was better than having to see once more on my mother's face that awful grey defeated look that seemed to age her in an instant, or to have to witness again her sadness and quiet tears. I grabbed the bowl and my sister's hand, and off we went.

I purposely avoided any of the Big Houses where the cooks were known to us and our mother and crept instead down the clean-scrubbed curving area steps of several others. 'Would you be after having any old dripping to spare?' I mumbled the words self-consciously at each kitchen door, at the same time marvelling at my new-found mimicry and hoping that very dark hair, greeny-blue eyes and numerous freckles made me look Irish. I also forced myself to smile my very best smile, complete with its slight gap between my two front teeth – a feature which, so I had been told, was considered lucky. Savoury cooking smells drifted tantalisingly past our noses as the kitchen maids said: 'No – get away with you.' Or 'Stop bothering us, we're busy.' And the doors would be firmly closed in our faces. It was not a bit like the times I could remember earlier in the Thirties when our mother, after dressing us in our best clothes, had taken us with her to visit kindly cooks after delivering clean laundry to the ladies upstairs. Always then we had been invited below stairs for a cup of tea, and our mother presented with a bundle or basket of food. There had been no shame attached to it at all. But this was proving vastly different. I just hoped than none of our friends would be coming through the Square on their way home from Hyde Park or Oxford Street or elsewhere and chance to see us.

I heard the clock above St Mary's Church strike the hour for one o'clock and knew we had to hurry. Soon our unsuspecting mother, in another savoury-smelling kitchen hardly a stone's throw away, would be untying the starched white strings of her own cook's apron and heading for home, and Father.

At the next house we called at, a tall, thin maid listened patiently while I said all that I was supposed to say. Then she turned back to the others in the kitchen and called out: 'Will you come and look at this – little girls begging on the doorstep!'

The next moment we found ourselves being stared at by an assorted small group of white-capped and aproned women, some with wooden spoons and suchlike still in their hands. They looked at us as if we were circus animals and I nearly shrivelled up with shame.

'What do you want?' the red-faced cook demanded in a rude and aggressive manner, 'Why are you out begging?' and 'Where are your parents?' And I had to recite the whole rigmarole again – this time stumbling over the words and almost forgetting what it was I was there for.

The cook clicked her teeth and they all tutted: 'It's disgusting in this day and age,' said one. The maid on the threshold turned back to us: 'Go home and tell your mammy and daddy they should be ashamed of themselves.'

Although tears of mortification were pricking my eyes and a big hurtful lump seemed to be growing in my throat, I still decided to try at just one more house. Joan wanted to go home but I pulled her along with me and knocked at the next house but one. The cook herself answered the kitchen door. I could see the big table inside was already cleared and being scrubbed, which meant that the upstairs luncheon must be over. I discarded the Irish accent and the concocted story for something in the woman's face made me want to tell her the truth: 'Mummy's at work and Daddy's been drinking, and there's nothing to eat.' My voice nearly broke as I began to gabble our tale of woe to that motherly cook.

'Come in my lovelies.' She almost gathered me and my sister into her strong-looking arms. She tipped the cat out of the cook's chair beside the fire and told me to sit in it. Joan sat on a three-legged footstool at the other side of the hearth. The surprised cat was quickly picked up and cuddled by Joan. Over the sound of its purring and the steamy song of the big tea kettle on the hob, I listened to the cook's concerned voice as she asked us all sorts of questions about ourselves. While she was talking she was also laying out, on two plates, some small oval moulds of minced steamed ham, accompanied by dark green buttered spinach and new potatoes.

As we were quickly eating this meal, balancing the plates precariously on our laps, for the table was still wet, I told her quite a lot about our home life. I also told her about the promised evacuation that we were both looking forward to if there was a war. At this point she stopped what she was doing, turned, and with her hands on her hips looked full at us: 'It would be the best thing that could happen to you,' she declared. Then she added, with a little shake of her head: 'When I was your age I too had a father who drank. I can tell you I was mighty glad when I became fourteen and could get away into service.'

When we left she put a neat package wrapped in grease-proof paper into my hands, which contained four thickly cut ham sandwiches smeared with mustard. 'See if you can get your father to get these down him – before your mother comes home,' she said knowingly. 'Tell him that if he doesn't Mrs Eggleton from the Square will be after him with her ladle.' We kissed her goodbye and promised to send her a postcard from wherever we found ourselves evacuated to – if that ever happened.

Father never saw Mrs Eggleton's sandwiches. We arrived home to find that he had gone out, and the gramophone had gone out with him. I quickly ran upstairs and hid the package under a pillow so that our mother, when she came home, wouldn't see the strangely arrived food and ask where it came from. I knew that she was going to be upset enough as it was. I did not want to add to her sorrows the shaming knowledge that her children had been out begging.

As the days became longer and sunnier, so my longing to be away from home and London increased, and it was the same with my sister. We became almost desperate for some sort of change – anything that would provide us with a short release from family worries. If it brought us adventure and excitement as well it would be marvellous, we thought. We would have liked to speed the whole thing up, but all we could do was watch and wait.

❦

We knew a girl who lived in one of the turnings off the other side of Baker Street. Her name was Audrey. She was not a best friend but she went to St Mary's School and she had a very jolly and jokey family. They always seemed to be laughing. Sometimes, if we were going to see the Wallace Collection on a Saturday, we would go home past her street and, if she was playing there, she would ask us in to have a cup of tea with whoever was there.

It was in this way we learnt that every summer the whole family went hop picking in Kent. That explained why Audrey sometimes came back to school much later than anybody else. Her family explained to us that by hop picking they not only got a holiday but they got paid for it, too. One day, on the spur of the moment, I asked Audrey's parents if we could go with them. 'Of course you can,' they replied in their jovial Cockney manner. 'You don't mind sleeping a bit rough, do you?' But when I told our mother the good news – that our holiday problem could be solved in such a simple manner – she was not a bit pleased. 'Of course you can't,' she said, very crossly. I was quite jolted because she was usually so very gentle and patient with us, even when she was tired.

❦

During those fateful weeks when the war clouds were gathering behind the scenes, lots of people seemed to think that nothing would come of it, but just as many seemed to believe that a war was inevitable. We sometimes pushed our way through the crowds of people who gathered at Speakers' Corner at the edge of Hyde Park. There, with the busy traffic milling past the Lyons Corner House and around Marble Arch on the one side, and with scores of men in view on the other side digging the deep trenches that were now criss-crossing quite a lot of the park, making black scars in the yellowing grass, we would stand beneath the shady trees and listen awhile to the various types of orators perched on their soap boxes or on step ladders or in miniature wooden pulpits. They were having a field day, for people seemed more than usually willing to listen to the words of anybody who seemed to hold a positive view in the midst of so much confusion and conjecture. Even in the ordinary streets men and women could be seen talking and frowning in puzzled-looking groups, outside shops, public houses, communal bath houses, libraries and other such places.

Whenever grown-ups spoke to us about the possibility of evacuation, they would say cheerful things like: 'Make the most of it if it comes off. Aren't you the lucky ones!' Or: 'If a war does come, it'll all be over in a fortnight and then you'll be back again in smoky old London.' I just hoped it would all happen while the weather was still nice. Joan hoped we would be taken to a farm, where there would be lots of animals to fuss over. I had a new swimming costume. It was made of pale-blue wool and had rubber buttons on the shoulder straps. It also had a canvas belt around the waist with a chromium buckle and was considered very smart. Our mother had cut it down for me out of an old one given to her for that purpose by Mrs Coburn, her regular employer. With the aid of water wings and a rubbery-smelling brand new swimming cap, white with blue spots, I was learning to swim at the Seymour Hall Swimming Baths opposite our home. I decided I would happily let the evacuation authorities transport me to the seaside for a little while, and there I would be quickly transformed into a two-legged mermaid. But when I talked it over seriously with my sister we thought it was more likely we would be taken to somewhere just outside London. We hoped it would be somewhere nice like Box Hill where the charabancs took us on the Sunday School outings. Every day when we woke our first thoughts were always about the same thing – whether or not there really was going to be a war. I watched the London scene eagerly for pointers as to which way the wind would blow, in much the same way that the farmers in our story books looked for weather signs in the sky.

There were many small indications of the way things were shaping up in the world, but all too often they were contradictory and took a lot of sorting out. An important sign was when our mother came home from work one day and told us that Mr Coburn, who still was a film director, had now been asked by the government to help make propaganda films about conscription and mobilisation. She had to explain to us what the words meant. I felt she was trying to prepare us for something. Yet all the while she was smiling in her reassuring manner.

Despite all the weird things that were happening in the world outside our home, my sister and I – and our friends – were unaware of any real threat to our way of life. That, we thought, would go on forever, like the British Empire and Britannia ruling the waves. Everyone knew that ours was the greatest country in the world, we thought, and therefore totally invincible. Yet some adults were beginning to go around looking definitely worried. It was all very puzzling.

Meanwhile one thing did stay the same. In the heat of the dusty summer city the question of whether or not we would be evacuated became of absolute paramount importance to us – and each day, as we indulged in the exciting but tantalising business of looking for clues, our worst fear and anxiety was that the whole thing might be called off.

In London the news boards of the newspaper sellers all had a rather ominous look about them, it was true. But still we had no firm clue and certainly felt no fear for, after all, they had always looked either over-ominous or over-optimistic. That seemed to be the way with newspapers. Yet more and more the wireless or the Movietone News or Pathe Gazette that we saw each Saturday morning at the Mickey Mouse Club were talking about or showing us pictures of Herr Hitler, over in Germany. But as they still often spoke of him with derision as 'Mr Shickelgruber' and joked about his goose-stepping soldiers, we couldn't tell whether they were really worried or not. Also, still fresh in our minds was the fact that just a little while before, in the previous September, we had seen pictures of the Prime Minister, Mr Chamberlain, waving a sheet of white paper and happily declaring 'I think it is peace for our time.'

Every day since I had been at school Mr Oliver had pinned the front page of *The Times* newspaper to the school notice board, and ever since I could remember it had been about one war or another – the war in China, the war in Abyssinia, the war in Spain. It seemed just the natural way the world was: like summer following after spring, and then during the summer holidays the sooty railings of St Mary's School getting a coat of fresh paint thus heralding the coming of autumn and a new school term.

The enormity of what might be lying in wait behind all the rumours, speculations and contradictions simply went over our heads. The testing of the new air-raid siren we had just found amusing. We watched with unfearful interest as workmen dug even more deep trenches for air-raid shelters in the park – they seemed to have no true reality for us, they were just one more aspect of the mysterious ways of grown-ups. Just a little further along down the leafy paths, where Hyde Park became Kensington Gardens and the fountains splashed all day with a sound like fairy bells, Peter Pan stood serenely on his tree trunk in the sunshine. His world of flying children and poor Lost Boys and a ticking crocodile was something we could identify with and understand. We knew what a crocodile was and so we could be afraid of it. We also knew what being lost meant, so we could sympathise with the poor boys. But we couldn't be afraid of an air-raid shelter because we didn't really know what it was. We heard a few things about 'refugees', but we didn't know what they were either – any more than we really knew what an 'evacuee' was. We weren't stupid, but we needed some kind of previous link-up if the new sights and sounds we were experiencing were to have relevance. My wooden pencil box had the words: 'Made in Czechoslovakia' printed on the bottom of it. To impress my teachers, I had long before learnt to spell it – so the word Czechoslovakia actually meant something to me. In March, it seemed, Herr Hitler and his Nazis had taken over the country which made pencil boxes.

But our ignorance didn't stop us from wringing every bit of excitement or adventure we could from the changing scene. We thrilled to the sight of the night sky being raked by practising anti-aircraft searchlights, with no fear at all of what might be about to happen. Later the trenches, dug deeply into the clay beneath Hyde Park, filled with seeping water at the bottom. On one particularly hot day Joan and I were reprimanded by the workmen for climbing down into one of them and running through the cool trench water in our bare feet. We had been having a lovely time, pretending that we were paddling in country duck ponds, or the sea.

There had not been much air traffic over London up until that time – maybe just the odd monoplane, so rare indeed that all of us would stop our play and watch it go out of sight as it droned lazily across the sky. Sometimes we would look up from our street games to watch an advertising biplane chug along close to the high chimney pots. Floating out behind it would be a long tail of flimsy material with the words: 'Zam-Buk Ointment' printed on it in big black letters. But now there were other things in the sky: the barrage balloons, looking like a herd of enormous silver elephants floating above us. Some children argued that they looked more like whales. Whatever they were they were very much appreciated by us. Somehow they didn't seem to belong to the world of grown-ups at all – they were too fantastic. In the mornings, as we hurried down Crawford Street with the strident peals of the school bell echoing over the rooftops and ringing in our ears, we would see them up above us, watching us and keeping us company. They were like friendly sky-animals and when the weather was fine their chubby bodies would be golden-pink in the early sunshine. In dull weather or rain, they would be silvery grey. In fact, depending on the light and the time of day, their hides would glint in a variety of colours as playful winds turned them slowly around at the ends of their long, steel, tethering cables.

At night, as we lay tucked up in our beds, we would gaze out of the window at the barrage balloons. When the moonlight was strong their silvery sides would reflect it, and as they moved in the warm end-of-day air currents rising from the streets and parks, the bright reflections would seem to flash on and off, as if they were twinkling out 'goodnight!' messages to us. Sometimes the barrage balloons would fly high under the stars. At other times they flew low enough to peep at us through the chimney pots. Some of their steel cables came down onto winches on the backs of lorries in Hyde Park.

In the park, even more anti-aircraft guns were being mounted and dozens of men were employed filling sand-bags. I noticed that the sandbags smelled of cats, even though they were new. Other men, and soldiers, were starting to pile sandbags along the outsides of certain pub-lic buildings: especially near the doors. Because they were laid on top of each other in a way that made them like steps or pyramids, they were very tempting to climb up. Boys in particular often had reddened ears from being 'cuffed' by soldiers or workmen.

Black-out material for curtains came on sale in Woolworths, alongside long, gummed strips of rough-looking 'curtain netting', which, according to the labels, was to be wetted and stuck on to window glass to 'prevent splintering'. There were also rolls of brown-paper sticky-tape that were to be stuck across the glass in square or diamond shapes, like leaded panes, for the same reason.

On the next counter were fancy covers designed to fit over the cardboard boxes in which the government had supplied everybody's gas masks. They were made of mack-intosh fabric or canvas and had nice broad shoulder straps which looked far more comfortable for carrying them than the string which most people had attached to their gas-mask boxes, and which cut into their shoulders. But most people couldn't afford to buy them. Some women, who made their own clothes, used up some of the spare pieces of material to make gas-mask covers to match their outfits

– in much the same way that many little girls, including us, had mothers who made them matching knickers to go with their dresses.

Another thing that was making it difficult to calculate the chances of a war coming was that our Aunty Alice had told us she would soon be off to France with her employers for a month or more. She was still nanny to the granddaughters of Viscount Falkland who we knew was an important man. Two villas were being rented in Le Touquet: one for the family and some friends and the other for the servants and the children. Already she was busily engaged in stitching certain items of nursery furniture into hessian wraps so that they could be shipped on ahead. Just as when they rented a villa in Torquay each year, they preferred the little girls to use their own things as far as possible rather than rented or hired equipment. I couldn't make it out. Surely to uproot the entire family and staff and set up house on the continent for more than a month was a strange thing to do if a war was really expected, I thought. And surely such high-ranking people as Aunty Alice's employers would be in a position to make a good guess at what was going on.

On the other hand, our mother came home from work one day with two small, brown, fibre suitcases that Mr and Mrs Coburn had bought for Joan and me as a 'going-away-present', just in case we were suddenly evacuated, they had said. They were also preparing emergency luggage for their own little boy, Richard, apparently. I overheard our mother tell Father that she was sure her worldly employers 'knew a thing or two'. She also said that at every private dinner party she had done recently the table talk was full of people's private preparations for a war.

We knew our mother loved us very much, yet she rarely cuddled or kissed us. As well as being quiet and gentle she was also a little bit reserved. So I found it a very telling thing when one day, when she and Joan and I were crossing over Oxford Street from the Mount Royal to Park Lane, she suddenly took our hands and, drawing us close to her, said 'Come along my little chickens.' I could hardly believe my ears – the endearment was so surprising coming from her.

Father was now working again at the Grosvenor House Hotel, and we had been on our way to meet him when he came off duty. He had recently been telling our mother that a lot of the rich Americans staying there were getting prepared so that they could leave for the United States at quick notice, should it be necessary. We were aware that one of the fairly frequent diners at his set of tables – his 'station' – was an American lady called Barbara Hutton and that she owned all the Woolworths in the world. They were called the 'Three-penny and Six-penny' stores and Joan and I would have fun trying to guess how many three-penny pieces and six-penny pieces she must have collected in her lifetime. But as we walked past the elegant buildings in Park Lane my mind was totally taken up by the fervent hope that Barbara Hutton had not been to the Grosvenor House for lunch that day. Father was always grumbling about her, or so it seemed to me. At work he was still called Charles and she always, apparently, insisted on being seated at 'one of Charles' tables' and filling up the rest of his station with her many friends. She liked his 'old-fashioned English courtesy'.

But he was always in a very bad mood after her visits. As he still received just 30 shillings a week pay, he relied on the tips he was given by his customers to make his money up to a decent living wage or, at least, an amount that didn't make him feel as if he was a serf. But he told us that she never, ever, tipped him – or anybody else as far as he could make out. Mother tried to soothe him on these occasions by saying that because she was a millionaire and one of the richest women in the world she probably had no idea of the struggle that most working people had in order to exist. But it didn't soothe him. I remembered him once exclaiming angrily: 'She and her crew have had me running around like a blasted flunkey for three solid hours and not a brass farthing to show for it!' At moments like those I knew that he loathed his job and was really quite miserable inside.

As the summer advanced I fancied I saw a subtle change coming over Father. Other children may not have noticed their fathers' moods but, because of circumstances, I had grown used to always keeping an eye on the way he was. I knew, for instance, that if he became rather quiet and engrossed in deep thoughts but humming to himself at the same time it could mean that he was about to go out on a binge. But now a quite different side of him was beginning to show. More and more I noticed him saying things like: 'If it comes to it, I think I'll be glad to join up and fight for King and Country instead of all this pussy-footing around as a waiter.'

In common with quite a few other men in the neighbourhood there was a new alertness in his demeanour. It seemed that the more 'serious' the newspaper headlines became, the more purposeful and jolly many of these men became – including our father. Whether this was them expressing their real feelings or was simply bravado, I had no way of telling. But I had the strong impression that they, too, were looking forward to some sort of adventure.

Our mother had taken to slipping her arms around our shoulders and giving us little hugs and squeezes at unexpected moments. I also frequently noticed her gazing at us, almost secretly, as though she was quietly photographing us with her eyes. As for my sister and me, we went along happily unaware that the world of our childhood was fast slipping away from us and would never come back again.

17

The Last Summer

In Mr Philips's sawdust-floored grocer's shop on the corner of Homer Street, women daily spoke to each other about the many preparations for war that were going on all around us. One question in particular was often mentioned: Why, they wanted to know, had all the canvas hiking knapsacks disappeared from the shops, just when they needed them for the possible evacuation of their children?

While they stood gossiping and exchanging views they often rested their wicker shopping baskets on the tall jute sacks of sugar which stood against the side wall of the shop. Now and then one of them would perch a small child on top of those soft and bulky sacks. Then the yellowed moustache of the white-haired Mr Philips would twitch and his face would turn dark red behind his gold-rimmed spectacles: 'Kindly remove that child from my sugar-sacks and stand it on the feet God gave it,' he would say between clenched teeth. The ruffled mother would then lift her child down and, as a rule, stand it by the row of glass-lidded biscuit tins which stood on the floor in front of the wooden counter. There the child would usually proceed to gaze longingly at the pretty biscuits on display and then dribble all over the glass. Or else it would go and play with the wooden tap of the big vinegar barrel, which stood on low struts in a corner beside the bundles of firewood and the paraffin. Failing that a child might amuse itself by playing with the neatly stacked iron weights of the vegetable scales, often pocketing the small, highly polished brass ones which were used for weighing ounces. Or it might try to scramble up the wooden stepladder that leaned against the high shelf which supported the big tea caddies and coffee bins. But Mr Philips's greatest worry seemed to be that small children would reach up to the counter top and get their fingers perilously near to the blade of the bacon slicer. He really hated children. I had once heard him tell our mother that all too often 'the little brats' would wet themselves while they were sitting on his sugar-sacks, causing him to lose several inches of his sugar stock.

After hearing this story I always examined our own sugar bowl very carefully, looking for anything suspicious. Not for nothing had my schoolteacher Miss Carpenter been telling us, for what seemed like years, about the importance of purity. I was by now in my parents' opinion, quite a 'finicky eater'. Also, after seeing the hordes of flies which buzzed around the whole carcasses of meat which hung on hooks outside the butchers' shops, and having grieved over the lambs which also hung there (with much of their woolly fur still on their little bodies and their heads still on to prove they were 'English' and not frozen meat transported from New Zealand) I now refused to eat any meat at all. As far as I knew I was the only 'vegetarian' in the district and thus considered an oddity.

Instead of meat I managed quite well on cheese, cut fresh with the wire from the inside of the round, and chose for myself the brownest of Mr Philips's 'chucky' eggs, which nestled in a basket of straw on his counter. My mother didn't complain, although she and Father sometimes joked about my 'contrariness'. The only time she had put her foot down firmly at my occasional fussy moods, which were a new thing, had been during the previous cold winter when, sitting at the table waiting for Sunday dinner to be served up, I had remarked that the cutlery was too cold to use and would somebody please warm it up. 'Even your father, at work, doesn't have to go to those lengths!' she rightly objected, while Joan piped up that I was becoming like the princess in the story of 'The Princess and the Pea' – all of which made me collapse into uncontrollable giggles that I, and not Father, should for once be the distracting centre of attention. After which I came happily back to earth.

That year, 1939, I had become eleven years old, and during the early summer I found that my thoughts were becoming very 'poetical' and I was beginning to daydream quite a lot. So it was that, while the whole of central London seemed hell-bent on bristling itself up with war defences and as quickly as possible, I did something, perhaps born of these same poetical thoughts, which almost earned me a stroke of the cane at school. Girls were rarely caned, but I came just about as near to it on that occasion as any girl could.

There was growing in me a great longing for the more gentle and lyrical side of life – for beauty and stillness. Even though this seemed to be in contradiction to my ever-growing desire for adventure, yet the two desires did not seem to conflict. The two-in-one seemed to be most satisfied when I conceived the idea of going for a stroll around Regent's Park in the very early mornings before going to school. Not only would this break the monotony but in so doing I would, I thought, be spiritually set up for the day. I merely had to start off a little earlier and then, leaving Joan to play with her own friends in the school playground, nip along Baker Street and enter the park by the Clarence Gate. I knew that, later on in the day, two of the favourite characters of all the children would be stationed at the park entrance. At the kerbside at the left of the wide gate would be the navy-blue box-tricycle of the neatly uniformed Wall's ice-cream man. 'Stop Me And Buy One' was the tantalising slogan on that magic three-wheeled vehicle, which housed frosty tubs and penny briquettes of either creamy vanilla or tongue-tingling lime-flavoured ice cream. But most popular with children were an assortment of delicious water-ices, each one encased in a triangular cardboard tube. The ever-helpful and always smiling ice-cream man would cut each one in half with a sharp knife so that a smaller portion could be purchased for a halfpenny. With care, such a portion could be made to last all the way along the main paths, past the quacking ducks and the hissing geese, and right into the children's playground with its swings and sand pit. Or even as far as the Tea Pavilion with its lovely sound of spoons tinkling in saucers, on the other side of the black bridge. To the right of the Clarence Gate was the official pitch of the Italian ice-cream man. The sleeves of his crisp white shirt were rolled back, revealing strong, brown, hirsute arms. He wore a bright-red waistcoat and a white-bibbed apron. On his head was a yellow straw boater and on his face was a curly black moustache, with the ends waxed into stiff needle-like points. The sight of his gaily painted red-and-yellow barrow was enough to turn a child's heart over. Four twisted brass poles looking for all the world like barley-sugar sticks supported a red-and-yellow striped awning. In the shade beneath it, the domes of two highly-polished brass lids stood guard over two wooden tubs of thick and custardy ice cream. The tubs were sunk into the work-surface of the two-wheeled barrow and beside the lids, standing like two gracefully arched displays of tall flowers, were stacked sugar-wafer cornets. The two ice-cream men appeared to be on amicable terms, even though they must have been arch-rivals.

But during that time when I went into Regent's Park before school in the mornings, it was too early for the two men to have yet taken up their positions and hardly anyone but a few quiet gardeners were ever encountered.

On the broad pathway inside the gate I would be greeted by soft grey pigeons, cooing and fluttering around my feet. Then I would let my gaze draw me into the tranquillity of the scene: vapoury mists rising above the empty boating lake, still reflections below the willows, the white shapes of sleeping swans on the shadowed island and hundreds of dewy flowers in the loamy beds, each one smelling of pollen and honey, and the early sunshine bathing each translucent petal in a pale golden light. It really seemed to me at that time that every plant and flower in the park had become more alive. They were not only drenched in sunlight but were also glowing with a light of their own.

It appeared to blaze out from within, like a mystical fire. I wondered vaguely why this should be so but was not at all disturbed by the new magical way of looking at things which I seemed to have acquired: it was rather pleasant being bewitched in that way every morning by plants and flowers and leaves and light.

But after I had happily wandered into school about half an hour late on five consecutive mornings – thus missing the morning prayers, the hymns, the register-calling and the all-important communal recitation of the multiplication tables – I was sent up to the headmaster in disgrace. Mr Oliver, after giving me a withering lecture about 'honouring and respecting' the school, which left me feeling ashamed, then told me that, had I been a boy, I would have been given three strokes of the cane and suffered the further penalty of having my name entered into the 'Caning For Serious Offences' book.

Quite soon after this incident I learnt that I had been awarded a scholarship, and that my name was, after all, to be painted in gold lettering on the high broad inner wall where all the achievers of honours for the school had been listed since the early 19th century. The thought of it gave me an awesome feeling, as if I was about to be buried in Westminster Abbey. But the best part came to me because of an old school tradition: apparently every time any of St Mary's pupils won a scholarship, the whole school was given a half-day holiday. When my turn came to bestow this blessing on my contemporaries I found myself extremely popular for almost a week.

During the two previous terms I had come top of the class in examinations, but that summer I found that I shared top marks with a boy called Francis Cameron, who was a newcomer to the school. His father was a Scottish engineer who was now working on a project in London, having brought his family down from Scotland with him. Not only was Francis studious and owl-spectacled but he had a very pronounced Scottish accent. The other boys picked on him.

One day, when Miss Carpenter was out of the classroom, they started on him again with their baiting and ridicule. At first I thought he was going to cry but he clambered up onto the seat of his desk instead. Then, tossing back his fair hair and with blue eyes blazing, he quickly pocketed his spectacles, put up his puny fists and yelled, 'You're all guttersnipes – come on you dirty English guttersnipes.' Just at that moment, Miss Carpenter, who was as English as tea and crumpets, came back into the room and heard what he said. Nobody said a word in his defence and he was sent up to be caned.

Later on, when the examination results revealed that he and I had the same ratings, Miss Carpenter announced this to the class. Then she said, 'There cannot be two children at the top of the class so, as Francis Cameron is a boy I am marking him in first place and Enid Elliott in second.' Francis smiled across at me with apology in his eyes. I managed to smile back but I was furious. It was only later I realised I had learnt something more about the world – it was that boys received both preferential treatment and harsher punishments. It levelled up. It was fair.

Towards the last days of that term, before we were due to break up for the summer holidays, the school Sports Day was held as usual in Regent's Park. The weather had 'held' and everyone in the school was in high spirits as the various teachers guided each class in long tidy crocodiles all along Baker Street, past the big shops and the bustling crowds to the park. There we clattered over the metal bridge and proceeded to the wide-open spaces beyond Queen Mary's Gardens.

Soon all the parents who could get away from their duties were present, sitting in deck chairs or on the shorn grass in their summer clothes, many of the women in pools of shade under paper parasols. Their presence was gradually swelled by crowds of other people – strangers, visitors to London, a few young men already in military dress or simply Londoners strolling through the park for some fresh air. They all seemed delighted to have come across a whole schoolful of children, wearing coloured braids across their chests and happily competing against each other in sack-races, three-legged races, wheelbarrow- or egg-and-spoon races, or simply just running the 50- or 100-yards sprint. Most parents, ours among them, brought picnics. No food, I thought, could taste better than those cucumber and egg-and-cress sandwiches. Nor any tea more fragrant than that poured, sweet and steaming, from dozens of brightly coloured Thermos flasks into aluminium cups.

The lovely weather seemed set fair to go on forever. The wide sky above us was blue and tranquil as an empty lake. Muted echoes of young men's voices floated over the trees towards us as, on a nearby grassy sward, the older boys of the St Marylebone Grammar School played cricket in the late afternoon sunshine. The distant hum of the London traffic in the background merely seemed to emphasise the peacefulness that was still to be found in the midst of so much tension, and preparation for war. The changes going on around us were speeding up – some so quietly that they had happened almost before we realised it. Elsie Grey's mother, for instance, did not appear to be the same woman who had wept into her apron after the attentions of the Means Test men. She was beginning to look and act in a way that was quite different from the way she was before. It seemed that because of the war-scare her life had been transformed, for her two eldest sons had been able to earn some money at last. They had enlisted into His Majesty's Forces: 'My Stanley's joined up. He's in the army now and my George has gone into the navy' she told everyone, her eyes shining with pride and relief. After having been poor and without hope for years, she was now suddenly as proud as a peacock and as happy as a lark. She had even had her hair Marcel Waved and had bought herself a new hat for Sundays, which had a saucy frill of spotted net veiling hanging down the front.

Even more men in uniform were appearing on the streets, and some saloon cars had been sprayed with matt khaki or grey paint, and bore mysterious stencilled markings like A.R.P., M.O.I. and A.F.S.

We knew a tall, lanky girl called Ivy Brown, who lived with her widowed mother in Molyneux Street. All the local children, us included, pronounced it as 'Molly-Knocks' Street. There was an old, dark, shuttered shop down there where boys and girls sometimes spent their halfpennies on tablespoonfuls of mustard-pickles wrapped in newspaper – even though forbidden by their parents to do so. But lately they were not even getting into trouble for it. Ivy Brown had often grumbled to us about the way her mother was so strict and demanding with her, and how she frequently wished she could escape for a little while. At first, like us, she had been excited at the prospect of being evacuated. But then one day, in a rather airy fashion and not really looking at us, she suddenly announced in a hollow theatrical voice: 'Just like the ivy clings to the wall – I shall cling to my mother if a war comes.'

We were right in the middle of playing 'hand-stands' up against a wall. We stopped playing and all stared at her in amazement. She then told us that her mother had clung to her the night before and wept all over the shoulder of her pyjamas because, she said, she couldn't stand the thought of her precious little one being taken away to 'God knows where'. While I wondered how anyone could refer to the towering Ivy Brown as their 'little one', Ivy admitted to us that she had been forced to agree to stay behind in London with her mother if the evacuation started happening. We were really sorry for her.

At the other end of the social scale, we learnt from our mother that plans were under way for Mr and Mrs Coburn's little boy, Richard, to be sent down to his grandmother in Devon if there was a war. It would be like a nice holiday for him in her big house by the River Exe at Topsham. We also learnt that some of his older friends might be sent away to America on a Liner. Our minds boggled: America was where Shirley Temple lived, as well as nearly every other film star we had enjoyed watching over the years at the Mickey Mouse Club.

It was there, on a newsreel, that we saw pictures of the first Anderson Air Raid Shelters being delivered to people's homes in London – and on the very next day we got ours. It was delivered to us on an open-sided L.C.C. lorry. It was all in bits. With the bits came an instruction leaflet. The eight giant pieces of heavy, corrugated, reinforced steel were to be fixed together using the nuts and bolts supplied and then sunk into a deep pit in the yard or garden. Father scratched his head in puzzlement as he stood in our paved back yard. He did not own so much as a trowel, let alone a pick and shovel. He was mightily thankful when four hefty workmen from the L.C.C. turned up the next day to do the job for him. Several of our friends were with us while our shelter was being put together. There was Ernie Willard and Kathleen Rock from Crawford Buildings, Lola Petit who lived in Gloucester Place, Ivy Brown from Molyneux Street and Freda Green whose father was manager of 'The Volunteer' opposite our school.

Part of our attention was fixed on the workmen and the other part of it was fixed upon the row of assorted neighbourhood cats who were sitting on top of the high yard-wall, watching the proceedings with interest. Our attention was, in fact, divided equally between the shelter and the cats – for we had all become 'cat-watchers'. This had come about because, in the middle of all the war tension, one of the evening newspapers had been reporting almost daily on the most recent antics of a Marylebone tomcat who, reputedly, had grown a pair of big, black, furry wings. Now, instead of slinking along the tiles at night he was flying around the chimney pots – or so the newspaper said. We had seen it there, printed in black and white. A fuzzy photograph of him had also appeared in the paper alongside an interview with the animal's owner. The man said that his pet had always had very bony shoulders, but that in the early spring of 1939 little furry stumps had begun to appear near the cat's shoulder blades which, by the summer, had sprouted into a fine pair of wings.

The paper then went on to say that the cat in question had, unfortunately, not been properly photographed by their own press photographer because it had flown off just before the interview. The owner was blaming himself saying: 'I shouldn't have given him his dinner.'

My sister and I, and our friends, were very excited about this cat. Several times we had been quite sure that we had seen his little furry body flying up high among the barrage balloons. We also now scrutinised every other feline's shoulders just in case there were any offspring or uncles or cousins showing similar family traits. The flying tomcat only lost his position of importance when our parents were suddenly instructed that, as from Monday 28 August, all of us children were to start reporting every morning at nine o'clock to our school. We were to be fully prepared and equipped for immediate evacuation. The authorities could not be certain of the exact day we would go, but we must be absolutely ready each morning, and have said our goodbyes.

18

The Moon in The Chimney Pots

On Sunday 20 August, Joan and I had attended Mr Green's Sunday School at the Paddington Chapel. Mr Green looked so sad that he might have been seeing us for the last time, I thought. There were about 40 of us there and during the afternoon he gave each one of us a white postcard. On one side was his name and address and a penny postage stamp. The other side bore our individual names followed by a blank space. If we posted our new addresses to him when we were evacuated, he said, it would enable him and the other Sunday School teachers to keep in touch with us by letter. He did not have a telephone. Neither did any other ordinary person we knew. Apart from the 'telegram boys' the postman was the bearer of most news, good and bad. Back at home Joan and I tucked the postcards into our new suitcases next to the similar cards which had been given to us, with almost identical instructions, by our parents. Nobody said anything about using secret codes if the place where we found ourselves was awful. It seemed to be tacitly expected that all would be well. At least, that was the confidence-boosting impression that I received.

There was an added twist to the way in which Joan and I were to be evacuated, one which made the prospect even more of an adventure into the unknown. Most of the London children would be going away under the protection of schools they had known ever since they were in the Infants. They would also be in the company of all their friends and with schoolteachers who had been in their lives for a very long time. But for my sister and me it was not going to be that way at all. We would be going away under the care of a school which was entirely new and strange to us. This was because of the scholarship – the 'Free Place' I had been granted at the Paddington and Maida Vale High School for Girls, or the P.M.V.H.S. (still quite a long name).

Ever since I had been told that I had won the award I had been in a mild state of excitement. Many times I had taken my sister for a walk with me along the Edgware Road, past the Grand Union Canal, and down Elgin Avenue in Maida Vale in order to look at the new school building which was in the final stages of being prepared. I understood that it would be ready for the beginning of the new September term. I now thought, gleefully, that when we came back to London again after being evacuated, it would be something to look forward to.

A letter containing a brochure and a curriculum had been sent to my parents by the headmistress, Miss Bracken.

She referred to the school as a 'select establishment for girls and young ladies'. The ages of the pupils there apparently ranged from eleven to eighteen years.

When my mother proudly showed the brochure to Mrs O'Brien, who had come over from Crawford Buildings to have tea with us at Shouldham Street, our old neighbour remarked: 'They're not schoolgirls! At eighteen, surely they're young women, fit to be mothers?' As most children of working-class parents left their elementary schools when they were fourteen, and then went out to work to help pay for their keep, my father had to sign a form promising not to remove me from the school before my studies were completed. These would include Latin, German, French and Greek, and something with the awful name of Trigonometry. If I was taken away from the school before my education there was complete, Father would be fined 'a minimum of five pounds' for wasting the school's time. As I could not imagine myself ever being fourteen, let alone eighteen, that part of the agreement did not worry me in the least. It was all part of the slightly dreamlike way our lives were shaping.

I had been told that the majority of the girls at the Maida Vale school had well-off parents who paid fees for them to go there. As I would be a scholarship pupil, the only money my parents would have to find was for my uniform and equipment. I felt rather guilty at adding a further financial problem to the ones our family already possessed, for the list of clothes and other things required was very long and every item on it was so expensive that the green-and-white uniform might as well have been trimmed with ermine. Yet my parents told me that they would cope – somehow. In fact they seemed quite pleased and proud.

For my part, I was more surprised than anything else at my achievement, for I was certainly still no swot or 'egg-head'. I had tried hard to win the award for two main reasons: partly to please my parents, and partly for the same reason for which I hoped to be evacuated, and that was for the sake of the adventure. I wanted the thrill of wearing a smart new uniform, for one thing.

My clothes had always been nice: either the once-expensive garments that had been passed on to me after having been worn by the rich children to whom Aunty Alice was nanny, or the pretty dresses that our mother made on her old treadle sewing machine. For the last two terms at St Mary's I had worn a navy-blue gym slip that she had cleverly made out of an old serge skirt given to her by Mrs Coburn. Many a time I had sat at my desk in it with a day of school stretching before me, thinking of all the interesting, exotic and elegant places my gym slip may have been to, when it was the glamorous Mrs Coburn's skirt.

I thought it would be very exciting, at last, to wear something that had actually been bought from a shop just for me, and which, I imagined, would go part way in transforming me into one of the schoolgirl heroines I read about in books by Angela Brazil, Rita Coatts and E.L. Haverfield. Those girls played tennis and hockey just as I soon would, and went to boarding school where, with their schoolgirl chums, they had midnight feasts in the 'dorm' and had spiffing adventures solving all sorts of mysteries which usually involved either slaying ghosts or saving the honour of the school. I could see it all happening to me: 'Well done, old thing!' and 'Enid has saved the day!'

What I really needed of course was a boarding school. But the one at Maida Vale was the next best thing, as far as I could see. Now that it looked as if Joan and I might be evacuated with the school as well, and be living away from home in something called a 'billet' – things were beginning to look really interesting.

The government had already issued the rule that brothers and sisters were not to be separated during an evacuation, even those who went to different schools. In such cases the youngest children must go away with the schools attended by the eldest in their family. When the threat of war was beginning to look really possible one of my major worries was that through some hidden clause or rule I would not be able to go to my new school after all, and would have to go back to, and away with, St Mary's. I thought it would be a terrible anticlimax because, in a small cloud of glory on prize-giving day, I had said goodbye to all the teachers, and thanked them for all they had done for me.

Sunday 27 August 1939 was destined to be the last day we would spend together as a family in London. But, of course, we did not know that then. Joan and I were joyful as always at the prospect of having our mother to ourselves for a whole day. We also looked forward to the added joy of having our father join us in the afternoon for a few hours when he had finished work. We were going to have a picnic in Hyde Park. Mother had filled the Thermos flask with tea, and a stack of bread and butter, wrapped in the waxed paper saved from our Post Toasties, was packed into a brown-paper carrier bag beside slices of homemade caraway seed cake. Our towels, woollen bathing suits and water-wings lay on top of the food to keep it cool. It promised to be a very hot day – the sort of Sunday when London became a dreamy summer city shimmering in a haze of heat.

When all was ready the three of us walked the familiar ten-minute route to Hyde Park, entering it from the Bayswater Road just below Marble Arch at the Stanhope Place Gate. There was a tall and ornately decorated drinking fountain on the right hand side of the gate which, according to an inscribed tablet, had been given to the citizens of London by an Indian prince. The exotic shape of it and the intricate carvings of the pink-and-grey marble and granite made it look like a miniature Moghul temple. It was, to many local children, a beautiful and magical link with one of the more mysterious parts of our Far Eastern Empire. After drinking icy water from the heavy metal goblet which was attached to the fountain by a chain, we stepped into the park.

It is only with hindsight I can realise that, with those few steps away from the Indian fountain on that last Sunday of peace before the Second World War, we were actually leaving behind us an era that was doomed to vanish and walking towards the one that was just beginning. For as we emerged from the shade of the trees and into the open spaces we saw that the air-raid shelter trenches, which the workmen had been digging at for weeks, were now even more extensive and deep. High piles of newly-exposed earth lay on the grass, drying out in the heat. Even more subterranean water had seeped from the clay into the new low levels of those dark slits in the ground and, even though it was a Sunday, all the usual number of workmen were still there, digging hurriedly in the sweltering heat. Most of them had stripped off their shirts and waistcoats and vests, but still sweated profusely in their thick corduroy trousers and hobnailed boots or wellingtons. Some of them wore makeshift hats made of handkerchiefs, knotted at all four corners. Right behind them we could see the big white shape of Marble Arch and, behind it across the broad expanse of thoroughfare, the Cumberland Hotel and the Lyons Corner House.

From the other side of the park near the barracks came the noise of big guns, as the artillery kept up their almost continual practice. The trunks of the trees seemed to reverberate to the sound. Turning right and following the pathway under the itching-powder plane trees, we made our way past the Ring, where well-groomed horses cantered by beneath riders who looked as erect and haughty as any I had seen in 19th-century engravings. To my eyes, those expressionless riders seemed so detached from the tense and anxious world of August 1939 that they might as well have been mere phantasms of the past.

Beside the cool fountains at the end of the Long Water we paused to listen to the sounds of Kensington Gardens: pigeons cooing on the ancient flagstones, the laughter of little children all mixed up with the gentle admonishments of nannies and the magical sound of water droplets plashing into the dark lily-padded pools. At the Serpentine Lido, Joan and I changed into our swimsuits in the green marquee, then let ourselves slip gently into the warm gnat-hovered water where, surrounded by scores of heads in rubber bathing caps, men, women and children, we splashily practised our doggy-paddles and breast-strokes.

Army lorries were on the broad path behind the lido, and men in the uniform of the Territorials were busy mounting even more guns. They were also doing other, more secret, things. We could not tell what, because they had cordoned themselves off from the public behind barriers of rope netting with thin strips of khaki material knotted all over it.

After we bathed we returned with our mother to Hyde Park and to the place, beside a clump of trees, which was to be our pre-planned picnic spot. There we would wait for Father. After his lunch-time duty he would be free for the afternoon. At about a quarter to three we saw his tall, long-legged silhouette striding towards us across the broad flat parkland with the shimmering green of the Park Lane trees by the Grosvenor Gate far behind him in the distance. As we had hoped, he brought his own contribution to the picnic – several small titbits that had been left over from the luncheon. He quickly divested his pockets of a number of stiffly starched white table napkins, all of which had 'Grosvenor House Hotel' embroidered in the corners. These he spread out flat on the short dry grass.

Laid before us we saw paper-frilled cold lamb cutlets, cold chipolata sausages and thin slices of smoked ham. All was ready for us to eat with our bread and butter and the lettuce. To follow this there were peaches, grapes and petits fours, and to finish up with there were Bath Oliver biscuits and some nice tasty Cheddar cheese. Everything looked as fresh and dainty as though Father had just served it up at one of his tables on dishes. 'There you are then, girls,' he said expansively to Mother, Joan and me, his extended arm sweeping across and then back from the tempting display, as though he was a magician revealing his latest trick: 'this little lot would cost you at least five shillings in the Grosvenor House, so tuck in.'

With the food comfortingly inside us we talked and laughed – not bothering to move from our pleasant leaf-dappled picnic spot – just happy to be together. But, slowly, the sun moved over the gold-tipped tree-tops beyond the Long Water. Faraway voices took on that strange echoey ring which only happens during the closing hours of an afternoon. The sound recalled for me the line from Thomas Gray's 'Elegy', which we had so often recited at school, and which only now, at last, seemed to be opening up its meaning: 'The curfew tolls the knell of parting day.'

The four of us, stretching the day as far as possible, stayed in the park till half past six. Then Father had to make a dash for it to get back on duty in time. We half ran and half walked with him back to the Grosvenor Gate where we kissed him goodnight. Mother and Joan and I then strolled slowly along Park Lane in the warm evening air, the fragrance of lime blossom drifting out to us from the still trees in the park. It was such a lovely evening that we lingered on the edges of the park for a long while. Then, to our surprise, after we had crossed the road by Marble Arch, our mother shepherded us into the marble-walled bustling foyer of the Lyons Corner House. The inside of the lower tea restaurant on that August evening was bright and wide and warm. There were black marble pillars, huge wall mirrors and feathery palm trees in pots all around the room. At one end, on a raised dais, was an eight-piece orchestra. All the musicians had flushed warm faces and wore full black-tailcoated evening dress. The joyful sound of Strauss waltzes and polkas could be heard well above the clatter of dishes, and the buzzing murmur of voices that came from 120 or more white-clothed tables.

Our mother, on seeing my expression, told us that there were at least two more Corner House restaurants of similar size on the floors above us, each one providing a different type of service. Every table I saw was laden with silver-plated tableware, cutlery, teapots, hot water jugs, tea-strainers, slop basins, milk jugs, sugar bowls and sugar tongs, cruets, ash trays, match-box holders, muffin dishes. All over the room was a wonderful silvery shine: even the small vases filled with fresh flowers that stood on every table seemed to be made of heavy silver plate.

The waitress who served us was one of the Lyons 'Nippies'. Her dress, shoes and stockings were black, but her frilled cap, pleated apron and crisp collar and cuffs were all made of a white material like organdy and her

8. Nippies at the Lyons Corner House.

cap was threaded with black ribbon. The atmosphere in the restaurant was gay and carefree: the happy music filled every corner. Although it was filled with ordinary people, like us, all eating simple things like tea and cakes or roes-on-toast, we were all treated with such good service and respect that, I was sure, everyone in there felt like royalty and that all must be well with the world. It cost one-and-ninepence for tea and toasted muffins for the three of us. Our mother told us that the outing, a special treat, had been paid for by our father. Apparently, he had pressed a silver florin into her hand as we left him. I realised that he must have had good tips at lunch time and I was happy for him. Following his instructions, the threepence change from the florin was given to the waitress. A very good tip under the circumstances. The smile on her face when she received it made me think of Father's oft repeated observation that: 'A good tip is the mark of appreciation which separates "service" from "servitude".'

When we finally came out of the close atmosphere of the restaurant, the risen moon was like a great silver ball in the sky, outshining the lights of the West End of London, which were beginning to twinkle. It was a waxing moon, just coming up to the full. As we walked home along Great Cumberland Place to Bryanston Square and then, turning left, into Shouldham Street, the moon seemed to be following us. The man in the moon had a big smile on his face. He seemed to be dodging along the high rooftops and peeping at us from between the chimney pots just as the barrage balloons did when they were flying low. The barrage balloons were not low that night. They were high up, over the park, reflecting the moonlight.

Within two nights the moon would be full. Only astrologers and astronomers would have known that it would be shining from that portion of the heavens known as 'Pisces', the gentle sign whose symbol had, long ago, been adopted by the early Christians in memory of their Prince of Peace. Only clairvoyants could have known that it would be the last full moon of peace time – a celestial marker that a way of life in Great Britain, and Europe – indeed the world – was fast coming to an end. The next full moon would be in Aries – the sign ruled by Mars, the god of war.

19

The Longest Goodbye

It was Monday, the morning of 28 August. Our small suitcases were all packed and ready. Every instruction on the government leaflet regarding evacuation had been either obeyed or carried out. Our nightclothes and two changes of underwear were in the cases with our new sponge bags, towels, hair brushes, postcards, stamps and other sundry items. There was more than sufficient for the stipulated one week's supply. Anything else ('should prevailing conditions require it', so the leaflet said) could be sent on later by parcel post.

Not only was our baggage labelled with our names and home address, but similar labels had been tied onto stout safety pins and then securely pinned to our 'going-away dresses' by our mother. This instruction had been in capital letters and underlined. By now everybody knew that there could be no forwarding addresses on our labels because nobody knew where any particular school would be going.

It was also compulsory for all children who, like us, were prepared and waiting to be evacuated, to carry their labelled gas masks with them at all times. Every morning when we reported at school, ready to be whisked away, we were also expected to have with us enough sandwiches to last a full day – and possibly into an evening as well. We were told that drinks would be provided at appropriate railway stations en route.

9. Gas masks.

Our mother had bought us new cardigans and pyjamas and had made us matching dresses on her sewing machine, from a long length of pretty summery material purchased in Selfridges' Bargain Basement. They had short puffed sleeves, shirred waists and dainty white crocheted collars which she had also made. From the leftover pieces, as a surprise, she had produced matching garments for Joan's two teddy bears and my double-jointed doll. Father had bought us a stack of new comics to read on the train. They smelled excitingly of new print and unopened pages: *Comic Cuts*, *Chips*, *Funny Wonder*, *Radio Fun* and *Beano*. To go with our sandwiches he had brought four speciality biscuits made of thick layers of sugar wafers from work at the Grosvenor House. They were as round and large as tea plates and the word 'Hungary' was inscribed on each in icing-sugar writing. 'Hungary biscuits for hungry girls,' he joked. He had also brought us home two champagne corks. The body of each cork had been hollowed out and an oval glass capsule slotted in place. Housed in each transparent capsule was a tiny dancing doll – a French cancan girl – kicking one leg on high from a skirt of red, white and blue frills. Captivated by their daintiness and uniqueness we tucked the champagne corks into our suitcases as lucky mascots. Joan left her teddy bears, Teddy and Tiddles, sitting on her bed, dressed in their new clothes, to await her return from the country.

I did the same with Anne-Gretchen, my beloved chinafaced doll. I had given her the second name of Gretchen because she had been born in Germany. At the back of her neck underneath the dark, ringletted cascade of curls, which were made of real hair, was inscribed the word 'Germany'. I knew very little of that country apart from what we saw on the newsreels. I personally had never set eyes on a real German.

I found it sad that, because I had won the scholarship, we were going to be parted from all our friends, both at school and near our home, for this adventure. Most of them would be going away with St Mary's and others with the school in George Street, but all of them would know lots of the others and even be best friends with some of them. It was just beginning to dawn on me that, because my sister and I were going away with the new Maida Vale school, where we knew nobody at all, we might just miss out on some shared fun. On realising this we had quickly got together with all our long-standing childhood friends to talk over our situation.

They agreed, with us, that we should all swop stories about our adventures when we got back again to Marylebone. All of us girls promised faithfully to keep our Brownie diaries up to date so that we would not forget anything. The boys implied they would be able to remember everything without having to resort to such 'sissy' acts as writing things down. Lola Petit suggested we should all pay tuppence to whoever came back with the best story. As so many adults had told us we would only be away for about a fortnight that is what we believed.

That week, the one that began on 28 August, was even stranger than any we had ever experienced before. On Monday morning we stood neat and clean and properly labelled beside our new suitcases. Our parents hugged us tightly to them as we kissed each other goodbye. Father's jollity was interspersed by quiet words and his hands stayed on our shoulders for a long time. I noticed how fit

and well he looked after more than two months of sobri-
ety and continuous employment. Mother's quiet ways
were interspersed with a forced jollity and nervous little
bursts of laughter at things which were not really funny at
all – like Joan running back into our bedroom at the last
moment to say something private to her teddy bears. 'Be
good girls' Mother called to us in a rather squeaky voice,
from the doorstep. 'Be sure to post those address cards to
us as soon as you get there,' Father's resonant voice echoed
as we turned the corner. We then got onto an Edgware
Road bus and off we went to report to the new school in
Maida Vale, where the great adventure would begin.

That evening we returned home again feeling tired and
bewildered, after waiting around all day at the school only
for nothing to happen. The same thing happened on the
Tuesday, Wednesday, Thursday and Friday of that week. It
was a great emotional strain on all of us. Each night Mother
had to make us some more cheese and tomato sandwiches
ready for the next day and to press and hang our clothes
ready for re-packing again quickly the following morning.
We could hear her thumping away with the heavy flatiron
when we were in bed. Father made up new stories to tell
us, and even though we were much more grown up now,
me being eleven and Joan nine, to our delight they were
all funny ones: the sort where chamber-pots were thrown
out of bedroom windows onto the heads of unsuspecting
burglars below.

Then the next morning our goodbyes would be said
all over again.

By the end of the week our parents seemed not quite so sad when they kissed us. It was as though they were beginning to think that we were not going to be evacuated after all.

That week of waiting was not entirely wasted, for it gave us the chance to get to know the names of a few of the girls and one or two of the teachers, all of whom were very conservatively dressed and genteel ladies. We also learnt that they were not referred to as teachers but as mistresses. But for the most part the new school was, to our minds, filled with rather vague and shadowy people. I was glad I had Joan for company. I realised she must have felt even more bewildered than I did, for although I was one of the youngest pupils among all those strangers she was even younger than I was. Nothing there was geared to the needs of nine year olds. None of the girls we met there came from the same background as ourselves either. They all seemed to come from homes in a much higher social stratum. We spoke reasonably well because our parents did, and they were strict about such matters. But the new girls we were meeting shared a manner of speech and a vocabulary that differed from ours in certain telling ways. Instead of saying 'my parents', for instance, they would say 'my people'. Consequently they would make remarks such as: 'I say, my people were most awfully surprised when I returned home again last night. Were yours?'

The bright, new, modern school premises were not yet quite completed and so we assembled daily in an ancient building in Elgin Avenue which was providing a temporary home for the school.

It stood on the remains of an old nunnery and was said, excitingly, to be haunted: with its pointed Gothic windows and doors and echoing arched corridors it was very easy to believe. Joan was not very keen on ghosts and kept very close beside me wherever we went. The classrooms looked empty and lifeless with no books out and no chalked writing on the easelled blackboards and all the stationary cupboards padlocked.

As it was officially still the school holidays there were no lessons and nothing much for us to do. For most of the time we amused ourselves in the sooty garden playground, which we considered a great improvement on the underground play area and back courtyard of St Mary's. There were also tall trees in the garden on which the leaves were just faintly beginning to change colour. At the end of each fruitless day Joan would pick a few marigolds and nasturtiums from the flower beds to take home for our mother and father. By the end of the week all our flower vases were full and Monday's flowers were beginning to wilt. Sometimes we were all assembled in the main school hall to listen to things. Sitting on bentwood chairs in neat rows we heard the headmistress, Miss Bracken, tell us that nobody knew quite what was going to happen to us:

'But whatever it is,' she addressed us in ringing tones, 'the most important thing for us all to remember is the good name of the school.' She then went on to instruct us that our uniforms must be worn correctly: 'Hats and gloves worn at all times in public, good manners and the correct use of the English language are also to be observed at all times, whatever the circumstances. You girls,' she went on, 'are the trusted emissaries of the school and must always endeavour to make a ladylike impression, wherever you may find yourselves.'

Joan and I were quite impressed and automatically sat up straighter. Nothing was actually said about war. The probability of it was implied rather than stated. All the mistresses carried on as though it was quite a normal thing for a whole school full of girls to be sitting in classrooms in the summer holidays with suitcases by their desks, gas masks slung over the backs of their seats, luggage labels pinned to their rather nice clothing and eating sandwich meals from greaseproof paper on the desk tops.

Once or twice an impromptu concert was arranged in the main hall. About half the mistresses and quite a number of the older pupils played solo pieces on the piano or violin. The majestically tall music mistress, Miss Hordern, sang 'I Vow to Thee, My Country' for us, from the dais. According to some of the pupils, she sometimes sang on the wireless, for the BBC, so we felt quite honoured. After this we all 'let off steam' with organised and highly ladylike community singing. It was all rather dreamlike. The prim and starchy headmistress and other lady teachers joined voice with their pupils in the rendering of such popular songs as 'Little Sir Echo' and 'The Lambeth Walk'. Discipline was obviously at its most relaxed. Despite all the various uncertainties, my sister and I were quite happy. In fact we rather enjoyed ourselves in a strange sort of way – soon adjusting to the odd 'limbo land' kind of existence in which we found ourselves, where everything was new to us, and time itself was beginning to have no meaning whatsoever.

Golden August turned to mellow September, the traditional month of transition. With hindsight it was as if the lovely spell of tranquil weather was trying to linger just a little longer, before it was time for the first morning mists and cooler winds to bring warning of the approach of a cruel winter.

On the first morning of that fateful month, Hitler's troops invaded Poland. On the next day, Joan and I said goodbye for the sixth time to our mother and father – only this time we didn't return home again in the evening.

20

Destination Unknown

We got to Paddington Station at about half past one in the afternoon, having been transported there by the red double decker buses which had lined up outside the school. As we all filed along beside the Great Western Railways train standing at Platform One, the massive black engine was already hissing and wheezing as every facet of it was made ready for the journey. It was almost as if it knew it had a part to play in the great exodus of the children of London.

Other engines standing at other platforms were doing the same thing. Crocodile lines of chattering children from other schools began lining up beside those other trains. The noise became enormous. It echoed in the vaulted glass canopy above the station and there was a kind of electricity in the air. We climbed aboard, settling our cases and gas masks in the luggage racks and scrambling for the best seats. Then, after a great deal more rattling and hissing from the engines and much wheel-tapping and shouting from the railway men, the steam-whistle shrieked and the great locomotive steamed out of Paddington.

For the first hundred miles of the journey our excitement was high. We dreamed again all our dreams of country farms and seaside towns, of orchards and duck ponds and beaches. During the second hundred miles we began to get fidgety and thirsty. We had read our comics and eaten our sandwiches. We just longed now for the journey to come to an end and for us to be given something to drink. During the last 50 or so miles boredom began, then weariness. Wherever it was that we were being taken to it was certainly a far cry from Box Hill. It was also a very long way from home.

We had passed many pretty villages and small country towns on the way, as well as countless farms and woods and cornfields. There had been dozens of places where, with our hearts in our mouths, we had hopefully anticipated that the train might stop and set us free to enjoy ourselves and be happy there. But the train didn't stop. It just whizzed through all the stations sounding its whistle as it did so and we just swallowed our disappointment. In the end we decided that the train must be taking us to somewhere really special. Then we closed our eyes and, listening to the never-ending '*tickety-tack, tickety-tack, tickety-tack*' of the wheels as they sped south west over the rails, we tried to doze.

Very few of us could have been really wide awake when the train at last began to slow down. Then it stopped – the engine issuing forth clouds of steam and wheezing again, this time as if it was sighing with relief. It was good to stretch our legs as, carrying our luggage, we were marched four abreast from the railway station to something called a Community Hall. It was early evening and crowds of people lined the pavements of the town to watch what must have been, to them, the interesting sight of several hundred schoolgirl evacuees from London who were coming to live among them.

I don't know what the other girls felt but, for my part, I was hugely disappointed. In fact I felt betrayed. I had thought we were going to be taken away to the country instead of which we seemed to have landed up in a town. Had we really come hundreds of miles and so far away from our parents just to end up in such a depressing-looking place? It looked boring! The low flat-faced buildings were built of some kind of stone that was a melancholy shade of grey – like wet pavements or old tombstones. And all the buildings seemed to be alike, especially after the varied architecture of central London. After all our months of glorious anticipation, this drab-looking place was such an anticlimax that I had to purse my lips very tightly together as we paraded past the lines of local people, or I would have shamed myself by weeping in public.

According to the signs at the station we were in a place called Camborne. When we got to the Community Hall I saw that a hand-printed notice saying 'Reception Centre' had been drawing-pinned to the door. Joan and I, being two of the youngest children there, were among the first to be prodded into the hall by a group of official-looking local people. Inside were hundreds of chairs in rows, separated by gangways – but we were told to go and sit up on one of a line of trestle tables over by a wall so that we could 'be seen'.

A crowd of aproned women stood in a far corner beside two tea urns. They eyed us speculatively before one of them came over to us carrying a tray of steaming mugs. The tea made us feel much better. Our suitcases were on the wooden floor beneath the tables and our legs swung over the tops of them as curiosity began to build up in us. Sitting next to us were two nice girls we had not met before. They were sisters, like us. The eldest was about my age. Her name was Yvonne. Her pretty little sister was younger than Joan and was called Rosalie. I fancied that when we got to know each other better we would probably become friends. Yvonne confided that she, too, was wondering why we had come so far, just to end up at what she told me was a tin mining town. She thought that being industrial it possibly wouldn't even be safe.

My mind was not so much on safety. I was wondering what had happened to our promised holiday. The other girls were gradually filing into the hall through the wide door, the eldest coming in last. Finally, when everyone belonging to the school was inside and all the chairs occupied and some girls standing, the door was closed. After quite a long spell of settling down during which time no one seemed to know what to expect, the door was opened again. This time to the people of the town.

I was becoming very uncomfortable on our high perch, for the trestle table was too broad for us to be able to lean back against the wall. Then I saw that a crowd of people were pushing their way into the hall. A draught of cool air entered with them. The men and women moved up and down the gangways looking along the rows. I could not make out whether we had been allocated to certain people chosen in advance or whether we were actually being chosen at random. Yvonne thought it was probably the latter because of the way the way they were looking us over. Their eyes darted backwards and forwards along the rows of waiting girls, seeming to be seeking faces that fitted their various preconceptions of what sort of girl or girls they wanted. Their brows were creased. Some of them stroked their chins or folded their arms. In burred accents we could not understand, they spoke to each other about us. Some whispered.

Still not knowing quite what was happening we tried to smile so that we would look attractive to some nice people. But it was difficult because it was almost impossible not to feel demeaned. It felt like being in a slave market or a cattle auction. Slowly the hall began to empty and only little groups of girls were left. Then those small groups started to diminish – thinning out like water vapour on a hot day. Soon nearly all the other girls had departed, taken to their new Cornish homes by people who wanted them. Probably there were hot meals awaiting them and nice cosy beds.

Joan and I sat among the remaining few children. Only Yvonne and her sister were still with us on the trestle tables. One or two others were scattered around the hall. My cheeks were burning. My tummy felt sick and my hands had become clammy. Could it be that we had been passed over, rejected? Or were some other people still on their way to the hall? It was growing awfully late. I did not dare to look directly at my sister but, glancing at her secretly from the sides of my eyes, I saw that she was looking very lost and miserable. I prayed that she would not start to cry. I thought of our parents – of our father, of the expression in his eyes when he had, oh so gently, kissed us goodbye that morning. He had always been so proud of us: 'The prettiest little girls in London' he had often called us. I was glad he could not see us now. Then I thought of our mother, of the scented folds of her soft, summery dress and the way her hair had brushed my cheek when she had held me so tightly to her before we left. By now they would have realised that we were not coming home, that this time we had really gone. They would be thinking about us, I knew, wondering where we were, trying to picture what we might be doing, worrying about us. Just then Joan turned to me and whispered nervously: 'If nobody wants us, does that mean we can go home now? Back to Mummy and Daddy?'

I was wondering what to answer when I saw that a middle-aged man, all on his own, was making his way slowly across the hall to where we were sitting. He was of medium height, thick-set, blunt-featured, and wearing a three-piece tweed suit. He came very close to us and then stood with his head held back at an angle so that his pale

10. Waiting to be chosen.

eyes were regarding us through half-closed lids. I felt very uncomfortable and really hoped that he was not about to claim us. Then one of the women helpers came over and signalled to Joan and me that we were to get down off the trestle table and go with the man. As we slid off it she said chattily to him: 'These four are all sisters, two lots of sisters who must not be split up. Come over to the door and you can sign for these two.' 'But I don't want these two,' he answered her, 'I'd rather have those two sitting beside them.'

My mouth must have dropped open – I didn't know whether to be mightily relieved or whether to regard his words as the final humiliation. I glanced at Yvonne. She was scowling at him. Her little sister Rosalie was looking at him with big round apprehensive eyes and pressing herself closer to Yvonne. I intuitively disliked the man and felt really sorry that our new friends seemed likely to have to go with him to goodness knew where. It was then I realised that the woman helper was speaking to him again, and what she was saying were the last words on earth that I wanted to hear: 'Those two girls are already spoken for,' she was telling him. 'That couple across the room are filling in the form right now. It's all arranged!'

With undisguised bad grace the man grunted and told us to wait where we were while he went over to fill in a form for us.

As we sat there waiting for his return I certainly gave no thought to the larger political issues which had propelled us into our present position. In history books, no doubt, we could be regarded as just two of thousands of evacuees who were taken from their parents to a place of safety. Also we could not know that our country was coming to the end of its last day of peace, or that a totally new way of existence was opening up for us, which would be full of strange happenings and world-shaking events and that everything in all our lives would be turned topsy-turvy. All I knew in the closing hours of that September day was that we were, simply, two London children who were wishing that we had not left home, who were wishing that our parents could have been like Ivy Brown's mother and refused to let us go. They had done what they thought was best for us. Like us, they could not be aware that we were destined never to return to our London home again.

It only took a moment or two for the man to register his details. As we left the hall with him he walked before us carrying our suitcases. Weary and fearful, and with a late evening wind fluttering the labels pinned to our clothing, we followed him out into the gathering darkness.

21

Epilogue

During the months that followed my sister and I were to find out, in the most dramatic circumstances, just what life could sometimes be like for children who did not have the protection of adults who loved them or truly cared about them.

In our first billet, the one we were taken to by the man on his own, who collected us from the Community Hall, we were soon to encounter both sadism and sexual harassment, and were only rescued when his wife had the sense to recognise what was happening. In our second billet, which was arranged privately by that same 'well-to-do' and 'well-respected' man who had so troubled and threatened us in the first, we were to experience troubles of a quite different kind. We found ourselves in Dickensian conditions of dirt, ignorance, near-starvation and the apparent indifference of anyone to our plight. The over-busy and war-strained teacher who was sent to inspect the

second billet was 'fobbed off' with tea and pleasant chat –
sitting in the smart, 'used-once-a-year' front parlour. She
did not look behind the scenes, or beyond the misleading
facade that was presented to her.

Because of our mother's great sacrifices to get me to
the high school, allied to the fact that I was still overawed
by it and did not know of anyone we could turn to, I did
not complain. Most importantly, we quite expected that
the war would end at any moment, and then we would be
taken home to London and our nightmare would be over.

By the time that our mother came down to Cornwall
to visit us unexpectedly, she found us cowed, mute and
apathetic from fear and neglect. We were also nearly a
stone lighter each, in weight, than we had been when we
left London. She went upstairs and looked at our bare

11. Nearly a stone lighter.

bedroom in horror – at the sagging and evil-smelling bed, on which the sheets were never changed, at the horse-hair stuffing spilling out of the battered mattress, at the bare boards of the floor without covering of any kind, and at the filthy windows without curtains. She saw that we had not been able to unpack our clothes since the time we got there and were literally living out of our suitcases because there was no other furniture of any kind in the room apart from a nail on the door, a tin chamber-pot under the bed and a stump of candle (our only light), which was stuck by its own wax to the wooden mantel shelf above the empty fireplace.

At the time the Government Billeting Allowance, paid to householders who took in evacuees, was ten shillings and sixpence for the first child and eight shillings and six-pence per head if they took in more than one. Added to this was a sizeable further allowance sent weekly by most parents, including ours. Some unscrupulous people, who did not themselves earn much, were taking in evacuee children simply to add to their income. The head of the household in our second billet was just such a man: he was employed, at a very low wage, by the man who had taken us into our first billet.

Our mother was at her wits' end with worry. She wanted, desperately, to take us back to London on the train with her, immediately. But, unbeknown to us, the citizens of London were expecting horrific air raids and gas attacks to be inflicted on them at any moment. Hundreds of empty coffins were being stacked up ready for use in every available public hall and other repositories, and government leaflets and posters were imploring parents not to bring their evacuated children home, but to 'Leave the children where they are.'

Mother angrily informed the school of our parlous and disgraceful situation. Then, after reassuring us that help would be coming quickly and giving us further words of courage – plus some secret money and Mrs Coburn's telephone number – she hurried back to London to tell our father about what she had discovered. They put their heads together and, without any hesitation, worked out an emergency plan for our deliverance. What they had decided was that, as they could not bring us home, they would come and join us instead. Even though our father did not relish the thought of looking for factory work in war-time Camborne, their main priority was that we should all be together, that we children would never again be left to the mercy of strangers and that, for however long the war should last, we should henceforth have their protection in a home of our own. They set the plan in action with amazing speed. Then, just as they were preparing to leave London, we had the most wonderful surprise – we learnt that Joan and I were to be re-evacuated with my school to Torquay, in Devon – the place from which Aunty Alice had sent so many tantalising postcards whenever her employers had rented summer villas there – the place where there were hundreds of good-class hotels which, now that a war was 'on', would be looking out for good, experienced staff. And so it was that, because of the great unhappiness and trauma that my sister and I had suffered, our small family was guided towards a bright new beginning.

Soon after the evacuation of Dunkirk, and when the Battle of Britain was raging in the skies, my sister and I had become the envy of most of the girls in my school, for we had been reunited with our parents in Torquay. The town still had the palm trees and the clement weather, but apart from that it had become like every other English seashore – highly fortified and blacked out. On walls and lamp posts were notices instructing the civilian population what to do, or rather what not to do, in the event of enemy invasion: which was to 'stay put' and leave the roads clear for British troops to get there in a hurry. But apart from the worrying war conditions, my heart was light: our 'lovely fortnight's holiday in the country' had opened my eyes. Although I would never forget any of the up-and-down and character-challenging experiences we had known in our London home, as well as the frequent financial poverty, I now realised that poverty of love, kindness or goodwill could be a million times worse. It had taken a war and an insight into a few other families' ways of life to make me aware that there must be countless adults and children who were starved of things that had nothing to do with financial security, but had everything to do with happiness. I hugged to myself the knowledge that, in the things that really mattered, we were lucky children indeed.

Our father now knew that he would be going into the Royal Air Force. But meanwhile he had become second headwaiter at a nearby five-star hotel: a position which quickly restored his self-respect. As most of our furniture was still in storage in London (there being a long waiting-list for a suitable vehicle to transport it) we had, in the beginning, no table to dine from. But we did have silver-plated vegetable dishes, a soup tureen and cutlery, which had been loaned to us by the friendly headwaiter where our father was now employed. So our first meal together since the war began was laid out on four wooden orange boxes – grouped together in the middle of the almost empty living room of the modest new home our parents were making for us. But the meal was eaten from silver dishes bearing the crest of 'The Imperial Hotel, Torquay'. Afterwards the four of us danced around the 'table', singing and whooping from the sheer joy of all being together again.

Later that evening our parents had told us that they had brought our much-pawned but beloved gramophone with them on the train from London, as well as all the favourite gramophone records. The gramophone was then set up on the orange boxes and Father placed our most worn and crackly record on the turntable. It was the one we had listened to countless times throughout our childhood, before the war came, often in the firelight while watching our parents dancing together. For us now, it was a sign that we were not just experiencing a wonderful dream – from which we would soon wake – but that the family really had been reunited and that now, with confidence, we could face the rest of the war. The night was drawing in and soon it would be time to black out the window with one of our few blankets. Beyond that window the moon shone down on a town that was still beautiful, but was bristling with war defences: from anti-aircraft guns to tank traps. Beside the silver sea, the lonely sands lay like coverlets over hundreds of army mines. Behind them, disfiguring the beaches from end to end, coils of barbed wire would now be rocking gently in the night breeze, and on the cliff tops and from look-out posts we all knew that hundreds of our men in uniform would be keeping an ever-watchful eye on our shore.

In the bare living room of our new home that night we were very aware and grateful that, so far, we had come through the war physically unscathed. We also thought of the millions of less fortunate families, just across the water, who were feeling the bite of Hitler's cruel regime. We prayed that it was not too late for many of them to be able to show each other, as we had, just how much they were loved. Then we listened to the voice of Al Bowlly, who was singing for us – and the world – 'Love is the greatest thing, the oldest yet the latest thing, I only hope that fate may bring, Love's story to you …'